INISVICKILLANE

L

...cheál Ó Dubhshláine was born in Kilkea, Co. Kildare, in 1942. He ... principal of Dún Chaoin National School from 1970 until the ...ing of 2003. He was awarded an honorary Masters Degree in ...cal History from Maynooth University in 1994. He was the author ... four previous books, two in Irish, *Óigbhean Uasal ó Phríomhchathair Éireann* (1992), *An Baol Dom Tú* (2000), and two in ...glish, *A Dark Day on the Blaskets* (2003), and *Are You Going Home ...? Memories of Old Kilkea* (2006). He died in May 2006.

Mícheál Ó Dubhshláine

Inisvickillane

BRANDON

A Brandon Original Paperback

First published in 2009 by Brandon
an imprint of Mount Eagle Publications
Dingle, Co. Kerry, Ireland, and
Unit 3, Olympia Trading Estate, Coburg Road, London N22 6TZ, England

www.brandonbooks.com

ISBN 9780863224126

Mount Eagle Publications/Sliabh an Fhiolar Teoranta receives support from
the Arts Council/An Chomhairle Ealaíon.

2 4 6 8 10 9 7 5 3 1

This publication has received support from the Heritage Council under
the 2009 Publications Grant Scheme

Cover image: Painting by Tomás Ó Cíobháin, reproduced by kind permission of
Ionad an Bhlascaoid, Dún Chaoin
Cover design: Design Suite, Tralee
Typesetting by Red Barn Publishing, Skeagh, Skibbereen

This book was first published in Irish in 2007 as *Inis Mhic Uibhleáin*
by Mícheál Ó Dubhshláine, ISBN 9780863223730

Contents

To my wife Áine, to whom I owe so much in so many ways,
and to Nicole, Donie, Sorcha, Sinéad and Breandán.

Fothram Fothraigh

For Mhícheál Ó Dubhshláine

Ní raibh ann ach tamall de lá geal álainn
Ach mheasas go rabhas ann ón tseanaimsir
Ag siúl, ag stop agus ag éisteacht
I measc na seanfhothrach ar an Oileán Tiar.

Stiúraigh máistir tofa na dtreoraithe sinn
Isteach sa tseanáitreamh i lár an bhaile
Ag léiriú, ag deimhniú agus ag sainmhíniú
Déantús na dtithe agus ailtireacht na haimsire:

Gach doras ag féachaint ó dheas,
An bhinn sa bhfothain i gcoinne an chnoic,
Gach scairt acu is a thóin le taoide,
Díon scolb a athraíodh chun peilte.

Thaispeáin an treoraí dúinn Scoil an tSúip,
An Scoil Náisiúnta agus seomra an teagascóra,
Tobar Flint gan glór ag triomacht,
Tobar an Phoncáin os comhair bolláin chloiche.

Shiúlas trí dhoirse agus d'fhéachas trí fhuinneoga
I measc na bhfothrach leis an spéir ar oscailt.
Chonac os mo chomhair peann agus dúch,
Seilfeanna leabhar agus cóipleabhair á mbreacadh
I dtigh Thomáis Chriomhthain leis an bhfardoras fuinte.

Chuala an ceol, an rince, na scéalta go léir
I dtigh Sheáin Lís taobh theas den seanbhaile.
Bhraitheas an teagasc, an léann, an fhoghlaim
Sna scoileanna ar dhá thaobh an tseanáitrimh.

Chuala an chaint gan cháim i measc na gcosán.
Míníodh dom mar a tomhaiseadh faid agus leithead
A raghadh chun oiriúint do thigh ar an gCeathrúin.
Tugadh thar farraige cúplaí agus cearchaillí
Agus buaileadh go cruinn, tomhaiste go géar
Ar thigh Mhaidhc Faight, caomhnóir na coille.

Ní raibh agam le feiscint ins gach tigh ar an mbaile
Ach clocha gan fuineadh agus simnéithe titithe
Ach b'fhuraist a thuiscint as lámhscríbhinní oilte
Go mbíodh anseo saoirseacht agus deatach as tinte.

Sheasas sa tseomra ab áille ar an mbaile,
Radharc mór chun na farraige agus cúng ar a chúl
Binn ard ar thaobh amháin agus ionad tine ina bhun.

Chóiríos i m'aigne leabaidh shocair déanta
Nuair a chonac san urlár barra rua miotail
Do chorraigh an staraí agus mhúscail as a shuan
Seaniarsma meirgeach do fhráma iarainn leapan.

Dhúisigh mo smaointe agus bhí seasta cois leapan
Seán Sheáin Uí Chearna an t-údar atá sínte le tamall
Ach anois ag caint, ag gáirí agus ag léamh m'intinní
Mar sprid sa tseomra leapan i bhfad siar
San Oileán Tiar agus mé ar séirse chun na farraige.

Domhnall Mac Síthigh

Introduction

A Day on the Inis

On that fine August morning in 2004, a little after eight in the morning, Danny Sheehy was waiting for me down at Dún Chaoin quay. Truth to tell, I felt anything but well that same morning, although I was keeping the best side out against the cancer that had been eating into me for the last six months. I was unsure of how much longer I would be around, but was taking the day for what it was, hoping another would follow. Danny, determined that I was going to see the Inis in this life, whatever about the next, had issued an invitation that was more like an ultimatum.

It didn't take him long to fit out the little boat, *Naomh Gobnait*, and then in we climbed ourselves. Danny woke the engine and the startled fulmars sprang from the cliffs of Faill Mór and made a few crooked rounds of the cove. The sea was calm, with a gentle eastern breeze, as we started away out to sea, cutting the waves before us and leaving a white trail of foam.

It was rough enough out on the open sea in the middle of the Sound. It always is, even on the calmest day. We left Liúir and the Seanduine behind us, not stopping even to toss a bit of tobacco to it as was the old fishing custom. We crossed by the Maoil Mór where the *Santa Maria de la Rosa* has lain for the past four hundred years. I felt every rise and fall of the little boat, with my backbone thumping against my belly, but I kept my grip. North of us we could plainly see Beginis, low, level and safe, and it occurred to me to ask–nay, implore–Danny to head for it and not bother with Inisvickillane. Some other day, maybe. But the courage held and I kept my grip on both sides of the boat, my seat on the petrol container and set my two feet solidly on the deck. A great splash of bitter cold seawater hit me square in the face. Though it was a fine morning, I didn't feel warm. Cancer is a cold disease. Danny pointed out An Bheannaigh to me, and I remembered Deálaí telling me long ago, and we both in the safety of sipping a pint in Krugers, that a child had been born there, his own aunt, as they were fleeing into the Great Blasket for the birth. Eilís, she was called, and everyone called her Eilís na Beannaí from the day she was born.

We spent a while looking at the huge grey cliffs, the dark green cormorants sunning themselves on the rocks with their wings stretched out to dry in the breeze. Inis na Bró was looming towards us. What an awesome sight were the Cathedral Rocks, An Charraig Scoiltithe (Split Rock) as the Island people call it. The Inis presented itself to us little by little: gentle island, high in the shoulders and low on both sides.

We drew in close to the pebble beach, Tráigh na hInise (Inis strand), but the sea was too rough to land. We then sailed over to the Léithrigh, another landing place with a cement pier and iron ladder to the top from the water. The stiff breeze was still too strong for the *Naomh Gobnait;* she was being smashed against the wall by the wind and waves, so much so that Danny was afraid that she would be damaged if left unattended for any length of time. He had expected a rubber dinghy to be at anchor there and that he could moor *Naomh Gobnait* and land in the dinghy, but there was no dinghy. Danny decided that it was best for me to land and that he would remain on board till my return. He had been on the Inis many times before, but it was my first trip.

He drew in close to the ladder. When the wave rose, I took my chance, jumped and grabbed the ladder and ascended to the top. There was still a steep, dangerous climb to the surface of the island, but I set out and gained the top without too much trouble. I lay back on the soft green sward trying to recover. I then looked at the length of Inisvickillane stretched out before me, under its cover of soft, silky grass. Uíbh Ráthach and Corca Dhuibhne and the many scattering of islands lay east and south. To the north of me was Tiaracht, threatening and fort-like, and the Great Blasket from Ceann Dubh in the west. The great Atlantic stretched right over to America. It felt like untouched land, and that I was among the privileged few who had set foot on it. The words of Seán Pheats Tom Ó Cearnaigh of long ago came to mind: "The place is full of fairies, night and day."

In or around an hour I took mooching around the Inis, taking everything easy, a while walking, a while sitting, stopping and examining everything, every nook and cranny, being all the time conscious of the nagging pain in my side and the heavy weariness. I saw Tigh na hInise, the little fields around it, the Tigh Mór at Gort an Earraigh, the huge cliffs and stones, the little early monastic settlement. The stories were right: there was magic about the place everywhere. Everything about it had its own story and was trying to tell it to him who would take the time and trouble to listen. And yet it is so small, no bigger than an average size farm: "Cuan Farm in the parish of Ventry or Inisvickillane," they used to say.

It hit me suddenly, the knowledge that I had to make some attempt to tell the story of the Inis. It was one hundred years since the Ó Dálaighs had closed the door on Tigh na hInise for the last time and moved over to the Great Blasket. I would have to try and tell their story, the story of those who had lived there, through whom the blood of life had run once, but now were for ever silent. They lived there, falling and rising again, all the time going on to the highest rock, taking the day as it came, fleeing from the shower, laughing and crying, full of love, of hope, of loneliness, of courage and fear. Before I left, I asked the patron of the island, Mocheallóg Mac Uibhleáin, and St Gobnait herself, patron of Dunquin, to give me space to tell their story.

Beannaím duit, a Ghobnait naofa,
Mar a bheannaíonn na naoimh, beannaím féin duit,
Is chughat sa a thánga ag gearán mo scéil leat,
Is ag iarraidh leighis i gcuntais Dé ort.

We started out into the great ocean again. I took one look back at the Inis, bathed in the bright sunlight of summer. Then I saw with my own two eyes an old couple, man and woman of advanced years, she with a shawl and he in his cap and blue jersey, up there on the cliff top waving goodbye to me. I stood up and waved back. It was then I felt the courage and hope surging up in me, and a new thought took hold. I would be granted the time and the opportunity to tell the story of the Inis. With the help of my family, my friends and neighbours, I would win. The cold shivers left me, and I felt the new blood rising to my face. I felt the surge of life and courage come back. I laughed out loud, my first real laugh since spring, when I had received the shock. The seabirds, the sea, the sun all around, and Danny laughed with me. The beginning of health is a laugh. I looked again at the Inis. The old couple had gone, faded away into the island again.

And Danny steered into Tráigh an Loinnithe in Beginis. We landed and drank strong tea on the bare rocks. It was the nicest tea I'd ever tasted.

Enough of that! To work.

* * *

Here is my poor attempt to describe the Inis on paper, immersed as it is in archaeology, history, folklore, stories and music. Hopefully one will come afterwards who will do it more justice than I can. Good luck to him. But at least I've made a start, and every start is weak. Any inaccuracy is purely my fault.

Chapter I

The Devil's Tail

When God created the world he said to the Devil, "What do you think of that?"

"You haven't finished it off yet," says the Devil. "You left it without a tail."

"Sure, I'll leave that much to yourself," says God to him.

And so he did. It was the Devil who made Inisvickillane.

And isn't it easy to see that for yourself.[1]

In the most south-westerly part of Ireland in County Kerry is Corca Dhuibhne, a peninsula stretching from Tralee west some fifty miles beyond Dingle way out to Slea Head and Dunmore, the most westerly point on the mainland of Ireland. Tossed there in the ocean by the hand of the Almighty is a fistful of islands called the Blaskets.

"There is grass growing on seven of these islands," Tomás Ó Criomhthain tells us in *Dinnseanchas na mBlascaod* (1935).[2] The other islands are mostly stones and bare rocks, continually battered by the storms so that scarcely a human foot has ever landed on them.

Five of the Blaskets had human habitation at one time: the Great Blasket, Inisvickillane, Inis Tuaisceart, An Tiaracht and Beginis. The island with the most inhabitants was the Great Blasket itself, with up to two hundred souls during the First World War, a number which declined until 1953, when the last door closed. Next in importance was the island of Inisvickillane, even though it is nine long miles from the mainland and is pretty bare. Still, water is readily available on the Inis and the land is rich. It yielded good crops of oats, cabbage, onions, even tobacco–against the law, to be sure. Potatoes were not so good there. The land was too light and the growth went into the stalk and leaves rather than into the tuber itself. Two hundred sheep could be reared there, fatter and better by far than those on Inis Tuaisceart or the Great Blasket itself. Even the Inis rabbits thrived there and were in great demand when sold in Valentia Island or Caherciveen. It was a great advantage that this island had fresh water. Without it habitation would be impossible.

These are the wells as told by Máire Mhaidhc Léan Ní Ghuithín, whose people were from the Inis:

Tobar na Maighdine
Tobar an tSúil
Tobar na Muice
Tobar na Cárthaí
Tobar Cuas na mBáirneach
Tobar Shéamais Dhonnachú
Tobar Chuas Mhadra
Toibreacha Chuas na nÉan [or, Chuas an Éin][3]

Let's start with the land itself. According to the experts the area due west of the Dingle Peninsula was under water next to a continent whose only remains are to be found near Slea Head. Around 414 million years ago, a massive volcano erupted somewhere near Inisvickillane and lava and ash was spread in an area twelve miles long and four miles wide. This is how Inisvickillane and the Blaskets were formed as well as Ceann Sraithe and the Mionnán Rock in Gráig. The island of Ireland rose up from the sea and the continent sank.

There is something about an island that appeals to us all–an island that is not so big that you would go astray there, still small enough that you would know every bit of it. You could escape into it from life and all its problems. That is, of course, unless you have to live on it, to be marooned there miles from the mainland, completely dependent on your own wits, with all your neighbours and friends far away. There are such islands round the coast of Ireland. One such is a magical faraway island on the coast of Corca Dhuibhne in west Kerry. Huge waves and breakers batter it every day of the year with the incessant cry of the seabirds as they fly overhead.

Inisvickillane is one mile in length and about half a mile in width. It contains 80 hectares (171 acres) and is 120m at its highest point in the middle of the island. The highest point on the Inis is 135.59m above sea level according to the Ordnance Survey. It is fifteen miles south-west of Dingle, nine miles from Dunquin and six miles from the Blasket quay, with two sounds of great strong tides, among the most dangerous in these islands. There are no trees or bushes growing there due to the lack of shelter from the salt-laden air.

Its position is 52 degrees, 2 minutes and 36.56 seconds north latitude and 10 degrees 36 minutes and 14.07 seconds west longitude.

"This island is the most interesting of the Blaskets from the geological point of view. There are many . . . stones there and, more importantly, basalt."[4]

To begin at the beginning–the name. You would imagine that to be simple enough, but in the case of Inisvickillane nothing is simple. The reason for the confusion is that some of the names stretch back near enough to two thousand years. Here is a list of some of the names it has been known by down through the years and how they were written down:

Inis Mhic Aoibhleáin, the official name in Irish
Inis Icealáin (Maurice Mhuiris) in the local speech
Inisícealáin (*Twenty Years A-Growing*, 1933).
Inisicíleáin (Robin Flower)
Inis 'ic Ileáin
Inismhicealáin
Inis Mhicealáin
Inis Ícíleáin
Inis Mhic Uileáin
Inis Mhic Uíleáin
Inis Mhic Uíbhleáin
Inis Mhic Uibhleáin
Inis Mhic Fhaoláin
Inis Mhic Fhaoileáin
Inis na Cillain (Macalister)
Inis Mhic Choileáin
Inis Mic Cillan (Ordnance Survey)
Innis
An Inis
Inniscollane (Windele, 1838)
Innis Makilaan (Whittle and Laurie's Map of Ireland, 1817)
Innishvicillane
Inish Vicillane
Inis-Mac-Keilane (Charles Smith, 1756)
Hynchemacyvelan (Registration Book, St John's Hospital)
Inish Mackillan (Petrie)
Innis Vick Killane (Kruger)
Deálaí's Island (in Uíbh Ráthach)
Oileán Dálaigh (the fishermen)
Inis Haughey
Oileán Charlie
Inisvickillane
An Chloch, and others . . .

15

After all that, it seems that the correct form is the basic Inis Mhic Uibhleáin. It is so described by Seán Ó Cinnéide in *Oidhreacht an Bhlascaoid*[5] and by Seán Ó Coileáin in the latest edition of *An tOileánach* (The Islandman). The official English version as on the latest Ordnance Survey map is Inisvickillane.

An Seabhac says: "The speech of the people–'Inis mhic-il-eáin,' with the emphasis on the vowel on the 'áin.' It is their opinion that it is 'mac Fhaoláin' or 'mac an Oileáin' that forms the second part of the name, but there is no way to certify that now."[6]

But then Seán Ó Cinnéide maintains that *"inis-ic-uíleáin,"* or, *"inis-ic íleáin,"* is the usual pronunciation by the Island people themselves and that it is thus pronounced by them in the documentary film, *Oileán Eile*, produced by Muiris Mac Conghail.[7] (This was the version accepted by the late Dr Pádraig Ua Maoileoin).

Although there are Inis Tuaisceart, Beginis and Inis na Bró, still if the Inis is mentioned in conversation, it is accepted that the reference is to Inisvickillane, as in *"Tá sé istigh san Inis."* (He is in the Inis.) That is: "He is in Inisvickillane."

Mocheallóg Mac Uibhleáin

Now the meaning of the name itself, and there are many versions of it. Does the word *beag* (small) have any bearing on it, e.g. *An Inis Bheag* (The Small Island). We must also consider Micil or Mícheál. There is an old Celtic tradition of naming high places after Saint Michael, Archangel, for example: Mont San Michel in Brittany; St Michael's Mount in Cornwall; San Michele in Italy and our own Skellig Michael. When place names and their meanings were first studied in the nineteenth century, it was common to use the simplest place name. With regard to Inisvickillane, it is beyond dispute, at this stage, that Inisvickillane derives its name from a saint of Corca Dhuibhne stock named Mocheallóg Mac Uibhleáin. It was he who established the monastery on the Inis and he may be buried there under the Leacht, which was the usual honoured spot reserved for the founder.

To get some idea of Mocheallóg we must go back many years, right back to the fourth or fifth century AD, even before Patrick came to our shores. The territory of Corca Dhuibhne then contained, as well as the peninsula, a portion that stretched across Dingle Bay to include a good part of the next southern peninsula of Uíbh Ráthach. To the north of Corca Dhuibhne around Tralee Bay and the coast of what is now north Kerry lay the territory of the Uí Fheabhra of the Alltraí tribe. Another tribe, the

16

Ciarraí Luachra, held possession of Sliabh Luachra, and the Eonacht held sway around what is now Killarney. The Corca Dhuibhne tribe had its own saints, holding them in high honour and esteem, among whom were Maolchéadair, Gobnait, Flann, Erc, Cuán, Fionntain and Mocheallóg Mac Uibhleáin. Very little is known about any of them today, but they were of great importance in the immediate locality in those early times. Seán Ó Cinnéide tells us of Mocheallóg's existence: "Inis Mór or the Western Island has achieved great, well deserved notoriety, but I really think that Inisvickillane was once held in even greater regard in the south of Ireland. We cannot say much about it now except that it was named from a Corca Dhuibhne saint, i.e. Mocheallóg Mac Uibhleáin."[8]

He goes on to say that Mocheallóg, one of the patron saints of Corca Dhuibhne, may have lived around the year 600 AD, though he may have been there even earlier, before St Patrick himself. There is a tradition that the area was Christianised before that bishop arrived. The feast day of Mocheallóg is given as 26 March.

According to the old manuscripts Mocheallóg, who was a monk in the early Christian tradition, had a number of foundations, the principal being on an island named Inis Labhrainne. Neither the site nor even the name any longer exists. It is mentioned in an early verse which describes the destruction wreaked by the Vikings on the principal monasteries of Ireland:

Inis Labhrainne ina liad
Ros Ailithir róairgseadh
Lios Mór gan cráifeach gan chrois
Imleach gan eaglais.

In it Mocheallóg Mac Uibhleáin is mentioned as the head of *wild* Inis Labhrainne, being among the most important monasteries in Munster.

It is said that it was one of the monks of Inis Labhrainne who first put to paper the saga of the Battle of Ventry (*Cath Fionn Trá*).

Inisvickillane is not mentioned in any other manuscript. But where was Inis Labhrainne?

Some of the authorities think Abhainn na Labhrainne was the old name for the small River Imileach that runs from the Slieve at the bottom of Caherconree, close to Mám na hAltóra, running into the sea at Inch, four miles east of Annascaul. It seems that there was an island at Inch beach, or that the beach itself was an island until late medieval times. Part of the sand dunes is still called *Oileán Inse,* or Inch Island. The island is marked on

17

some of the first very early maps of the area. Both Breandán Ó Ciobháin and Seán Ó Cinnéide, who have carried out extensive studies, are of the opinion that it was here, at Inis Labhrainne, that the monastery of Mocheallóg was situated. *An Seabhac* thinks that the monastery was situated at nearby Cathair an Chruitire, another early monastic site near the same Inch beach. Some of the authorities even think that Inis Labhrainne is an earlier name for Inisvickillane itself, and that it was on the Inis that Mocheallóg had his chief foundation. A peculiar aspect of the question is that the Blasket Islands and the Inch beach area seem to be linked together parochially going back many years. The Blaskets and Fahan, across the Sound at Slea Head, and Inch are part of the old parish of Baile an Bhóthair, and existed as such right up to the nineteenth century, although they are separated by up to twenty miles. It may be that the connection goes way back to pre-Norman times to the time of Mocheallóg himself.

Charles Smith (1756) writes: ". . . they [the Blasket people] pay tithes to a very distant parish called Ballinvohir."[9] until 1200–1220 AD. Thus:

Sciant (&c.) ego Ada Dandno dedi (&c.) Hospitali sancti Johannis extra Novam Portam Dublinie, fratribus & sororibus ibidem deo servientibus, pro animabus patris et matris mee & Agnetis condam uxoris mee & pro animabus omnium parentum meorum, tam predecessorum quam successorum, unam marcam argenti de redditu quam Ricardus de Marisc(o) mihi debet annuatim de Insula de Hynchemacyuelan ad duos terminos anni, scilicet ad Pascha dimidiam marcam & ad festum sancti Michaelis dimidiam marcam. Habendam & tenendam sibi libere & quiete in puram & perpetuam elemosinam in de Mar(isco), Gilberto Cum(in) clerico, Johannes de Cusinktun' clerico, Thomas Dandno, Nicholao Dandno, Willelmo de Workeshale & multis allis. (1200–1220).[10]

Dandno, a Norman, tells us in this Latin document that he bestows a silver mark, the yearly rent of Inisvickillane due to him annually from Richard de Marisco, on the Hospital of St John the Baptist, without the New Gate in Dublin, for the soul of his father and mother and all his family, the money to be paid at Easter and at the Feast of St Michael. The Hospital of the Priory of St John the Baptist was the first public hospital (in the modern rather than monastic sense) in Dublin, in St Thomas's Street, and the name still exists in St John's Lane Church, the name of the Augustinian Church on the site.

When the Normans took over the area, the lands on the very west part of Corca Dhuibhne were granted to Geoffrey de Marisco, nephew of

Strongbow himself, and then passed on to his son Robert, and through him to other Normans, including Dandno, and eventually settled with the Fitzgeralds, who leased out the Blaskets to the Ferriters.

So this way-out island was in the possession of Dandno, and was of value to him. It is thought that the monies came from the pilgrims' fees on their visits to the Inis, which was a pilgrimage centre. Such fees proved to be a valuable source of finance from visitors. Some came seeking cures or performing penances to seek God's forgiveness for their sins, while others were just medieval tourists out to see the world. And there were many tricks to part the pilgrim from his money, from boat fees to lodging fees to the sale of badges to hang around the neck to proclaim to the world that you had performed the pilgrimage, as well as fees for confessions, pardons and indulgences to shorten your stay in Purgatory. It illustrates the importance of the Inis, even after the arrival of the Normans, that the people continued to visit it and that the Normans thought it worthwhile to have possession. Indeed, according to Professor Peter Harbison, it would seem that the whole of Corca Dhuibhne was one huge pilgrimage area stretching by sea from the Skelligs to Illaunloughan to Inisvickillane to Ventry Harbour. There the boat was left and the rest of the pilgrimage performed by foot or on horseback on Casán na Naomh (the Saint Road) by Kilcolman and Kilmalkedar, right to the great terminus on Mount Brandon.

As *An Seabhac* writes: "It would seem that the Inis was a pilgrim island in the old days and that was enough to attract the attention of the Normans to Inis Mhic Uibhleáin as far back as 1200 AD."[10]

It is certain that the Vikings made attacks on the Inis as they did on the other surrounding islands from around 800 to 1000 AD. It is mentioned in *Cogadh Gael le Gaillibh* that they laid waste the sister monastery, Inis Labhrainne, as well as Valentia and the Skelligs as early as 810 AD. They didn't get away scot free, however, because it was reported that on one occasion they left more than 400 dead on the battle site. They did leave their mark on the complete area, even extending to the place names, and the name Blaskets itself is believed to derive from the Viking language, meaning shell. The name of another of the Blasket Islands, *Inis Tuaisceart*, may also derive from the family name Oscar, as in Tuscar Rock. We also have the name Smerwick, meaning the Butter Harbour, where the Vikings made frequent stops to rub butter into their boats. It was Brian Boru that put a stop to them in the year 1014 at Clontarf, and those Vikings who didn't flee settled down and remained law abiding, so much so that many of the monasteries came to flower again, including Inisvickillane.

Chapter II

Place Names

The first source we have for the Inis place names is from John Ganley, who was sent there in 1840 to prepare an account of the island for the Ordnance Survey. He states in a letter to G.A. Leask in Dublin dated 13 October 1845: "The correct names of the rocks are now marked on the sheets on the authority of the person who has charge of the Island. He was not able to give me their meaning in English, but he has always heard them called so from his infancy." It was either Seán a' Mhúraigh Ó Guithín or his father Tadhg who gave Ganley this information.

But when it comes to the Inis and any of the Blaskets, the master of them all as regards information is Tomás Ó Criomhthain (Crohan). He deals with the last half of the nineteenth century and the first quarter of the twentieth, when he flourished himself and was a frequent visitor to the Inis. His collection is to be found in *Dinnsheanchas na mBlascaod*, first published in 1935, reissued in 1999.

Another rich source is to be found among the pages of *Fiche Bliain ag Fás*, or *Twenty Years a Growing* (1933), by Muiris Ó Súilleabháin (O'Sullivan). Muiris, however, is not always exact in his information, being more of a storyteller than a historian.

Another valuable source is *An Seabhac's Triocha-céad Chorca Dhuibhne* (1939), of which he says as regards the Inis place names: "Seán Ó Criomhthain and Dálach of the Inis came to my assistance as well as Seosamh Ó Dálaigh, Dunquin."

A later source for place names is a map of Inisvickillane published in 1984. Eoghan Ó Riagáin prepared the map, Charles J. Haughey collected the names from the Ó Dálaighs, Tom and Paddy, and Éamonn Ó hÓgáin edited the work. The great advantage of this map is that both names and locations are included, though a greater number of names would have been welcome.

Another valuable source is *Ar Muir is ar Tír* (1991), by Muiris Ó Catháin (Keane). Muiris and Paddy na hInise were contemporaries and friends on sea and land. Muiris, who was from the Great Blasket, was often on the Inis with Paddy na hInise, hunting or fishing, and mentions many of the place names.

A number of articles by Seán Ó Cinnéide, as stated in the list of sources, the last of which, *Logainmneacha*, was published in *An Caomhnóir*, December 2005, contain valuable information on the place names of the Inis.

The most direct contact with the Inis and the names was provided again by Muiris Mhaidhc Léan Ó Guithín, RIP.

Apart from the name Inisvickillane itself, there are many place names throughout the island that make a wonderful collection in a place so small. Some of the names are so ancient that we can only hazard a guess as to their meaning. Some other names date back to the settlement of the Guiheens and the Ó Dálaighs and others in the early nineteenth century, while a few of them are of more recent vintage. The great number of names show the love, the familiarity and the connection the people who lived there had for the Inis, and the intimate knowledge they had of every nook and cranny, every fence and stone, so much so that they almost became extensions of themselves.

So, we will begin in the north-west corner of the Inis, close to Inis na Bró.

An Mharcaíocht: A sharp headland jutting out to the north-east into the *Bealach Caol* (Narrow Strait). The meaning of the name is not known.

Cuas na Marcaíochta: A cove close to it to the east.

An Léitheach/An Léithreach/An Léirtheach: Another headland to the east of an Mharcaíocht. Also known as *An Léithligh*.[1] Meaning is not certain, though one of the meanings given is "steady," according to Tomás Ó Criomhthain.[2]

Cuas na Léitheach, or, *Na Léithreach*: The creek to the west.

An Rinn Chaoil (The Narrow Point): The small headland close to the strand, the landing place for the Inis.

Cuaisín na mBáirneach: A short distance to the east of the strand. From here people could collect beach food and shellfish. The Cove of the Limpets.

Cuas na Bó: The Creek of the Cow, probably the female seal.

Cuas Hannraí: Henry's Creek. No account of who Henry was.

Cuas Bhun na Steipe: The Creek at the End of the Step.

An Cuas Dubh: The Black Creek. There are four creeks here in the cliffs east of the little beach.

An Cárthach: An ancient word, with various explanations, maybe from "*Cáth*" meaning "chaff," as winnowing was done here.

Dún Scilín Rua and *Dún Scilín*: Two headlands that project into the sea to the north-east of the side of the Inis. There is no account of either. *Dún* is fort, but there is no account of *Scilín*. This is a spur that runs out from the Inis a little. Grass flourishes there because there is no way to cut it. Seabirds land there all the year round, and when the time comes they build their nests and lay their eggs there.

An Cuas Nua: The New Creek. To the south-east of Dún Scilín. In the old days, boats used to race to here. In more recent times, the seals have decided to set up and give birth here, and that's why it got that name.

Fód an Fhiolair: The Eagle's Sod, or Place. A name from the time when the eagle had a nest in the Inis, up to about 1890, according to Thomas F. O'Sullivan: "A pair of eagles nested on Inistooskert up to seventy years ago, when a man named Pádraig Ó Catháin succeeded, at great risk to himself, in reaching the eyrie, and in bringing away three eaglets, which he sold for £1 each."

In 1870 a pair of white-tailed eagles used to breed on the Great Blasket, but they had ceased to do so in the next decade.

The last eagle was seen on the Islands about forty years ago.

In 1888, the late Dr Kane, Annascaul, wrote in reference to the Golden Eagle:

> *A few years since the bird could be seen in every mountain range in the locality. In my shooting excursions, I have seen twelve in a day. Their nests were made in a very high cliff overlooking a mountain lake. They bred there for years within recollection. This year (1900) a pair returned to their former breeding ground.*

Cuas an Droichid and *Mionnán Chuas an Droichid*: The Bridge Creek. This is a fine cove for seals, which used to be killed and eaten. Tomás says, "It's often I ate seal taken from here, caught by my own father. The seals are still there, but no one bothers them today." To the east of the cove is the Mionnán, i.e. cliff rock, or crown.

An Uille Gharbh: The Rough Angle. It is incorrectly named Illaungarriff rather than Uillegarriff on the Ordnance Survey map. It's here the eagle made his nest for generations, but for years now there is neither nest nor eagle. "I do not remember," says Tomás, born 1856, "ever seeing an eagle either in the air or on land."

Speir na hUilleann Gairbhe: Part of the cliff and a small headland. The *Speir*, or "Spur", is the farthest point east of the Inis.

Na Fir Ghorma: The Black Men or The Blue Men. Three stacks out in the sea. Dark blue moss grows on them, because the sea almost covers them completely in the winter, so they remain dark blue, from which they get their name. They have the same appearance as each other, so one would think they were three men standing on board a ship.

An Cuas Fliuch: The Wet Cove, from the continuous rush of water that enters and exits there all the year. Very difficult for the swimmer that enters in pursuit of the seals.

Mionnán an Chuasa Fhliuch: A rock outside the *Cuas Fliuch*.

Bas an Chuasa Fhlich: Part of the cliff rock between *Cuas Fliuch* and *Cuas an Éin*. *Bas* means "the palm of the hand." The stone is like a palm.

Com na bPortán: The Glen of the Crab. *Com* is a valley with a recess, i.e. comes to an end. The English word is "Combe."

An Poll Garbh: The Rough Hole. Two creeks south of *Speir*.

Mionnán Lic Bhuí: The Crown of the Yellow Flagstone.

A rock in the sea on the east side of the Inis. Marked "Minnaun Rock" on Ordnance map. *Mionnán* can mean a rock, but can also mean a crown, e.g., *Mionnán na Gráige* looks like a king's crown.

Leac na bhFiach: The Flagstone of the Shag, to the south of the Mionnán. *Fiach*, or *Fiach Mara*, is a shag, from their landing on it. Also as in *An Fiach* and *Máthair an Fhiaigh*, close to Sybil Head.

Cuas an Éin and *Rinn Chuas an Éin*: The Cove of the Young Seal.

The Rinn is the point farthest south in the Inis. The cove is alongside on the east side of it. It is the best place in the Inis for seals. There is a large pebble beach there, and the water seldom goes that far to it. Seals used to be drawn out of it with ropes to the land above, a very difficult task. *Éan* is the word for a "young seal."[3]

An Tóirneach: Thunder Rock. The largest rock in the sea on the south side of the Inis. It is named Thunder Rock on the Ordnance map, a name that was never heard in the area. *Tóirneach* = thunder.

Bealach na Tóirní: Thunder Sound. The strait between Rinn Chuas an Éin and the Tóirneach.

Mionnán na Tóirní: The Crown of Thunder.

Poll na Tóirní: A rock beside the Tóirneach a little out to sea. There is a large hole right through it, which is said to have been caused by thunder and so the hole is called *Poll na Tóirní*. Birds congregate on this rock, and on a sunny day you wouldn't be able to count the number of seals sleeping there. Very often the islanders used to surprise and kill them while they were sleeping.[4]

Uamhain na gCeannaí: This creek is broad on its inside. There are caves here and there inside in it, so many that the seals can hide in them and not be discovered. So the place is called the Caves. Seals can be drawn out with ropes from the land. The significance of *Ceannaí* is not understood.

An Muilcheann Beag and *An Muilcheann Mór*: Two rocks a short distance east of the *Tóirneach*. They are called Milkaunmore and Milkaunbeg on the Ordnance map. Probably named from *maol* = bald.[5]

Dún na Geannaí: A small headland. The meaning is unknown.

Rinn Sheáin 'ic Éamainn: The Point of Seán 'ic Éamainn. This headland goes down to the water. It is named from Seán Mac Éamainn, who had a mishap here when a stone from a rabbit warren fell on him, or so Tomás thinks.[6]

Mionnán na Ladhaire: This is a rock with two flagstones rising out of it like two branches from a tree. *Ladhar* can mean a fork where two branches meet.[7]

An Gleann Briste and *Mionnán an Ghleanna Bhriste*: The Broken Glenn, and the Rock of the Broken Glenn. This is a creek called the Glen and a rock outside it called the *Mionnán*, a thick high stack.

Mící the Peeler: A stack in the cliff in the shape of a person wearing a policeman's cap, and it was from the cap that it got the name. "Peeler" was a nickname for a policeman in the nineteenth century, so named from the founder of the police, Robert Peel. It may also mean Mící the Pillar. The only fully English name on the Inis.

An Cuas Dóite: The Burnt Creek. Probably used to be set on fire early on in the year.

Daingean Uí Mhuirchearta: Moriarty's Fort. A headland between *Cuas Dóite* and *Cuas Dóite na bhFaoileann Beag*. It is not a fort, but it may be named from one of the Moriarties of Dingle who were part owners of the Inis at the beginning of the last century. A ferret belonging to Moriarty went into the rabbit burrow but never emerged, and so gave it the name.

Cuas Dóite na bhFaoileann Beag: The Burnt Creek of the Kittiwakes.

Speir Rinn na bhFaoileann and *Rinn na bhFaoileann*: The Point of the Gulls. A headland by the cliff. The eastern point of the headland is the *Speir*. *Speir* = spur of rock. A good stop for the sea birds during bad weather, or any time their bellies are full.

Cuas a' Mhadra and *Speir Chuas a' Mhadra*: The Dog's Creek. A dog was chasing a rabbit. The rabbit made for the creek, but the dog jumped at him and held him in his jaws, and they both fell to their deaths into the sea.

Cuas Mhuiris 'ic Aonghais: Muiris 'ic Aonghais' Creek. Muiris fell to his death here.

Cladach Mhuiris 'ic Aonghais: At the bottom of the creek, and, *Oileán Chladach Mhuiris 'ic Aonghais*: at its mouth.

Cuas a' Chaipín: The Cove of the Cap.

Faill na gCalaidhe: A creek that is cut well into the land. There may have been a landing place here.

Mionnán Fhaill na gCalaidhe: At the end of the headland between *Cuas Fhaill na gCailidhe* and *Cuas a' Tarraic*.

Cuas a' Tarraic or *Cuas a' Tarraig*: *Tarrac* = tarrang, small rough waves that break in over the rocks.

Spur Chuas a' Tarraic: A rocky headland to the west of Cuas a' Tarraic.

Cuas na Rón: Seal Cove. On the western side of the Spur.

Oileán na Leamhan, *Raca Oileán na Leamhan*, and *Fochais Oileán na Leamhan*: These are rocks west of the Spur. Inishvickillane Rocks on the Ordnance map. *Oileán na Leamhan* means the island of moths or butterflies, and though it is a very bleak spot for moths, it seems that they are found there. There is one species of moth that can be had on the Inis and the Tiaracht called the Yellow Shell Moth, *Camptogramma bilineata isolata* (Kane). Usually this moth is yellow and is to be found on the west coast of Ireland and Scotland, but there is a particular dark brown type that can only be found on these two Blaskets. Kane first noticed them around 1893 on the Tiaracht and J.E. Flynn discovered the same moth in Inisvickillane in the year 1953. According to Henry Huggins, 19 of them were seen and 9 were caught on the Inis between 1961 and 1964.[8] Muiris O'Sullivan in *Twenty Years a-Growing* calls this rock *Oileán na Leann*, which could mean the Island of Beer, aptly named as Muiris Mór Ó Dálaigh found a barrel of rum there once.

Seán Sheáin Í Chearnaigh tells us: "That is on the west side of the Inis. It is full of holes and they are not moth holes, the sea can be heard flowing through these holes on a fine night."[9]

This place is also well known for seagulls' eggs according to Muiris Mhaidhc Léan Ó Guithín.

Cuas na nGabhar: The Creek of the Goats. A little north of *Oileán na Leamhan*.

An Banc Fiain: The Wild Bank. A great fishing bank at the mouth of Dingle Bay, east and south of *Na Feoibh*.

Tóin na hAirne: At the north end of the Inis. *Ára* means kidney (plural *airne*), but it is very doubtful if that is the meaning here. It is part of the Inis that is separated from the rest of the island. There are also small lumps here like sea pink clumps that may be compared to the kidneys, another possibility. Seán Ó Cinnéide thinks that perhaps *Ára(inn)* like in the Aran Islands in Galway and Donegal may have been a previous name for the Inis before it was named from Mocheallóg.[10]

Cuas Thóin na hAirne: In this creek a female seal once spoke to a man who was just about to kill her. She had just returned from the sea and was nurturing her young. "Ah, don't kill me yet until the little one has drank his fill." But the man would not listen and killed her immediately. No sooner had he done this than the sea rose in a swell, and he remained there himself as he was unable to swim.

Inisvickillane harbour/Inisvickillane beach: This harbour is three and a half miles from the most western point of the Blasket known as *Ceann Dubh* or *Béal Capaill*. This harbour is a beach: this place is not safe in the depths of winter.[11]

Leac na Roilleog: Here is a nice description of this place written by Seán Sheáin Í Chearnaigh after he paid a visit to Inisvickillane:

> The beach was full of seals and they looked for all the world like soldiers drilling. There were big and small seals and a few bull seals amongst them looking like officers with their heads in the air keeping an eye out for the others. When they heard us coming towards the beach, they headed for the water, sending spray up over the Inis and squealing like the old witches long ago . . . We landed Paddy on Leac na Roilleog and he killed a big fat seal. He wasn't an old seal but a yearling seal. There were thousands of them around, and we remarked that it was easily known the islanders had left as otherwise they wouldn't be as abundant.

Poll na Mine/Poll na Mine Buí: This was used as a storage place by the Inis family and sometimes a man might sleep here. Seán Sheáin Í Chearnaigh again:

> "We beached the *naomhóg* and brought some of our goods over to Poll na Mine Buí. This is where the hunters kept their store of maize meal in the old days. The little house is about a half mile from this place."[12]

An Fhaill Ghlas: The Green Cliff. A great high cliff above the *caladh*. Large stones and rocks fall down very often. They often used to break and damage the boats below, and the people also, if they were in the wrong place. There is a long difficult climb to the top.

An Rinn Chaol: The Narrow Headland. This is on the outside of the strand. If the boats are unable to land the people on the strand, they attempt to land them at this spot. The Léirtheach is outside it.

Log na bhFiolar: The Dip of the Eagles. It is in the centre of the western half of the Inis. Eagles used to land there and there was often someone waiting in hiding to try and capture them.

Cnocán na Tine: The Hill of Fire, above *Cuas Dubh*. Not far from the old house, on the edge of the cliff facing the Great Blasket.

An Steip: The Step. A small shoulder runs out on this hill, which is called the Step. The strand cannot be seen from the house, so any time they need to know what is happening on the strand, someone says, "Go on the Step." Then there will be news immediately from the strand to the Step and from there to the house.[13]

Fód Sheáin Liam: Seán Liam's Sod. *Fód* can mean the place where you meet your end, and that is how it got the name.

Garraí na Cárthaí: Two little fields above the cliff just over the Cárthach on the north side of the Inis.

Barra na Mionnán: The top of the cliffs on the east side of the Inis.

There are some fields in the centre of the Inis in which crops grew when people lived there. There are names on them still:

Páirc an Earraigh: The Spring Field, because it was the first field to be sown in the spring. A fine field. There was always something growing there.

Cúlóg a' Ghréithre: Meaning forgotten.

Garraí Sheáin Uí Ghuithín: Seán Ó Guithín's Garden. Seán Ó Guithín's Garden, and it was he who broke it. It was probably Seán Mhuiris Liam Ó Guithín.

Gort na bPléar or Gort na bPiléar: The Field of the Bullets. In this field the well-off people used to practise gunfire after dinner, firing at small targets to see who had the best shot. The Inis and the seas around it were a favourite playground for Lord Ventry and his friends in the nineteenth century, as evidenced by C.P. Crane, the Kerry magistrate, about 1880:

> *A trip to the Blaskets was always looked forward to with the greatest pleasure. The bird life was exceedingly interesting, for on these islands could be seen the puffins in large numbers and the "Mother Carey's Chickens" [petrels] nested in the holes under the rocks.*

And again he describes the sport:

> *Days of sailing and shooting and pollack-fishing followed, and then a trip to the Blasquet Islands to shoot rabbits . . .*

27

We soon came to an anchorage between Inishvickillane and Inishnabro islands, and, rolling ourselves in blankets lay down in the little cabin of the "Mask." The slight roll of the boat and the lapping of the waves on her sides soon lulled us to sleep.

At about 3 A.M. there was a change and evidently a great swell outside. I felt myself occasionally at an angle of 40 degrees in one direction and about 40 in the other immediately after. However, I jammed my back against the side and fell asleep once more until 5 A.M., when F. de M. (Frederick de Moleyns, afterwards Lord Ventry) awoke me and told me it was time to go ashore.

We were broadside to a very heavy swell; nasty squalls were coming off the islands, the sky had a dirty appearance, there was "white water" in the bay and high waves oceanwards dashing on the cliffs of Inishvickillane. We landed, however on Inishnabro and shot and ferreted some sixteen rabbits, during which I shot very badly (finding all the rabbits going up and down with the heave of the sea) and got very hungry, we returned to the "Mask" for breakfast.[14]

Gort Beag an Lín: The Little Flax Field. Flax grew on the Inis also. It was extensively grown in the area during the eighteenth century and used for making sails.

Gort Mór an Lín: The Big Flax Field. It was said to be the finest flax field in the whole of Corca Dhuibhne.

Garraí an Scaibí: The Scabies Field. A disease that comes on sheep is called the scabies. Perhaps sheep who contracted the disease were penned off here to avoid spreading it.

Dhá Gharraí Challair or *Garraí Chollier/Dhá Gharraí Challair*: Collier's Two Gardens. George Collier, from Dingle, had the Inis for some time along with Michael T. Moriarty from Dingle. They had sheep and dry stock on the Inis.

Garraí na nGamhan: The Calves' Garden.

An Loc: The Dip. A low-lying garden, often used for penning sheep for dosing and shearing.

Garraí an Ghabáiste: The Cabbage Garden.

An Caraball: The Great Rock.

Garraí Bholláin an tSeithe: "The Garden of the Standing Stone of the Skin." In front of the house is this standing stone on the south side. The skin of an old cow was placed on top of the stone, where it remained for a long time drying in the sun because there was not a grain of salt in the Inis to cure it. Hence the name.[15]

Garraí na Cárthaí: Everything that needed winnowing or threshing was brought here for that purpose. It is a fine open windy place.

Cúlóg (an) Ghriaire: A man named Gregory spent some time in the Inis, and he reclaimed this little field.

Garraí an Stáca: In this garden was stored the hay, the oats and the turnips. It was close to the house.

Gort an tSíthigh: Sheehy's Field. He spent some of his life on the Inis and broke in this field. A Brian Sheehy is mentioned as living on the Inis at an early date.

An Móinéar: The Meadow. A great field for grass always.

Garraí na Champions: This is not the ancient name of this garden, but was named so when the "champions" (a type of potato) arrived and were sown in this garden. They were later called *seaimpíní* in Irish and were introduced in the year 1880 as the old seed had weakened. Ballads were composed to mark their introduction, such as "When the Champions Grow."[16]

An Gort Caol: The Narrow Field.

Béal na Lice: The Mouth of the Flagstone. This is at the top of this field. There is a cave under it, and it is never wet there.

Garraí na Mearbals: The Marbles Field. From the English word marbles, the small flat stones that can be found here in small heaps date back to the time the field was taken in.

Garraí an Tobac: The Tobacco Field. Tobacco used to grow in this field as good as could be found in Ireland, very handy during the winter months when it was in short supply and difficult to get.

Gort Dhiarmada: Diarmaid's Field. We don't know who he was.

Garraí na nOinniún: The Onion Field. Onions grew wonderfully in this field and were always sown here.

Gort na nGamhan: The Calf Field. Calves were kept here.

Garraí Loc an Gheamhra: The Green Corn Field. Rich green grass grows here every time of the year. *Geamhair* means fresh green corn in the early stages of growth.

An Gort Fliuch: The Wet Field. There is always water breaking out here. Seldom was anything sown in it as it was too soft.

An Chladach Bhuí: The Yellow Strand.

Tobar na Cárthaí: Cárthach Well. It is not difficult to get to this well down in *Faill na Cárthaí*. It is not sure where the name comes from, ranging from the possibility of there being a Saint Cárthach to it being an ancient word for a whore, to balance out Tobar na Maighdine, the Virgin's Well. It is worth noting that Tobar na Cárthaí never goes dry, unlike Tobar na Maighdine.[17]

Seán Sheáin Í Chearnaigh describes Tobar na Maighdine and Tobar na Cárthaí during a visit to the Inis with Pádraig Ó Braonáin, Paddy Mhicil Ó Súilleabháin and Paddy Beag Ó Dálaigh:

> Myself and Paddy Beag brought them back to Tobar na Maighdine (visitors from England) and they filled the big barrel with water . . . There is another well west of it called An tSrúill, but the best drinking water is found in Tobar na Maighdine. The old people used to say there was another well on the other side of An tSrúill long ago, but a woman washed some clothes there and the well had moved in the morning. That well is now down in An Chárthach in a big huge cliff. It is nearly impossible to get to it. You'd need to be a goat. I've often been there, but then Islanders are like goats when it comes to cliffs.[18]

Poll na Ré/Poll Ghrey: An interesting name, maybe from *Ré*–the moon–as explained by Muiris in *Twenty Years a Growing:*

> Indeed, Pádraig, why is that hole called the Hole of the Moon? I'll tell you why, says Pádraig, gazing into the hole; do you see the way the hole is turned to the south east?–I do, says I.–Well, says he, there is no other hole on the Inis that is turned in that direction, and on that account, when the moon is rising above the mountains of Uíbh Ráthach, it casts a fine light right through that hole, and that is why it is called Poll na Ré.[19]

But there may also be a second explanation, equally interesting, to be seen in a letter from George Thompson, Muiris's friend:

> You will remember Poll na Ré, so called, according to Maurice, because the full moon shines straight through it. (P. 62). But there was another version according to Tomás, son of Pádraig Ó Dála, the name was not Poll na Ré, but Poll Ghrey, referring to Mr. Grey, an Englishman who once visited the Inis.[20]

It would seem a distinct possibility that this is the Mr Grey mentioned as giving the shed to the Ó Dálaighs, especially as there were very few other visitors to the Inis at that time. We know nothing more about Mr Grey. Perhaps he had a special interest in seals or seabirds and watched them from this hole, thus giving it the name, which is worth remembering.

Chapter III

"There Lie Buried Holy Men"

Inisvickillane is a very fine island. It is six miles from the quay on the Great Blasket. There is a graveyard there with five graves where people are buried. There was a chapel there and the ruins are still to be seen. It is said that St Brendan was there and that eleven families lived there once. There was a mother and child living in one of the houses. The wind blew down the house and they were killed inside and they are buried in the graveyard there.[1]

You can see Inisvickillane from the Conor Pass Road coming into Dingle, and it can also be seen from Inch strand on the road to Killarney. If you look at it on the map, it would remind you of a puck goat lying down, with a mile between his tail and his chin. It is a lonely island where the silence speaks loudly. Yet it is the richest of the Blaskets, with good land for sheep and crops, plenty of turf for fuel and rich fishing grounds all around it. The climate is soft and kind, if very wild. Often the bad weather passes over, and the heavy clouds do not release their load until they hit the mountains of Mount Eagle or Márthain. It was those advantages that drew people to live there for many years.

We know nothing of those who first settled there. They have left no word after them, but they did leave remains in their wake that make it well worth our while to examine them to find out something about those people.

The most ancient relic on the Inis is the Dún, the promontory fort. It can scarcely be seen, but the fortification ditch crossing from one side of the Inis to the other at its narrowest point can be made out. There are many dúns such as this around Corca Dhuibhne, but this one, along with Dún Laoi in Inis na Bró close by, are among the most westerly examples in Europe. It is a very big dún. It is not certain what function they filled, but there are two possibilities. The first is military: that they were defensive fortifications against an enemy who might invade from the sea; or else that they might have been erected to provide a foothold for an invading force; or even that they might have been erected to provide a lastditch stand for those who were being driven out of their land into the sea. Others say they have no military significance at all but were purely of ceremonial and

31

religious importance to the people of the time, and that they were never occupied. It is even unsure as to when they were built, with dates varying from around 500 BC to 400 AD or even later. We do not know either if there was permanent occupation on the Inis at the time of the Dún. The first permanent type of occupation that we are sure of was that of the monastic settlement of early Christian times.

Charles Smith, writing some time before 1756, says:

> There stands in it, the ruins of an ancient chapel, in which an old stone chalice, and a baptismal font also of stone still remain; likewise a small cell or hermitage, being an arch of stone neatly put together without any mortar or cement, which admits no rain through its roof. There is one of the same kind at Fane in Ventry parish, in a ruinous condition, and another entire one at Gallerus . . .[2]

It was these holy people who left the most lasting mark on the Inis. It is difficult for us to imagine the reason why they picked out this lonely spot for their monastery. It must have been difficult to live there. Though not as high or as difficult to access as the Skellig, it must have been difficult to sail there in the frail, skin-covered craft of those times, and to land, especially in rough seas. But there was something there they needed: its removal from the hustle and bustle of everyday life. They sought the quiet spots that they might concentrate exclusively on getting to know the Creator without any obstacle between them and Him. The Inis was just right for that, as were the other islands on the south and south-west coast, islands like the Skelligs, Illeanloughan, Church Island, Inis Tuaisceart and Illauntannig. You could live there: the basic necessities could be procured. There was nourishment for animals and the fruit of the sea, the air, the land and a patch for vegetables and crops–enough to get by. It is probable, even, that the land was not as fertile as it later was, but became thus through the dedicated labour of the monks down through the years, drawing seaweed, draining and making trenches and terraces, and softening the soil through cultivation. Monks can afford to think in long terms. If you fall in the field, another monk will take your place. It is likely also that the monks pressed some of the pilgrims into work, in particular those who had insufficient money to pay for their stay.

So, it provided the basics, and there could be complete communication with God the Creator. They could give their lives over entirely to the love of God, the greatest source of satisfaction in life. They could adore him through his wonderful messengers: the sea, the wind, the islands, the fish, the animals and the birds; and even the difficult things like the fog, the storm and the continual rain. Indeed, it may have been that there was a confederacy between all the small island monasteries, stretching from the Skelligs west: one great spiritual, natural movement. We get some idea of the life of the monks in a spot like the Inis from a poem which, although it is supposed to have been uttered by St Colmcille, is, in fact, from much later than his time. It still captures the feeling of the little monasteries:

Meallach liom bheith in ucht oilein	Happy I'd be on a rocky headland
Ar bhinn cairrge	Secure on some island
Bhfaicinn ann ar a minice	To be watching the inconstant
Féith na fairrage.	Pulse of the sea.
Go bhfaicinn a tonnta troma	To watch the great waves
Os lear luchair,	Of the brilliant ocean
Amhail chanaid ceol dá nAthair	Seem to hymn the Father
Ar seol suthain.	In their eternal surge.
Go bhfeicinn a tracht réidh rionnghlann	As they break on the rockpoint
(Ní dal dubha);	In thrilling white
Go gcloisinn guth na n-éan n-ionadh	As strange bird calls
Seol go subha.	Float on the air.
Go ro sgrudainn ann na leabhair	To study awhile just those books
Maith dom anmain;	Good for my soul;
Seal ar sleachtain ar neamh n'iomhain,	A spell contemplating heaven,
Seal ar salmaibh.	A spell at psalms.
Seal ag buain duilisg do charraig,	A spell collecting duilisc on the rocks,
Seal ar aclaidh,	A spell at fishing,
Seal ag tabhair bhidh do bhochtaibh,	A spell feeding the poor,
Seal i gcarcair.	A spell in my cell,
Seal ag sgrudain flatha nimhe,	A spell studying saintly men,
Naomhda a cheannach;	Holy this exchange–
Seal ar saothar na badh forrach,	A spell at not too heavy work;
Ro badh meallach.	At these I'd be happy.[3]

There is little that can be said about the monastery on the Inis, and there are many questions without answers. How many persons lived there? Were they there on a permanent basis, or did they just come for the summer season? When was the monastery founded? Were women among its community? Were there lay brothers as well as ordained monks? Was there a school there? What work did they do besides praying? How independent were they for their existence, or did they depend on the mainland? How many people are buried there? Is Mocheallóg himself buried there? When did the monastery come to a close? We don't know if we will ever have definite answers to those questions. Again, archaeological excavation, such as that done on Illeanloghan from 1992 to 1995, would provide many of the answers.

There is no enclosing ditch around the monastery as is found in almost all like monasteries, such as Inis Tuaisceart, Illauntannig or Reask. It would seem, indeed, as though the complete island itself comprised the monastic enclosure and that the cliffs provided the natural defensive ditch. Perhaps there may have originally been such a ditch, but stones being of so much value, the ditch was robbed to provide field boundaries and shelters.

Not much of the monastery itself remains, but of that which does we may include:

The Oratory
The Ogham Stone
The Clochán or Beehive Hut
The Font
The Cresset
Cross Slabs and Grave Markers
The Well
The Leacht
The Graveyard

1. The Oratory

This is situated on good land. It has a rectangular plan, just as at Gallarus, the best example of its kind. It has no roof, nor is there any memory of one. The average height of the walls is 1.75m. It is completely built of drystone, and there is no corbelling: i.e., with the stones sloping in towards each other to meet at the top. That proves to be a peculiarity, as corbelling can be plainly seen in the sketch that John Ganley drew of the "Oratory in Inishvicillane" on the 6 September 1845 as part of the preliminary work for the Ordnance Survey Map of 1850. This gives rise to a question which we must discuss below.

The walls are above 1m in breadth. The door is in the east wall, again which is very exceptional as most other oratories have the door in the west wall with the altar on the east side, facing in the direction of Jerusalem. The door in the east gable where the altar would be expected to be is 1.2m in height and 0.5m in width. The sides of the doorway do not narrow in towards the top as is also usual in such oratories. There is a small narrow window in the east gable, and the window-sill is 1.1m from the ground. It may also be that there was a window in the south wall, but we cannot be sure with the amalgamation of stone that is present. There are two long flagstones on the outside that appear to have been lintels and a number of other flagstones that may have been window-sills. Underneath the window on the inside is a flagstone measuring 60cm in width and 7cm in thickness, which may have been an altar stone.

Charles Smith, the historian, was the first to write of the oratory, in 1756. John Windele paid it a visit in 1838, and it is strange that he makes no mention of the oratory at all, which might lead to the question: was it there at that time?

John Ganley says in the Ordnance Survey Names Book that there is a small ruin there, 15ft × 9ft with a grave in the centre.

Gorge V. Du Noyer, an archaeologist, says that there was an old ruin there in 1856, but that it had fallen so much that it was not worth making a picture of: "There are some ancient ecclesiastical remains, but so ruinous as not to afford a subject for a sketch."[4]

It was known at that time as St Brendan's Oratory, but it would not seem to have any connection with St Brendan. The Normans having accepted Brendan as patron, the old native saints seemingly having been pushed aside, may have led to the association of the Inis monastery with Brendan.

In 1892 the Ancient Monuments Protection Act mentions that there is the ruin of an oratory on the Inis.

In 1901, Macalister, the archaeologist most associated with Corca Dhuibhne at that time, paid a visit to the Inis but makes no mention of the oratory at all.

If the oratory was so much in a state of ruin in 1856 that Du Noyer did not think it worth making a picture of, but still that the Ancient Monument Protection Act makes mention of the oratory and *clochán* with a stone roof in 1892, what is the explanation? Could it be that the oratory had fallen into ruin in 1856 but that the Ó Dálaighs had rebuilt it, so that it was back again in 1892 when the Ancient Monuments Protection Act mentions it? It was well known that the Ó Dálaighs were excellent craftsmen with stone and with wood; it could cause them little effort to rebuild the oratory. There are still examples of their work; the house they built on the Great Blasket, and the turf shelter there also, as well as the boat shed they built at their new home in Baile na Rátha, amply illustrate their building competence. All those points seem to suggest that there are many questions yet to be answered regarding the oratory at Inisvickillane.

2. The Ogham Stone

This is the most precious monument associated not alone with the Inis, but with all the Blaskets.

These ogham stones date from about 350 AD to about 600 AD, by which time the Roman alphabet had taken over all over Ireland. These standing stones with the ogham markings on them are to be found as markers on the graves of important personages like chieftains or saints, though there is also the opinion that they may have been border markers between two territories.

They are to be found in a band from Cornwall right up through Wales and over St George's Channel to Waterford, into Cork and finally into Kerry, where they reach their high point in production and artistic merit. There are about 350 to be found in Ireland, about one third of the entire production in Kerry, and about 60 of these in the Dingle Peninsula. The ogham stone of Inisvickillane is the most westerly one in Europe. Most of them have connections with monastic sites, and some of them have cross forms etched on them, which connects them directly with early Christianity.

The inscriptions on them consist of combinations of short lines, some horizontal, some slanted, formed against the corner of the stone and read from the ground up. In some cases, the inscription continues over the top of the stone and down the other side. The letters themselves are based on the Roman alphabet and are simple to read once the code has been deciphered, though of course, many of the inscriptions have been damaged and worn, and so are difficult to make out.

The ogham stone on the Inis is 1.05m × 0.15m to 0.18m in width. The stone itself is of the Lower Silurian bed on the Inis itself, which shows that craftsmanship and artistic endeavour were practised there, and that there were people there who were able to produce such work. There are four various types of crosses etched on the four faces of the stone, one of which is far clearer than the others. This face may have been placed downwards in the earth for many years, thus protecting it. One of the crosses is of the swastika design used by Hitler as the symbol of the Nazi party. Here, however, the swastika symbol is of Christian or maybe even earlier origin, portraying the rising sun at the beginning and then the Cross of Christ, which even later developed into the St Brigid's Cross.

When John Windele saw the ogham stone for the first time in 1848, it was laid on the ground: "It lay in front of a rude *clochán* locally called St. Brendan's cell." Windele made a rubbing of it on that occasion and showed it at a talk he gave to the Cork Archaeological Society on 3 January 1849.

(CO?)BB(A?)AVI VLATIAMI MAQ . . .

These are the letters etched on the stone according to Macalister. They are neatly and carefully cut, and it would appear that they were made by a long-handled rather than a hatchet type tool. As regards the meaning of *Cobba mac mhic Vlatiami mac*–Cobba is the name of the person to whom the stone is dedicated. We have no idea as to his identity. We can say nothing about him except that he died, that he was an important person, and that he was loved by those who lived on the Inis who wrote his name in ogham. *Avi* means *grandson of,* and can still be found today in the Irish form Uí or Ó, as in Mícheál Ó Dubhshláine, meaning Mícheál the grandson of Dubhshláine.

Flaitheamh would seem to be the family name of Cobba. There was then and is still today the family name Flahive, and there was a small town in mid-Kerry, a little to the north of Firies, which is called Máigh Fhlaithimh or Molahiffe. It was an important centre for mid-Kerry in olden times. Cobba lived around 1,600 years ago. As Professor John Rhys states: "As far as the Ogham is concerned, there is nothing to prevent our assigning it to the 5th century; but it may, perhaps, be older."[5]

That means that it is a very early example, perhaps even before Patrick, which would further indicate how early Christianity came to those parts. Fr Kieran O'Shea is also of the opinion that Mocheallóg was one of our first saints in Kerry: In his newly published book, *The Diocese of Kerry;* "Present scholarship dates the earliest Ogham Stone to the 4th or 5th centuries and this may indicate that Christianity here predates the arrival of St. Patrick."[6]

John Ganley also noticed the stone and mentioned that it was in the north end of the graveyard at that time. When Macalister visited the Inis in 1902, however, the stone formed the lintel of the doorway of the oratory,[7] which further lends itself to the idea that the oratory was rebuilt. The stone did not remain there for long more. It was taken and removed to Trinity College in Dublin.

Professor Rhys writes: "One day last Autumn Dr Mahaffy sent me word that his friend Lord Cork, the proprietor of the island, had presented the stone to him, and that I could now study it in Trinity College, Dublin."[8]

There was a fuss about the transfer. Some maintained that the stone was safe from being damaged in Trinity, and was easier to access by scholars of archaeology:

> But the stone does not appear to have been removed from the island a day too soon, not to mention another consideration–it would have been the case of one eye on the stone and the other on the rolling billows . . . Visions of a night or a week of exposure would not leave me in the best of humour for studying Ogams or anything else . . .
>
> At any rate, no more unfavourable conditions for close study of Ogams can well be conceived, unless they happen to involve the presence of the whole body of an antiquarian society after a champagne lunch.[9]

But not everyone agreed. Foley, who wrote his *History of Kerry* about this time, states: "Steps are being taken to compel Prof. Mahaffy and the Commissioners of Irish Lights to restore the stone to its original site at the Church at Inisvickillane."[10]

But Foley did not succeed, and the Inisvickillane ogham stone is still in Trinity College and can be seen by the public in the same room as the famous *Book of Kells*, one of the most precious possessions of the nation. Thousands come to visit them both, but few think of the faraway island from where the stone originated. Charles Haughey made an attempt to have it removed to the National Museum in the 1980s and brought the matter up in the Dáil, but he, too, was unsuccessful.

Mr Haughey had a replica made of it and had it erected in its old position on the Inis, in front of the oratory: "A new replica of the Inismhiceáláin ogham stone specially made under the direction of Dr Pat Wallace of the National Museum was erected at the Monastic Cell."[11]

If so, it became clear that the new stone was not as hard-wearing as the old one. It was hard to beat the early Christian craftsmanship: "Ogham markings not weathering well–markings fading."[12]

3. The Clochán

This is no longer to be seen either. It was an example of the type of hut that was and is plentiful around Corca Dhuibhne. They have the shape of a beehive and are often called beehive cells. They are also built to the corbelled style, the stones gradually sloping in towards each other till they meet at the top. There is no need to use any timber, making it an appropriate building method for a treeless peninsula. Smith says about it:

. . . likewise a small cell or hermitage, being an arch of stone neatly put
together without any mortar or cement, which admits of no rain through
its roof. There is one of the same kind at Fane in Ventry parish, in a
ruinous condition, and another entire one at Gallarus . . . The Irish say
that those cells were erected by the first missionaries, who preached the
gospel in these parts.[13]

There is a fine illustration of this *clochán* drawn by G.V. Du Noyer in
Lives of the Irish Saints by Canon John O'Hanlon, which was published in
the last half of the nineteenth century. O'Sullivan was of the opinion that
the *clochán* was still there in the 1920s, but he was wrong because, at that
time, it had been cleared away: "The island contains the ruins of a Church,
an almost perfect *clochán*, and the foundations of numerous other cells."[14]

He calls it St. Brendan's Cell. Doubtless it was disassembled and the
stones used for building or for field divisions. All that is left is the circle in
the ground with some rough rocks where it stood. It would seem that there
were more examples of the same around the site, but that they met the
same fate.

4. The Font
This consists of a stone baptismal font that was placed inside the oratory
until about 1985. Just about half of the original vessel remains, the rest
having been broken at some earlier age. It is indeed miraculous that it
should have survived for so long. Charles J. Haughey took it into his home
for safekeeping, and it is there still. It is only 0.18m to 0.2m in height and
0.25m across. A little light cross has been inscribed on the outside of it.

5. The Stone Chalice or Cresset and Cover
This consists of two pieces: a stone vessel and a circular stone cover in the
shape of a disc, which is part of the set.

It was at first thought that this was a chalice and paten used for the
celebrating of mass in the time of the monastery, but it is now thought that
the vessel is an oil lamp and that the cover was for extinguishing the light.

Smith is the first to refer to it, in 1756: "There stands in it
[Inisvickillane] the ruins of an ancient chapel, in which an old stone chalice
and a baptismal also of stone still remain . . ."[15]

Ganley had heard of the existence of the two pieces when he came to the
Inis in September 1845. But he could not find them, and he thought they
had been removed: "There was formerly a stone chalice and plate in this

old ruin. They were destroyed by some person who visited this island about three years since."[16]

But the person who had taken the pieces was F.K. Burton, and he placed them in the safekeeping of the National Museum of Ireland in Dublin. They are now on loan to the Museum in Ballyferriter.

They are described in the *Catalogue of the Petrie Collection,* by W.F. Wakeman, the first person to make a study of them: "Cup from Inish Mackillan–the Western Blasket, procured on the spot by F.K. Burton Esq. R.H.A. and presented to Mr Petrie."[17]

They consist of:

> A small stone vessel tapering to the top and empty inside to hold the oil. It is 17.6cm in height and 12cm across.
> A small hard stone in the shape of an egg, with a small cut in the surface.

It is thought not to be a chalice because it is too heavy, and the base is too unlevel for it to stand on an altar. One side of it is levelled off, so that, perhaps, it could be hung against a wall. Moreover, the Church ruled from early times that the mass chalice could not be made from material such as stone or wood but had to be made from a precious metal like silver or gold. It used to be the custom in former times, when a station mass was being celebrated, to include some object associated with the faith from earlier times on the altar. It may be thus that the pieces acquired the tradition of being chalice and paten.

There are also many similar examples from the Continent of Europe that are certainly oil lamps. They are given a date from the mid tenth century to the mid twelfth century and may date back to the post-Viking monastery. There are about forty-six such examples from all around the country in existence from different monastic sites. They are called cressets. The cresset was filled with oil, and a wick made from natural material like wool was left to hang over the edge and lit. Such forms of light were used up to the end of the nineteenth and beginning of the twentieth century in the homes of Corca Dhuibhne, fish and seal oil being the fuel. Cresset stones are also to be had in UK and Scandinavia, as well as on the Continent.[18]

6. The Cross Slab
There was another ancient flagstone on the site also which is now missing, and it is not known what happened to it. It used to be inside the oratory

resting against the south wall. It would have been a burial stone, but, because of the Latin inscription, would not be as old as the ogham stone. It was Macalister who first brought it to notice in 1949. He describes the flagstone with a small cross inscribed on it with these words:

ORO DO MACRUED Ú DALACH

That is "Pray for *Macrued Ú Dalach.*" *Oro* is the old Irish word for prayer, from the Latin, *orare,* to pray. Clearly this inscription dates to the Christian period. It is a strange coincidence that the person we are asked to pray for is a Dálach, or Ó Dálaighs, and that it was a family of that name who, together with the Guiheens, are most associated with the Inis in much later times.

Macalister also mentions that there was another stone there that had a simple two-lined cross inscribed on it.[19]

7. The Well

Ganley, in 1845, tells us: "The well is not called by any particular name. It was formed in the earth and lined with stones in order to collect water as there is no spring on the island. [As he thought.] The church is not called after any saint and is similar to the oratory in Bally Wiheen [Reask, probably] and Kilmalkedar."[20]

It would seem from that account that he is referring to Tobar na Maighdine, the Virgin's Well. We do not know how it came to get that name; probably it was dedicated to the Virgin Mary. It is not a good well for water today except during wet weather. Perhaps it was in better condition in earlier times. Caoimhín Ó Danachair includes it in his list of holy wells of Corca Dhuibhne: "'Well' on 1842 map. Inisvicillane, Vague tradition of a former holy well."[21]

Of course, there are other wells on the Inis also, the best of them being Tobar na Cárthaí, or Carthach Well.

8. The Leacht

This is a simple, well-built, rectangular drystone structure with an edge of standing stones. It measures 7.45m north-south and 2.35m east-west. There is a small lintelled passage about half a metre high and wide, stretching into at ground level for a distance of 1m. There is a thin flagstone standing on the right side of the passage, with a stone cross standing on the north side. It is still not certain what use a *leacht* was put to, in spite of some excavation having taken place at Reask and Illaunloughan. It may be that it was the burial place of the founder,

Mocheallóg himself, and that it is a shrine erected in his honour, something that would add to the attractiveness of the monastery as a pilgrimage site. There are similar structures, ten of them around Corca Dhuibhne, like the Skelligs, Gallarus, Reask and Illauntannig. They all have a cross slab erected close by. It may also be an altar for the celebration of mass outside on the occasions when there may have been a good crowd present. It may also have been rebuilt as part of the penitential station connected with the pilgrimage, where people stopped to perform some of the devotions. They were afterwards used also as burial places, called *cillíns* or *ceallúnachs*, for unbaptised children or bodies washed in on the tide. The most recent work is the excavation done at Illaunloughan Island beside Port Magee, which shows they date back to the eighth century.[22]

Paddy O'Leary and Lee Snodgrass spent a good part of the summer of 1976 on the Inis examining and studying the remains there. They believe that much of the monastic buildings were destroyed for the stones to build field fences. This was done to keep in sheep and to protect the growing crops. Sheep were very important in the Inis economy when people came to settle there in the eighteenth and nineteenth century. Building and mending fences was an on-going occupation. Paddy na hInise tells us: "There was no place suitable then to shear the sheep nor to catch them except a place down in the cliff which was too dangerous. I had to construct a suitable place myself and spend my own money on it as well as drawing the stones on my back a good distance from home."

So, although the Inis is very rich in archaeological remains, there has been much change there and many of them are missing. Even the layout of the oratory itself is complicated. Excavation is the only way to find out further information. That will take time.

9. The Graveyard

There is a little graveyard beside the monastery with some graves, five or six at least, with grave markers on them. There may be more which can no longer be seen or from which the markers have disappeared. This shows us that the monastic settlement was securely based and that they were there for the long haul. There is no evidence for such a settlement on the Great Blasket, for example, but rather a small patch called Rinn an Chaisleáin (Castle Point) where unbaptised children or those who died in bad weather and couldn't be brought to the mainland were buried.

Chapter IV

Early Recorded History

In the year 1199, the Normans arrived in Corca Dhuibhne, and it wasn't long before they had most of Munster in their possession, including north and west Kerry. The Fitzgeralds, or the Geraldines, gained possession of Corca Dhuibhne and they passed on possession of the Blaskets to the Ferriter family. The Ferriters were a Norman family and had a castle at Baile Uachtarach, below Sybil Head, from where they could keep an eye on the seas around. The rent payable to Fitzgerald, the Earl of Desmond, was two falcons, to be paid annually. A peculiar rent, you might say, but hunting with birds was a very popular sport for the gentry at that time and the Blasket falcons must have been famous; the island terrain must have trained them well for that sport. It would seem that Inisvickillane had its own rent of the silver mark, on account of the lucrative pilgrimages which were still being made there.

We do not know how long these pilgrimages continued nor how long the monastery remained open on the Inis, but it would seem that, like many of its type, it came to an end in the middle of the sixteenth century with the religious problems arising from Henry VIII's dissolution of the monasteries. It is a long time before there is any further mention of the Inis or the Blaskets, though it would seem there was some habitation, at least on the Great Blasket, during the seventeenth century and that they gained some notoriety during the Williamite Wars of the 1690s, so much so that they were depopulated. David Dixon tells us of this in *Old World Colony:*

> Parts of the region, specifically south Kerry, fell completely outside Williamite control at times, passing back into the hands of tories and raparees. These men beyond the law, some operating in large brigades, were aiding, as well as being aided by, French privateers, which operated along the south-west approaches between Bantry and Dingle. As a result of local intelligence the French campaign was highly successful; more than twenty vessels were captured in the waters off Bantry in the course of a year, or so a hostile source claimed in 1694. It was later claimed that the Blasket Islands were depopulated

by order of government during Anne's reign to deny French ships ready access to provisions. These episodes–of consorting with privateers, cattle rustling, robberies, intimidation and incidents of physical assault–lasted until at least 1705 in the roadless peninsulas of the south-west . . .[1]

But it would seem that this depopulation did not continue for a long period, as there is mention of the Blaskets again in the 1730s in a letter from the Earl of Cork and Orrery to his friend John Kemp in 1735. The Earl of Cork had possession of the Blaskets from the last half of the seventeenth century:

> I have been today to view the Blasques, Earl's Quarter & Ballyferriter: the two first are in the parish of Dunqueen, which is divided into four parts: Mullin's Quarter, one, Ferriter's quarter is another, the Blasques and Earl's Quarter, which both belong to me, make up the four. . . . The Blasques are about nine islands in the sea, five of which are habitable for cattle: but, indeed, there's but one, wherein any human creature lives. In this I saw some tillage and a few cabins, from whence, during the time I was looking at the island some poor creatures ventured into a boat with rabbits for sale. Nothing, sure, but necessity could force 'em to trust to so tempestuous a sea; the sight of which shocked me so much that I hastened to Ballyferriter; but not without leaving my hearty prayers for the rabbit-merchants. Ballyferriter, as well as the Blasques & Earl's Quarter was formerly held by Capt. Edward Ferriter.[2]

Charles Smith give us our next account of the Blaskets in 1756 in his *Ancient and Present State of the County Kerry*. Smith did not himself go into the islands, but stood on Dún Mór head and describes what he sees as well as what he has read and heard:

> They formerly belonged to the Earls of Desmond, who gave them to the family of Ferriter, and who, by joining in the rebellion of that unfortunate earl, forfeited them to the crown. They were granted by letters patent, dated at Westminster, 27 June 1586, with several other lands of the said earl, to George Stone, of Kingston, in the County of Surrey, gentleman, and Cornelius Champion, gentleman, who conveyed the grant to Mr. Henry Billingsley, who sold the same to Sir Richard Boyle, knight, then of Galbally in the County of Limerick, afterwards Earl of Cork, and these islands, with several other lands

granted to the said Stone and Champion are now the estate of the right Hon. John, Earl of Cork and Orrery, by his father, the said Richard, Earl of Cork.[3]

The Inis is included in the Tithe Applotments Book, no. 12, Parish of Ballinvoher, All Saints Day, 1825. This was compiled to impose monetary tithes on the fruit of the land all over the country. Before this it was paid by a tenth of the crops, but now was to be paid in money.

This is how Inisvickillane stood: "*Inisvickelane, Tenant's Name: Laurence Wren, Total Tithes 15 shillings and six pence.*" Not too bad, one might say.

Then there was the time when it seemed that the Inis and Inis na Bró might be developed as a safe harbour for the British Fleet stationed in the south. The seas were deep enough and the area of strategical importance. It never happened, however, and we can only imagine the difference it would have made: "Plans to develop a harbour between Inisikillane and Inchibroe safe enough for the British Fleet."[4]

Our next reference is the *Griffith Valuation*, Tenure Book, Parish Dunquin, 1850, or thereabouts, that laid out the amount of money payable by each household to support the Poor Law System:

Inishnab[r]o and Inishvickillane.
Occupier John Guiheen,
Immediate Lessor Edward Hussey.
Head Landlord, Earl of Cork.
Content of Farm Acres 171. Roods 3 Perches 11.
These two Islands used to be £30 per annum. But the rent at present is not properly known as the party who occupies them may pay what he pleases (no other person would live there).
Inishvickillane is worth about £22 and Inishnabro £3 per annum. Dated 24th September 1850.

There is this mention of the Inis in the year 1882 by an English visitor: ". . . a beautifully green and rather low island. A herdsman lives here, tending sheep for the proprietor–by no means an enviable position, as communication from shore is often cut off for a long period."[5]

Another valuable mention is made by Fr John Casey, parish priest of Ferriter, who carried out a survey in 1835 at the behest of Daniel O'Connell:

Census of the Parish of Ferriter, 1835, Revd. John Casey, P.P.
Innisvickillane

Timothy Guiheen	*2 Males*
	4 Females
Total	*6*[6]

It would seem that this Timothy, or Tadhg (Tadhg Liam), was the head of the household on the Inis at this time. He was the brother of Seán Liam Ó Guithín. There was at least one other brother, Muiris Liam. Tadhg had taken over the running of the Inis because Seán Liam was in America at the time when Fr Casey made his survey.

Here are the population statistics of Inisvickillane that we know of:

Year	Source	Population
1756	Charles Smith	0
1835	Fr John Casey	6 (2m. 4f.) Guiheen
1837	Lewis	2 households
1841	Census	3 all male
1850	Griffith's Valuation	John Guiheen tenant
1851	Census	8 (3m. 5 f.)
1861	Census	3 (2m. 1f.)
1871	Census	8
1881	Census	12
1891	Census	7 (4f. 3b.)
1901	Census	6
1905	J.M.Synge	1 (Muiris in winter)
1911	Census	0[7]

From medieval times until the late eighteenth century we have no definite evidence of habitation on Inisvickillane. (The same would be true of the vast majority of the islands along the west coast of Ireland.) But from the 1750s on, the population in the whole nation began to increase, leading to a shortage of land for both grazing and cultivation. This forced people to rise higher and higher into the surrounding hills and mountains to sow their potatoes and oats as well as encroaching into the lower soft lands where there might have been a fertile patch. The evidence is there still in the so-called "famine beds" that can be seen both in mountainy and boggy areas. In the same way, habitation extended to the offshore islands where a marginally better standard of living could be eked out through fishing, beach collecting, hill for turf and grazing for sheep, without the direct depressing dominance of landlord and priest.

Although we have definite information of just two families inhabiting the Inis in the nineteenth century, there is a strong Blasket tradition that there were more families, although that might seem strange on so small an island. Still, that would have been no different from on the mainland, where many families occupied tiny holdings and very many householders were completely landless. Field names, such as Gort an tSíthigh (Sheehy's Field), suggest that a Sheehy family lived there, and Tomás Ó Criomhthain says: "This was a man who broke this field, and spent some of his life there, and so the name continues on the field still."[8]

The Baptism Register of the parish of Ferriter, recording baptisms from Inisvickillane, agrees with Tomás that there were other families there, and even adds to it:

Year	Child Baptised	Parents
1808	Catherine Guiheen	John Guiheen & Mary Duane
1817	Brian Sheehy	James Sheehy & Joan Bowler
1822	Gobnait Shea	Denis Shea & Ellen Guiheen
1827	Margaret Shea	Denis Shea & Ellen Guiheen[9]

Seán Sheáin Í Chearnaigh also refers to the tradition, though he increases the habitations even more: "Muiris's grandfather could remember ten house-gables there although there is now but one."[10]

There is even a suggestion of twenty-one houses. George Thompson points out: "On page 106 of the Irish edition, Pádraig Ó Dála says that at one time there had been twenty-one houses in the Inis. According to other sources there have never been more than two or three. Pádraig must have known this as he was born there. So I think too this must have been Maurice's mistake."[11]

Thompson was referring to the account by Muiris in *Twenty Years a' Growing*:

> Up we went to the house. It was a small low cabin with a felt roof, plenty of ruins around it with weeds and nettles growing in them.
>
> "It looks, Pádraig, that there were many people living here at one time."
>
> "Indeed, my man," says Pádraig, "wasn't there twenty-one houses here at one time, and he opening the lock on the door at the same time."[12]

Robin Flower says also that he was told by the islanders that there were numerous houses there at one stage:

In the old days as many as five or six families have lived on this island, planting crops and herding sheep and fishing. The soil is so rich, too rich they say for potatoes, which send up here so luxuriant a leafage that they exhaust their strength in that effort, and few potatoes come under the ground. But it is good earth for cabbages and onions and the like, and they say that even tobacco has been grown here.[13]

If there were numerous households, then it must have been way back in early times, perhaps even a faraway echo of the monastic times on the Inis or the time before the rising of the Earl of Desmond. However, there are many references to two or three households there, such as in the following sad story, which refers to *"Raghadsa 's mo Cheaití,"* one of the best known local songs:

Red Jealousy Is a Deadly Disease

In the old days, there were two households in one of the Little Blaskets, in the best and the biggest of them, Inisvickillane; and because there was much movement by people in those days fleeing from poverty, these two families took possession of the Stone for themselves, a half each. There were then two houses in it, and two families, each with its own sheep, and each recognising its own from the other's.

Both were married. One man was dark and plain, but had a wife that was one of the finest-looking women in Corca Dhuibhne in her time. The other man was one of the best-looking men going to the fair of Dingle; but not so his wife. People used say that she must have come across the sea to Ireland from some other country, as there were so many colours to be seen in her countenance.

Yes indeed! Then the bee stung them and the trouble began. When the sheep were having their lambs they used be falling over the cliffs and would even take some of the lambs and the older sheep with them—and the men used to have to be out before daybreak to prevent it, because it was then they made for the cliff. Life on the island had become very difficult for these men.

The woman with the handsome man, didn't it strike her that he was not going to stay with her, as the saying goes, 'Woe to the poor man with too pretty a wife.' It's the same story with the woman who has the handsome husband and she herself to be plain enough.

One morning—wasn't the fine handsome man missing.

She searched inside and outside, but he had vanished without a trace, [as she thought] with the fine wife of the other man, and she herself to be forsaken by him. She arose and went as far as the other house. He wasn't there.

She asked the woman of the house had he been in to her since morning. "He was here. He left as you arrived just now."

She went away.

When the men arrived home having done the round of the island, driving the stock away from danger, the handsome woman was there, but the other woman was not to be seen anywhere around her own house.

Séamus, the handsome man, went to the other house.

"Did you see herself?"

"She had been there in the morning, she hadn't stayed long," and the woman thought she had gone home.

But she was mistaken.

Then they started the search all around the Inis, but no trace of her dead or alive.

One of them went up as far as Cnocán na Tine (Fire Hill), looked down and there she was below in the sea swimming as alive as ever and she singing away her long, sweet song.

Frost and snow lie on the branches

As I walk all alone.

They all ran down to the strand and getting a hook and rope, ran to the water's edge and threw it out to her. But she just ignored the rope with no thought of returning to land or saving herself.

Go home and tell that I will not go with you.

They returned to the top–and there she was–drifting away out from the land–and she reclining on top of the water, just fading into the distance from them as though she were all the time on dry land.[14]

It would seem that this put an end to there being two households on the Inis:

About three weeks afterwards the husband left the Inis and nobody knows where he went or what became of him. The master of the Inis got to hear of what happened, that the man whose wife had drowned had taken off, and he made the decision not to put the second household on the Inis ever again. One shepherd would now have to do the work from then on, except that he got the pay of two.[15]

Of the Shea family mentioned living there, we have no account. The family most associated with the Inis in the first half of the nineteenth century is the Guiheen family, and, indeed it even seems that they were related to the previous inhabitants, both Sheehys and Sheas. In the Baptismal Register for the year 1808 the baptism of Catherine Guiheen, daughter of John Guiheen and Mary Duane, is recorded.

We don't know when the Guiheen family first settled there, but the indications are that it was late in the eighteenth century or the beginning of the nineteenth.[16]

Chapter V

The Guiheens

Charles Smith tells us directly that no one lived on Inisvickillane at the time he wrote, *c.*1756, but that cattle grazed there:

> Near the great island, are three small ones, the first is called Beg-Innis, i.e., the little island, which is a very fertile spot, consisting of about sixteen acres, that will fatten thirty bullocks every summer; the grass is mostly clover, and cinquefoil, and is constantly enriched by the spray of the sea, which always leaves a considerable quantity of salt behind it. The other two, are used likewise to fatten cattle, but they are smaller.
>
> The second of these in magnitude they call Innis-mac-Keilane, or Mac-Keilane's island; it lies seven miles W. by S. from the head land of Dunmore. As it stands too far out in the great western ocean, and the lands being low, and too bleak to afford shelter to inhabitants, there have been none here for many years past.

Muiris Mhaidhc Léan Ó Guithín recalls the family tradition that the family had always been there. But what does *always* in this sense mean? Probably as far back as can be accounted for in the folk memory: "I have often heard that the family of Guiheen had always been living on the Inis." And Tomás tells us:

> For generations before this the Inis was not without a shepherd, and they were all shepherds . . . More than a hundred years ago there were two families in it and two houses. They were small narrow houses, and because life was tough those times, poor people who had nothing welcomed the chance to go in to live there, and just as soon as one person left there would be a race among them to see who would get there to fill the place.[2]

People thought that it took a special sort of individual to live there, people who would be prepared to be alone, and able to take life easy:

> There was an understanding between the shepherd and the owner of the Inis that he would have enough space to sow, have two milk cows as well as eight pounds a year.

51

There were two households there—there's one there still—with a shepherd in each house, one watching during the night and the other during the day . . .

It was run by the agents of Lord Cork, and it was he who would put the stock there, and it's he would put the two shepherds there. He would send them everything they wanted because he used have a boat from the Great Blasket serving them, relations of their own. They had wives and families there, too, and a small boat to go in and out any time they wished. The Islanders were very envious of these two shepherds because they had no need to buy anything, and they had nine pounds to put in their pockets, sow and harvest as much as they wished, two milk cows and as many sheep as they wished. They used to sow a great amount of oats, potatoes and onions, and many other vegetables besides, but they had to be out at all times of the night guarding them because the rabbits used to do a great deal of damage to the crops on them. But they didn't mind. They had plenty of help and were willing to work.[3]

And the Inis fairies didn't bother them one bit: "It is said that this Inis is a great place for the good people, or the fairies, as they are also called, but no matter what fairies or ghosts that were to be seen, the shepherd had to be out about his business until sunrise. That was his duty and he had to perform it."[4]

Seán Mhuiris Liam is the first of the Guiheen family in the Inis that we have any definite account of. He seems to have been a hard worker and well able for the duties placed on him, as well as being of very independent spirit. He made a journey to Dingle, to the house of Bess Rice, the agent for Lord Cork, to pay the rent. (They must have had to pay a rent at that time.) But life was tough, and he had only half the rent. Bess would not accept it from him and told him she'd take nothing short of the full amount. Bess Rice reigned with a strict hand over her tenants in those famine years. (See Appendix III.)

Seán turned to her and says he boldly, "You'll take it when you get it again," and stormed out. Bess relented almost immediately; she sent a messenger after him asking him to return, that she would accept the half. But Seán refused to return and continued on home to the Inis.

He then herded all his sheep together on the Inis and transported them to the Great Blasket to his own people to care for. Then he and the wife set off for America and went working for a farmer who owned many sheep. Seán was very good at shearing, having spent most of his life at it, and sent home for his shears, which was duly dispatched to him. He was in great demand in that area as a sheep shearer and did very well for himself.

We don't know how long he spent in America, but when he returned he had a fine store of money. Whatever difficulties existed with the agent were ironed out, and he took up residence again on the Inis, at least for some time, because, it seems, he soon handed over the tenancy to his son and headed off back to America again.

The story does show the independence of mind of the Guiheens and the confidence they had in themselves in very hard times, and also, that the post of shepherd on the Inis was one of some importance.[5]

We have another brief mention of the Inis and her people by Du Noyer, the archaeologist who visited the island in 1856 in search of antiquarian remains.

Unfortunately, like similar visitors of the time, he leaves us little detail of the people who lived there:

> The island is systematically farmed and always stocked with sheep. A family of six or eight people inhabited it at the time of my visit. These people assert that during one stormy season their fire went out, and not having the means of relighting it, they were reduced almost to starvation. They, however, supported life for a period of two months by the use of sheep's milk alone.[6]

We have another account of an event that happened in the time of Seán Mhuiris Liam as related to us by Tomás's neighbour, "the old hag next door." Seán Mhuiris Liam had a piece taken from his leg by the bite of a seal.

> "Indeed, I well remember," said she, "wasn't I on the Inis at the time. Seán Mhuiris Liam was a young man at the time when the seal took the big lump out of his leg. The father, Muiris Liam, killed another seal, and applied a fresh piece of the seal flesh to it. He made it fit exactly the piece that had been taken from Sean's leg. He put it back exactly as you would put a cork into a bottle. He tightened it well with a bandage and left it like that for seven days," said she.
>
> "And when it was loosened then," said my mother, "how was it?"
>
> "The hole was full up of natural flesh, and the piece of seal laid aside," said the old hag.
>
> "And how long after that was it healed completely?" said my mother.
>
> "The day the bandage was taken off, he went walking on the Stone,

with no covering on the leg, but it exposed to the sun all day. And the skin had grown back on the evening of the same day," said the old hag.[7]

The reason for the old woman telling the story was because a similar mishap had befallen Tomás in a struggle with a seal on a strand on the Island, which had left him in danger of losing the leg. The advice was heeded, and though it was stormy November, a crew was quickly gathered, and the eight-oared seine boat, *An Collach Dubh*, set sail for Inisvickillane. The man on the Inis saw the boat approaching:

> The man on the Stone thought it was a wreck boat from a ship which had gone down, either that or that half of all his relations had died, if they were our island boats, and he was out in the water up to his waist at the slip as the boat came in, as there was a great swell. He asked them straight away what had brought them on such a day.[8]

The situation was explained and:

> The man from the Stone brought the boatmen to his house, and he was good at that. Needless to say, he gave them food, every sort that was in the house, and when they had eaten, he called on some of them to go with him to search for a seal. Four went, and they searched every hole in the Inis, but failed to find any seal.[9]

But they didn't give up. They couldn't possibly return to the Island empty-handed. There was one more hole left, a very dangerous one that would need a good long rope. That proved to be no problem. There was always plenty of rope on the islands. So they set out again, and Tomás's uncle and the Guiheen of the Inis—we are not sure whether the Inis man who came to their aid was Seán Mhuiris Liam or his son, Seán Óg—went down on the rope and brought out a fine seal. They then set off home in the storm with the seal and made no stop till they arrived home on the Island and applied the lump of seal meat to the wound, which had the desired effect within a short time.

Seán Mhuiris Liam Ó Guithín married Máire de Mórdha (Moore), probably from Dunquin. They had seven sons and four daughters. The four daughters didn't travel very far for husbands. All married in the Blaskets. Their son Séan a' Mhóraigh, or Seán Óg, married Léan Ní Chearnaigh (Kearney) from the Blasket. One of their daughters married another Cearnaigh from the Blasket.

Moll married Diarmaid Ó Sé (O'Shea), Tomás Ó Criomhthain's uncle. Cáit married Muiris Ó Dálaigh from Dunquin.

Eibhlís, who was born in 1851, married Eoghan Mór Ó Súilleabháin (O'Sullivan, "Daideo"), Muiris Ó Súilleabháin's (*Twenty Years a Growing*) grandfather. Eoghan lived until 1933.

All the sons went to America except Seán Óg (Seán a' Mhódhraigh), who spent all of his short life on the Inis. He was drowned in 1873.[10]

Back in the Inis, life was good by the standards of the time.

Seán Óg and Léan married and settled down in the old home on the Inis. It was then that Seán Mhuiris Liam and Máire de Mórdha decided that they would return to the States and leave the concern to Seán Óg.

Seán Óg's family included Pádraig (born 1866), Máire (born 1868), Seán born 1870), Cáit (born 1871), and Mícheál (born 1874 on the Great Blasket, as we will see).

As the family were still young and he was often in need of help in looking after the sheep and cows, saving the turf, fishing and the likes, some of his relations on the Great Blasket often came over to help and stay for a while. Seán had a small boat and often used to do a bit of fishing. George Collier, the agent, had given it to him so that he could row around the islands fishing, row over to the Blasket or bring the lambs to Inis na Bró to wean them from their mothers.

One day Seán decided to go to Dingle in the little boat, a fine long journey in by Slea Head into Dingle Bay. He started out one fine summer's morning rowing alone, and continued without stop until he reached Dingle. The people on the quayside saw him arriving and wondered that he had come so far alone in so small a boat. They helped him draw up the boat on the quay and asked him if he had any story after his long voyage.

It was he who had the story, and a very strange one it was: "He said that from the time he had left Inisvickillane until he arrived at the mouth of Dingle Bay, there was a dry road through the sea, with three men walking on it, and whatever pace he went at in his boat, fast or slow, they kept the same pace on the road. And he wondered much at it."

That was his story, and it made him very afraid and shocked. Such a vision was a sign that could not be taken lightly. There was no way he would return in the little boat. He remained a few days in Dingle until a vessel that was going fishing out that way took him and his boat back home. He decided never to row alone to Dingle again.[11]

This strange event seems to have happened early in 1873, though we have no record of it, except that we know that Eilís Ní Dhálaigh (Eilís na

Beannaí) was born in 1873, by which time the Ó Dálaighs had moved into the Inis and life had changed very much for the Guiheens.

One day some time after this strange happening Seán Óg and two of his helpers, Mícheál Ó Ceárnaigh (Kearney), another relation, and a man of the Dunleavys went in the little boat transferring lambs from Inisvickillane to Inis na Bró to wean them from the mothers. There is only a distance of a quarter of a mile between the two islands. They brought tackle with them to do a bit of fishing on the way back. They landed the lambs successfully and then rowed away to fish. They never returned. Something went wrong–what is not known–and all three were drowned. It was afterwards thought that they had gone down at the Laoch, a rock between Inis na Bró and Ceann Dubh at the back of the Great Blasket. Even when the sea is calm, strong waves break over it to the south of Inis na Bró out from Cuas an tSaibhris.

Back on the Inis, Seán Óg's wife, Léan, waited for their return as she prepared a meal. She was expecting a baby and had her four children and Seán's mother, Máire de Mórdha, there with her. The time passed and the men failed to return, and the women slowly realised that something had gone very wrong. They spent a very anxious night on the Inis. They lit the fire on Cnocán na Tine (the Fire Rock) to raise the alarm and let the Islanders know that they were in serious trouble. The fire was seen by the Island people from the hill, and they knew that help was needed urgently, because the fire was only lit in cases of great necessity, mostly in case of death:

> The Islanders put a crew together, and they set sail, making no stop or stay until they reached the unfortunate miserable island, with the wife of the man and the old woman, her mother-in-law, and two or three children, God save us!–and the three men who should have been there were not to be found, and their boat was found upside down floating below the house. The boat had disappeared the previous evening, and wasn't it awful to think that the two women lived through that night on that lonely island without one of the neighbours near to lend a hand. No one understood how they drowned or what ever happened to them, except that the body of the boy was found way over east of Dingle a good while afterwards.[12]

There is no reference to the drowning in any of the local or national newspapers. Kerry newspapers of the time have frequent reports of similar events in England and America, copied, no doubt, from foreign publications, but no reference to such a great local tragedy forty miles away from Tralee in our own county. Was it that the Blaskets were so far removed and isolated that the tragedy went unnoticed except by the small community whom it affected? There is no record of the event in the Parish Register either, because the bodies were missing.

As could be expected, this tragedy dealt a severe blow to the Inis and the Great Blasket community, as they were all closely related. Seán Ó Duinnshléibhe (Dunleavy), the Island poet, had a mind to compose a lament, but was prevented from doing so by the Guiheen family, though the drowned men would have been highly praised. The Guiheens preferred to mourn alone and not draw attention to themselves. As Peig's son Maidhc Ó Guithín said:

> Duinnshléibhe was going to compose a lament for my grandfather when he was drowned on the Inis, but my grandmother would not let him. He was a great poet.[13]

There was no chance, of course, that Léan could remain on in the Inis with her children and the old woman. So it was soon arranged that they would change over with Muiris Ó Dálaigh and his wife Cáit Ní Ghuithín, a sister to Seán, the drowned man. The Ó Dálaigh family, Muiris and Cáit, would set up on the Inis and Léan, her family and mother-in-law would go back and live on the Great Blasket. So it happened. They packed up their few possessions and made their way down the cliff path, bidding a tearful farewell to the Inis. Léan hadn't long removed to the Great Blasket when she gave birth to a boy, Mícheál, known as Maidhc (Mike), also called Maidhc Léan from his mother, who now had to rear him single-handed. That was in 1874. Most of us knew some of Maidhc's family, who lived at Barr an Bhóthair, Baile na Rátha, Dunquin, after they left the Blasket in 1953. There was Seán Mhaidhc Léan, Máire Mhaidhc Léan, who was married to Laurence Larry Ó Ciobháin (Kavanagh), and Muiris Mhaidhc Léan who lived in Baile na Rátha, till he moved to Ventry to live with his niece, although he still returned several days a week to his old home for some time.

Muiris remembered hearing talk of the tragedy when he was young: "When they found the boat the cork was missing from it. That was the only thing that was wrong."[14]

What Muiris meant is that it was a wooden boat with a cork in the bottom for draining and drying it out when on land. While the three were on the sea, the cork must have come out of the hole, and the fishermen were unable to cover the hole quick enough to prevent the boat's submerging and sinking.

Tomás mentions the swap over: "There was hardly two months passed before a new group went to live on it, a man with a fine family that were mostly girls."[15]

The vacancy on the Inis had been filled immediately, and the custom that some relation of the previous inhabitants would fill it had been upheld: "The three were never found . . . but the dead are of no use to the living, and the master came and gave the job to the only sister [sic] of the drowned man . . . the widow and her family lived on the Blasket from then on."[16]

Cáit and Muiris Ó Dálaigh must have been very reluctant to take up the position and transfer into the Inis. But, of course, Cáit would have been no stranger there, where she had been born and reared. But there would be a hard, tough, lonely life ahead of them, full of hardship, risks and danger, no neighbours to call on, no priest nor doctor and, on top of that, Cáit expecting another baby.

Chapter VI

Muiris Mór Ó Dálaigh

Way back in the early years of the nineteenth century, Séamus Ó Dálaigh from Bailícín, Dunquin, married Nóra de Lóndra (Landers), and they went to live in a little house in Baile an Ghleanna. They lived there through the famine years.

There is no other event that happened in Dunquin during these terrible years remembered as much as the story of Bríde Liath Ní Shúilleabháin (Sullivan) from Coumeenole in the same parish of Dunquin, some mile or two from Baile an Ghleanna. It is the story that most recalls the suffering and sacrifice the people endured.

Bríde was one of the Sullivans, and though she was married we do not know her husband's name, as women kept their maiden names. She was well known as a spinner of wool and travelled around the parish and into the Blaskets plying her craft.

Then the Hunger struck, and Bríde's husband died, and each of her eight children were taken from her, one after the other, by death, until she was left with only one, a very beautiful girl: "The finest and most beautiful girl in Kerry for years."

Bríde was happy and grateful that God had seen fit to leave her this last daughter. But it wasn't to be. The hunger of the famine was followed by the dread disease cholera, and it took away Bríde's last daughter.

The people, terrified of this disease and afraid that they could take it from each other, remained indoors. There was no one to help Bríde to convey the girl to the graveyard, dig the grave and bury her in God's earth. She had to place her trust in God and make the journey, a while stumbling, a while resting, carrying the body of her dead daughter on her back tied on with *súgán*, straw rope. As she went down through Baile an Ghleanna, she had to cross the stream at the stepping stones. Nóra de Lóndra saw her from her own door as she crossed. She was filled with pity and mercy. She went to the basket where she was storing next year's seed potatoes and put them among the embers at the edge of the fire that they might be baked for Bríde on her return journey.

Bríde continued on her sad journey that went, at that time, up the Clasach road and then across to Baile na hAbha graveyard, the old

Dunquin graveyard by the church. Just inside the gate she dropped her load. She hadn't the energy left to dig the grave. Just then some of the Baile na hAbha men approached. They had seen her arriving the Dead Road, and they couldn't but come to help her bury her daughter. When they had filled in the grave, Bríde remained behind to sing her lament, long, soft and sweet:

> Sleep soundly in eternal repose, my own family and my kind husband. There is no chance that you will be awakened until the sea fills in from the north and the raven turns bright white. Be not afraid, my family, that you will be endangered by hunger or thirst! You will have sufficient of the Stream of Glory to quench your thirst today. I leave you sleeping here in God's grace till the Angel blows the trumpet on the last day.
>
> She bade her daughter farewell as well as her kind neighbours, and started on the long road home to Coumeenole, heavy hearted and lonely, with nothing left in life for her. She crept along by the hedge at the roadside. Nóra de Lóndra was waiting for her at Baile an Ghleanna by the stream. She approached her, took her by the hand and brought her into her own home, put her by the fire and gave her the baked potatoes she had prepared with a drop of milk:
>
> "Indeed, my love to you, Bríde. Yours is a sad story, and it is the hard cruel world you have to face, but come in for a moment and sit, and if it was in the corner you must stay, then remain till morning, and welcome."
>
> Bríde answered:
>
> "Indeed, thanks to God, for potatoes, that Did not leave you in Baile na hAbha!"
>
> The words she uttered and their meaning are discussed to the present day. But whatever meaning may be taken from them, it is certain that Bríde had done a mother's share with her whole family.
>
> When Bríde Liath returned home, hadn't the people of the village burned her house to the ground before her. It was the only way to ensure that the evil disease that lived therein would also be burned. Bríde had no further reason to remain on in Coumeenole. She left the place and never returned, but took to the roads, a day here and a day there. She was very skilled at spinning, and she was always welcome wherever she went. She lived to an old age, over ninety it is said. Wherever she is buried, it is not in Baile na hAbha, because: ". . . no sod was ever again lifted from that grave."[1]

Nóra de Lóndra and Séamus Ó Dálaigh did not stay long in Baile an Ghleanna after that. The famine had lain very heavily on them, and they wanted to make a new start. It was time to run. They raised their sails, left the old home and headed for America. They were getting on in years a little, but they had their family raised, and they had courage and hope in God.

A good part of Nora and Séamus's house could be seen until recently on the banks of the little stream with its toes in the water, as Seán de Lóndra from Seantóir told me. Nóra was originally from Baile an Chaladh in the parish of Dún Urlann, and she was always remembered there. One night in Kruger's pub forty odd years ago, a row erupted during a card game. Seán de Lóndra, or Seán Kelly, as he was called, was involved. Things threatened to get out of hand into a full-blown row. Seán spoke up strongly to the company and told them that anyone from Dunquin had small cause to fight anyone named de Lóndra from Baile an Chaladh. Everyone stopped on the spot. There was no need to say anything further. Enough said. That was the end of the dispute.

They all said afterwards, and there were wise men among them, that Seán de Lóndra was completely correct and that everyone in Dunquin had good reason to defer to him.

Séamus Ó Dálaigh married Nóra de Lóndra from Baile an Chaladh on 3 February 1818. Their first child, Máire, was born in December 1818. Their first son, Tomás, was born two years afterwards, 1820. They had another son, Seán, in October 1823, and a daughter, Eilís, in January 1825. The last of their sons, Muiris Mór Ó Dálaigh, was born in October 1827, and he was baptised by Fr John Casey, the parish priest, on 14 October.[2]

Muiris Ó Dálaigh was close to thirty years of age when Dunquin church was being built. He was very strong, as were many of the Ó Dálaighs, including his son Paddy na hInise and Paddy's family after.

It is told of Muiris Mór that he was at the building of the church. The people of the parish were all working there voluntarily, digging foundations, shifting earth, drawing stones and building. Some of the stones came from Baile an Teampaill on the site where they worked, from the ruins of the old houses that had stood there and had been evacuated during the famine. Some other stones were drawn from inside the Gleann Mór (Big Glen), where the stones remained from another deserted village, while still more were being drawn from a small adjoining quarry called Job Long's quarry. The stones were being drawn by barrows. These were not wheelbarrows but rather hand-barrows, flat barrows with two handles on each end that two men could carry. There was another man named Breeny working there, a stranger who had come into the parish as a tenant. This man had acquired a rather bad name, particularly around women, that he was constantly watching them so as to do them harm. The women of the parish were particularly afraid of him:

> Breeny was a great workman, very strong. Muiris Ó Dálaigh, a young man, was working there at the time. Muiris was the son of Eoghan [recte, Séamus] Ó Dálaigh who lived in Bailícín. He had not married at all at this time. As he was working he noticed that Breeny was being unfair to a young lad who was working on the barrow with him–he used to fill the barrow too full. Muiris told the young lad that they would swap over, and Muiris was too much for Breeny by the time the day was done.[3]

Muiris also gave a spell working over in Cuan farm in the parish of Ventry, the property of the Earl of Cork. We don't know how he got to know the beautiful girl from Inisvickillane, Cáit Ní Ghuithín, or Cáit a' Mhódhraigh as she was named from her mother. (She was the daughter of Seán Mhuiris Liam Ó Guithín and Máire de Mórdha, who had probably been from Dunquin. They married on Shrove Tuesday, a traditional day for marriages, 12 February 1858. They went to live on the Blasket in a little cabin that it is thought was just above and to the right side of the Púicín Buí, the *clochán* or beehive hut that is still there. They settled down happily there. A little of the cabin remains there still.[4]

Muiris Mór was a sore loss to Dunquin, according to Tomás: "It is from the parish of Dunquin that the Dálach came when he was a young man and there wasn't in that parish a finer man than he. A widow woman that was here took him in as a *cliamhain isteach* [a man who married into a household] to her daughter, and they spent a long while of their life together."[5]

Muiris's sister Eilís, or Nell, as she was called, who was two years his senior, went into the Island also about the same time, having married Mící Ó Catháin (Keane). One of their sons, Peats, became the King of the Island afterwards.

One of the greatest difficulties relating to the Inis was the difficulty of landing there. The strand was difficult and awkward, and the way to the top risky and dangerous, particularly to animals. Efforts had been made as far back as 1870 to improve the situation when a vote was passed at the

Dingle Presentment Sessions, with Hon. E.A. de Moleyns, chairman, Captain Rowan, Messers Edward Rae, Edward Hussey, H. Hussey, M. Ferriter, M. Connor, T. Flaherty, J. Bowler, N. Fitzgerald and P. Real on the committee, that a road would be constructed round Slea Head, at the cost of £1.10 a perch. A second vote allowed £40 to build a slip and landing place on Inisvickillane.

It was reported at the meeting that: "The fishermen, both from the island and mainland were all in favour of it; and one stated that the work already done there was the means of saving his own and the lives of thirty-two other fishermen, who were caught in a storm."[6]

The vote was passed, £600 for the Slea Head Road and £40 for the Inis slip, and the notice placed in the local papers: "For making a landing slip and passage thereto in the island of Inishrickilane [*sic*], £40.00."[7]

Was the slip ever constructed? If yes, it has not stood the rigours of time and weather, nor does there seem to be any further reference to it. Paddy na hInise says some sixty years later: "I keep up the quay every year and if it wasn't for that no boat could be brought in there."

And again: "I asked the Government to repair the quay for me, but they didn't do it, although they did not refuse me."[8]

Another small indirect improvement was the erection of the Tiaracht Lighthouse and the lighting of the lamps. The building of the lighthouse on such a bare rock was a wonderful feat in itself. This work began in the summer of the year 1864, and the work went on for the next two summers. The tower and the houses for the lightkeepers were erected 263ft above the sea. The building stones were cut from the rock of the Tiaracht itself.

John D. Nagle refers to the Blaskets, the Ó Dálaigh on the Inis and to the lighthouse that is in the process of construction in his article for both the *Liverpool Echo* and the *Cork Examiner* in August 1866:

> Were it not that the Blaskets lie a few leagues to the north of vessels going to and from America it is not known what destruction they would have caused to life and property; but the new lighthouse now being built on the one called Tearacht (which is an island of 758 feet above the level of the ocean in a conical form like a sugar loaf) will when completed avert in a great measure the sacrifice of human life and the destruction of valuable property . . . the only inhabited one of these islands save for a shepherd and his family on the western island which lies up to eight nautical miles west of Dunmore Head.
>
> The islanders chiefly derive their living from the hidden treasures of the deep by fishing with the seines and handlines. Though the

majority of them are in humble circumstances, of what I might call farmers and poor fishermen, they have been the most generous and hospitable people on the face of the earth. I mean to shipwrecked mariners and fishermen who may be caught inside by rough weather. I could give several instances to prove this assertion.[9]

The light first burned on May Day 1870, and from then on a streak of light was cast regularly every minute across the sea, even lighting parts of Inisvickillane and Inis Tuaisceart. It wasn't that it made any difference to the life on the islands, but it was a contact with the living world. Also, the lightkeepers used call in to the Inis on their way back and forth to their headquarters on Valentia Island. It would seem that the Inis people were of great assistance to the lighthouse people also.[10]

Paddy na hInise mentions one occasion when he was of assistance to them: "There are signs between myself and the people on the Lighthouse in the Tiaracht and when they are in any difficulty I go over to them. It was us who brought up the man who fell over the cliff this year."[11]

They understood each other and knew that there was little between life and death on both rocks; something similar happened again on the Tiaracht in 1913 when one of the lightkeepers fell over a cliff when he was trying to drive goats home to be milked. One such incident happened on a winter's night in the last century when Seán Tom Ó Cearnaigh, Seán Mhicil Ó Súilleabháin (Sullivan) and Seáisí Ó Cearnaigh were out fishing mackerel. They saw a rocket being fired by the lightkeepers, and they knew there was something wrong and that they needed assistance. There were no telephones on the Tiaracht in those days. They headed for the Tiaracht. It is ten miles from the slip on the Blasket to the Tiaracht, ten miles of rough, heavy sea. They arrived on the Tiaracht where one of the lightkeepers had fallen down a cliff while tending to his goats, and he was unconscious. They wanted to remove the injured man to hospital in Caherciveen and then to collect another lightkeeper from Skellig Michael to be brought to the Tiaracht to replace the sick man. They managed to lower the sick man by rope and brought him to the Blasket Island where the woman looked after him for a while. Then they headed out to sea again for the twenty miles to Caherciveen. They brought the sick man to hospital and then headed for Skellig Michael and brought the lightkeeper from there to the Tiaracht, arriving there in the evening after sunset. They still had ten miles to go to reach home. They spent two days and two nights on the sea, which is a feat in itself. Three pounds each was their reward.

The lightkeeper returned to the Tiaracht where he recovered. There were plenty of lightkeepers and sailors who were well looked after on the Blasket when the good people lived there.[12]

But from 1870, the light could be seen from the Inis, and a new place name, well known to fishermen, came into being: a rather strange one–the Light.

"We'll go as far as the Light," they might say to each other, meaning they would row out until the light would catch them.

And the Light would be the last glimpse that many an emigrant would get of the old land as they steamed on their way from Queenstown to New York. The lighthouse remained manned until the spring of 1988, when it became automatic and the men left.

Anyhow, after Cáit's brother Seán drowned in 1873 and they were offered the Inis, Muiris and Cáit discussed the new twist that had presented them with the chance of a new life there. They would be independent. There would be no rent. The land was good. They would have £8 a year payment. They came to the conclusion that they would take the chance on going in. But Cáit laid down one strict condition for Muiris–keep away from the sea. One widow in the family was enough.

There were definite advantages to living on the Inis, wonderful advantages in those tough times:

> There was the understanding between the shepherd and the one who
> owned the Stone to give him enough land to cultivate two milk cows,
> and eight pounds a year. And if the master paid the Stone a visit in
> the season, he would not go there empty-handed, and there was many
> ways he could be of assistance to them if he was happy with them.[13]

It used to be said in those times that the family who had potatoes, fish and milk would never be hungry. Those were to be had in plenty on the Inis and even other products that meant there would be nothing wanting. They were good conditions for those times, on islands or on mainland. If Muiris were to stay away from the sea, they would give it a go. And he agreed. Wasn't it only a few years since five from Dunquin were drowned in the *Body*, the Baile na Rátha seine boat that was returning from Beginis loaded with seaweed. He understood the danger on the Inis and was happy to stay away from the sea. You would have to have mastery over it or else it would have mastery over you. It was a game of life and death, and it was often that death won the game.

It would be beautiful on the Inis when the bright sun of summer shone on Gort an Earraigh and Log na bhFiolar, but it would be different when there were days and weeks when you could not put out your head with fog, wind or rain with a north-west storm blowing. You could be stuck there for five or six weeks by the bad weather without sufficient food. They had heard the story of the sheeps' milk that had kept the people alive on the Inis for three months. They had heard also the dread story of Inis Tuaisceart, where the man of the house died and his wife had to cut up his body in pieces to take it out from the partly underground beehive hut in which they lived.

Given all that and even with Cáit expecting her baby, shortly after (about two months, according to Tomás Ó Criomhthain), Muiris Mór, Cáit and the family and the two cows moved to the old two-roomed house left vacant by the Guiheens.

> . . . a fine family, mostly girls; he [Muiris] had no man's help except himself. He was a fine man, a man that thistles or fairies wouldn't frighten. When he went in he had intended to stay away from the sea, to be sowing and reaping for himself on the top of the Stone, mind his flock, to kill enough rabbits for himself, pay a visit to the Island once every three months and bring back a full boatload of food from the Blasket that would do him for three months. The wife was the one that mostly left the Inis when anything was needed because it was she who feared the fairies and not him. He lived those first years on the Inis and he didn't have much to spare.[14]

New life began on the Inis. There would be smoke from the chimney in Tigh na hInise, dogs barking, hens scurrying and scraping around inside and outside the house, a couple of pigs rooting in the mud, sheep all around in front of the house, the two cows and the goats, children's clothes drying on the line, a stack of turf at the gable, crying and laughing to be heard again around the Inis. Muiris Mór would have been about forty-four years old and Cáit in her early thirties:

> The Dálach accepted the post without much delay and gathered together his few possessions. A boat went with help, and everything was brought over in one day. The master of the Stone sent him two sacks of yellow meal. There were a couple of cows on the Island, and he took them with him as there was always the grass of two cows for every herd that ever went there.[15]

We do not know when the house on the Inis that is there today was built. The Guiheens built it at some stage before the famine. The walls are built of dry rough stones without any mortar. The walls were plastered on the inside, but it doesn't appear that there was ever plaster on the outside, which is unusual for Blasket homes, where they were plastered outside and then whitewashed. There were various timbers in the roof, wreck that came in on the sea from time to time. There was a thatched roof on it at first, but towards the end of the nineteenth century, felt and tar were introduced, which were very much welcomed on the islands, as they could stand up much better to the storm than the thatch. The floor consisted of trampled clay on which fine sand would be shaken to keep it clean and dry.

If Muiris and Cáit had up to a dozen in the family, it is hard to imagine where they all got space to lie down at night. (The measurements of Tigh na hInise at the time of Griffith's Valuation about 1850 were 20ft in length, 13ft in width, with walls which were 5ft in height.)

There was but a kitchen and a bedroom. How must life have been for them in bad weather when they could not look out the door? They must have had the great gift of patience and a great understanding of each other. But that was family, in the proper sense of the word: all the members living peacefully and happily together, all under one blanket. The mother gave the love to them all and saw to their needs, and the father also gave love and worked to provide for them from morning till night. Both mother and father would teach the children the basic skills of life through example: milking the cows, cleaning the home, fishing, cutting the turf, sowing the crops, music, prayers, charity and respect for the neighbours.

Still, visitors were always welcome, whether scholars from England or Dublin studying the archaeology or nature; the people from the Great Blasket coming to hunt the rabbits, the seals or the seabirds, or fishing; or the people from Uíbh Ráthach trying to get a living from the sea. Others who were always welcome were the people from Gráig, Tioramháin or Clogher, who came for the lobster season. They would share what they had, regardless of how small the house was. They would all sleep on mattresses stuffed with seabirds' feathers, stretched in the kitchen or in the one bedroom. Eibhlín Bean Uí Shé remembers her father telling her that Cáit used to sleep in the doorway between the kitchen and the bedroom. Her father was a tailor, the Tailor Lynch, and he went in one year with a suit of clothes he had made for Paddy.

R.M. Lockley also slept in the house when he visited the Inis in August 1936: "A mackerel net had been folded to make a bed for me on a bench by the turf fire in Inisvickillaun house."[16]

It wasn't long before Muiris got in on the work on the Inis and was settling down nicely. As Paddy na hInise said years afterwards:

> My soul, I remember the day when my grandfather kept a beautiful garden here! Let me tell you he farmed the Inish a thousand times better than they do the Blasket to-day. You would scarcely credit that there is not a bull in the Blasket to serve the cows? They have to be taken to the bull at Dunquin in one of these giddy canoes. My grandfather always kept a bull here. He had a grand farm with four cows and many asses, and a flock of sheep. The fields were full of good oats, wheat and potatoes. If it were possible I too would prefer to live here as he did, always, but there's no peace with the young folk–they will be tearing off to the fairs and the races and the cinema of Dingle.[17]

It is not hard to imagine how difficult life must have been for the Ó Dálaighs in these early years on the Inis: "There used to be a shepherd on Inisvickillane at that time, Muiris Ó Dálaigh his name, and he had a good life there, that is when his own family grew up; until that his was only a hard life."[18]

They were not there long when they had their first crisis. It appeared as if the baby were going to come on early. Cáit became anxious and frightened. What would happen if there were any complications? She made up her mind quickly; it wasn't time to delay. The fire was lit on Cnocán na Tine (the Fire Rock). By some accounts, there was always dry wreck wood there, covered and laid aside for emergencies. Soon the black shape of the *Collach Dubh* appeared on the horizon, and it wasn't long before it sailed into the Léithreach, the cove by the headland. They left the Inis, Cáit with her helpers making their careful way down the cliff path, she with a rope tied around her, gripped by Muiris in close attendance. They set sail for the Blasket, three men rowing at their best, throwing the white foam from the boat's prow. Muiris and Cáit's grandson, Deálaí, takes up the story more than a hundred years later:

> I had an aunt called Lís na Beannaí. Her mother, my grandmother, was being brought out from the Inis to have her baby. Coming west from the Inis they were. They had to bring her into the Beannaigh, and it was there the baby was born. The Beannaigh is part of the Island. I never knew Lís na Beannaí. She went off to America when she was still a young girl. I never met her. But I named my first child after her.[19]

They survived the crisis. The mother came home with the new little baby, and life continued on for the bigger family. They were all there far from anywhere, depending on the land. But Muiris Mór was a great worker, and his courage never failed him.

"He was accustomed to hard work. He used to have oats and potatoes and every other sort sown, including even tobacco."[20]

It was far from hunger, but fine, fresh, healthy food that made them strong and energetic: "They used to have meat too, the sheep that would fall into the sea, or would become clifted, plenty of rabbits, birds and seals, and every other food that the people used in those times, and on account of eating such strong food, every man of them would be as strong as a horse."[21]

As well as fish caught from the rocks, seabirds' eggs and milk, they had their own vegetables growing: cabbage, potatoes, onions, turnips and oats for bread and porridge. If there was little to spare, there was no shortage. They all went around barefooted, dressed out in their own homespuns.

Muiris Mór and Cáit may have had up to seven children before they left the Blasket, although Tomás mentions that they had ten while still there. Eilís seems to have been the seventh child. They were all girls up to this, except one boy, Mícheál.

According as the family were growing, they were lending a hand more and more, and life was getting a little easier. Two things happened then that improved their lot, as it did in many other households by the sea. The *naomhóg* or canoe made its appearance around the Blaskets about 1880. It had come from the Maharees, where it had been developed by three families there: the Hartneys, Goodwins and Learys. The *naomhóg* proved to be much more efficient to small communities that the old heavy, eight-handed boats. They were small, light, easy to manoeuvre and could be handled by a crew of three or four.

The second thing that helped on the islanders was the new fish, the lobster. Great demand for lobster as a gourmet food grew among the rich in England and France. Good money was to be had for the lobster, and they were found to be very plentiful in the shallow waters around the Blaskets and, in particular, Inisvickillane. Again, the *naomhóga* were very suitable for that sort of fishing, in and around the rocks. It was from Uíbh Ráthach that the culture of lobster fishing came to the Inis and it came at a very suitable time for the Ó Dálaighs.

The *naomhógs* were very well represented all along the coast of Corca Dhuibhne, but came to an end there. Very few of them were used by the fishermen of Uíbh Ráthach. According to the Report of the Union of Caherciveen of the Congested Districts Board for the year 1892, the only *naomhógs* in the district were in Valentia Island:

> There are in this district 330 men and seventy-eight boats employed in fishing and carrying turf and seaweed; the boats are all open row-boats, from twenty to thirty feet long. There are no canoes in this district. Of the above, twenty-one men and seven boats carry sand and seaweed alone, chiefly for manure.[22]

But then, as regards Valentia Island, it states:

> Portmagee employs 64 boats and 268 men, and Valencia 45 boats and 158 men; total, 109 boats and 426 men. In Portmagee both wooden and four and six-oared open boats and canvas canoes are used, fishermen, as a rule, prefer the canoes as being handier and lighter. This is the most southerly point in Ireland where canoes are used.[23]

Dr. William Petty (1623–1687), a Cromwellian settler, introduced the seine boats to Kerry, particularly in south Kerry, where he held sway. He was presented with a huge territory of about 270,000 acres in the Kenmare area in return for compiling a national survey of the land to be planted. This he did, with a force of 1,000 foot soldiers. He then got to work and proved to be a genius in creating wealth and industry. He established iron and copper mines, as well as developing woods, fisheries and the seine boats:

> He established salmon, herring and at Kenmare, Ballinaskelligs, Dursey and Killmakilloge. The big seine boats still used in the bay were his introduction. He introduced the special local system of "sweeper" nets used to surround salmon by means of a seine boat and a smaller boat, a "follower." Seine boats are now used for the local sport of seine boat racing.[24]

It is clear that the seine boats were long established in Uíbh Ráthach and that most fishermen had no desire to try the new *naomhógs*.

And it seems that it was from there that Muiris got to know about lobsters and *naomhógs*. The story goes that one day when he was on the hill after the sheep, he saw a boat full of lobster pots. He went down to the slip to meet it and speak to the men on the boat. They understood each other as they all spoke in Irish:

70

They were from Uíbh Ráthach, and they wanted to get permission from him to fish for lobsters around his island, and that all would get his share . . . He was willing . . . lobsters were plentiful around the Stone, and that was the first time any equipment ever came to the Inis to fish them . . . Dálaigh had an old stocking full of yellow gold and silver from them at the end of the season. They went home and the next year they came again.[25]

"Although he had spent a while up on the Stone without going to sea because his wife wouldn't let him, Muiris broke his pledge to his wife about staying far from the sea."[26]

The lobster fishing went from May to September. A great deal of work was needed at that type of fishing. The lobster pots had to be made, a skill in itself. Willow rods were used, of which there was a great shortage in the Blaskets and surroundings because of the rough weather. Even in Dunquin and the parishes around, it was a scarce commodity, growing only in sheltered patches. The fishermen used to have to travel to places like Annascaul to fetch them and then pay for them. They had to be brought home then and steeped in a stream to soften them and the pots made. They had to be completed before the sowing of the potatoes. Then they had to have ropes to draw them from the bottom of the sea. Salted fish was the usual bait that was fixed in the pot.

The Ó Dálaighs then tried to grow the willows on the Inis with some success: "There are three fishermen in each *naomhóg* that fishes lobster. They fish twenty pots at least, and they try to have about a dozen to spare, because there is often the storm during the season and the pots are scattered away never to be seen again."[27]

Twice a day they would draw the pots, morning and evening. In the case of the Inis, that would mean a trip right around in the direction of the sun, east to west, so that, as they would say, they were returning home from the moment they started rowing. The catch would then be transferred to the store pots, large floating wooden boxes where the lobsters would remain alive until the boat from France or England would arrive.

That was Muiris's new job, but, as usual, his courage stood to him. Besides, the family was growing, and some of them were able to take care of themselves and to help him on the sea as well. The money from the lobsters was a godsend to pay the outstanding bills in Long's of Dingle. The standard of living improved for everyone on the Inis. They lived better than many, whether on the Blasket or on the mainland itself.

Lobsters were plentiful in those days. It wasn't long until boats from France came and offered a shilling for every lobster for the year. So it was until there were five boats blowing their horns at the Blaskets looking for lobsters. We spent a few years like that, no fisherman ever short of a shilling, with the boat arriving at the end of the house to us, and gold to be had for our fishing, as much as we caught.

A couple of boats came from Uíbh Ráthach to Inisvicillane at that time. They included the Inis man and his two sons, because they had their own *naomhóg*. Muiris Mór Ó Dálaigh had a good life in the Stone from that year until he left it.[28]

This was another golden age on the Inis during these years, years of plenty, and it wasn't long before the Ó Dálaighs took to repairing the *naomhóg*, making oars, and patching the canvas. They had to make do themselves. The next step was to make them themselves, and the Ó Dálaighs became masters at the craft. As well as that, their share of the cattle, the sheep and the pigs were thriving. It is Tomás Ó Criomhthain again who gives us such a fine account of those days when Inisvickillane was his Tír na nÓg. He was a young man, a fisherman himself, and the crew often called into the Inis for a break, to get water or just to visit. Tomás was very happy to visit, with good reason. There was a crop of beautiful girls there:

> But the great demand came for the sort of fish called lobsters (a shell fish): there was a great demand from England at that time, and the family of the shepherd had grown up by that time and had their own boat.
>
> At that time I used often to be there, because we would be always fishing around there, and if we had caught nothing to bring home we would pull in the boat, because that was the order we had got from the old couple in the house.[29]

You would think it was then that Tomás got to know the Ó Dálaighs, but that doesn't seem to be the case. When Muiris Mór and Cáit were newly married, the next house to theirs directly across from it was the house of Daniel Crohan or Daniel McCrohan, father of Tomás Ó Criomhthain. Tomás was called Tomás Dhómhnaill by the islanders, after his father. In that case, the two families must have known each other well, and since there was only three or four years between Tomás and Cáit, the eldest of the Ó Dálaigh children, they also must have known each other very well. In 1873, about the time the Ó Dálaighs went to live on the Inis,

Cáit would have been thirteen or fourteen and Tomás about eighteen. They probably even attended school together on the Island.

The Inis family gained the name of having big hearts, an echo back, perhaps, to Nóra de Lóndra and her treatment of Bríde Liath Ní Shúilleabháin in her time of trial. They loved having people visiting them, made everyone welcome and shared everything with them.

> The people used to say that these were the best couple that ever stood on the Stone, and they had a special reason for being nice to us. They had five sons and five daughters, the finest family together that two parents ever had.[30]

The Islandman (Tomás Ó Criomhthain) is not given to lavishing praise on those he knew but, more often than not, was quick in finding fault, whether it was deserved or not. But not so in the case of the Ó Dálaighs of the Inis. All he needed was an excuse to praise them to the skies:

> So, I'm going to mention Muiris Mór Ó Dálaigh, and anyone that asked me about him, as to what sort of a man he was, I am strongly of the opinion that as far back as I can remember, I cannot remember a finer man in every sort of way. He was a man for the strand, for the boat and for the hill. He was the man for the street, for the pub and for the bench. He was kind and generous in every manner. There were other fine men at the time, and there still are, but the Dálach Mór was a man who never said, "I'm exhausted" no matter how hard the burden of the day fell on him.[31]

There was no end to their generosity to all:

> There is no one who ever lived there that anyone who ever visited them had nothing but the kindest and best reports of them. It is often that fishermen had to seek refuge there when the weather was too rough and they unable to go back home, because they have every sort of hunting there, between fish and birds and rabbits and seals and they to be had plentiful around this Stone, and they were continually there and often unable to get off, and very frequently there used be four and five boats together there, and maybe, they would have to spend three days altogether there without leaving.[32]

They had learned the old system of the islands, to depend on and support each other. Maria Simonds-Gooding remembers noticing it years later when she got to know the islanders on her journeys to the Island:

It also made great sense of man's potential. Community living in its purest sense, brings out great qualities. Wherever it is left in the world it usually means hardship, where by pulling together, sharing the ups and downs, they survive.

I remember sitting one long evening by a fire on the Island and asking an islander how it was they lived like one family, all helping each other. His answer was that they had to do it. If neighbours had a row in the morning and were not speaking to each other–they would be speaking by the evening because they couldn't survive otherwise.

In the sixties I often spent a few weeks at a time with the islanders who were on the Great Blasket to shear sheep. We cooked and ate together. Everything was shared, it was their nature without question.

The Island, though often ravaged by storm and the elements, endlessly threatening rough seas and inaccessibility, has nonetheless a warm and good feeling about it, enveloping and freeing the spirit.[33]

For Muiris Mór and his family, the good life continued for a while:

The following year, the Inis man's family had grown: and two different crews from Uíbh Ráthach came fishing there. The son went with one crew, and he himself went with the other, and they made good money. The man from the Stone was, every year from then on, himself and his two sons, fishing there continually until one of the sons went to America, and a while after that another one left, and when they saw that was where they were heading, although there were twelve of them, between sons and daughters, they had slipped away from them little by little until only the one son was left to them at this time, and because there was no chance of getting a wife on this backward island, the last son made up his mind to leave it. They all decided to leave it, as there was only the father, mother and son living there in the end.[34]

Chapter VII

The Trip to Dingle

Muiris never had any wish to leave the Inis. He was happy there, putting in the day doing his chores. Even if it had the name of being visited by the fairies, he had no fear of them alive or dead.

> When the Dálach accepted the post to be shepherd on this rock–a distant island in the middle of the great ocean–he promised himself that he would not retreat from dead or alive, from strong or weak, and on account of that his courage was all the greater.[1]

Cáit it was who, now and then, made an effort to get away and have a trip to Dingle, "And every time they needed anything from the west it was herself who travelled."[2]

She would usually bring one or two of the family along, that they might see places and meet people, particularly the girls when they began to grow up, that the farmers might see the fine girls and have an eye to marriage with one of them:

> The Inis woman remained for a week on the Great Island and, when there was anyone going to town, she went there with her two daughters, that they would experience the outside. It's many a person who might be in need of a fine woman that would not have a great deal of dowry, as there wasn't much in the line of dowry those times except with well-off people.[3]

Tomás tells of such a trip the Inis woman and her daughter Cáit, Tomás's girl, made to Dingle with two fine pigs for the fair. Diarmaid, Tomás's uncle, and Tomás himself had promised that they would come to the Inis and fetch the two pigs for the Saturday market. All they really wanted was an excuse to go to the Inis, and to Dingle:

> There was no fair that time except on Saturday. When a fine day came during the week when the Ó Dálaighs planned to take over the pigs, it was early enough in the morning when my old uncle came in to me
> . . .
> "Yerra, what hurry is on you today?" says I to him.

"Sure, my boy, it will be a fine day today. We will go and fetch the pigs," says he, "and, it is likely," says he again, "that you'll be in no way lazy going there, whoever else will be," says the uncle.

"Yerra, why all this?" says my mother–it was she who answered first.

"Well, bad luck to you, if that's how it is!" says he. "Aren't all the girls on the Stone losing their heads after this lad, and they are there, all beautiful," says he.

"Be out in two hops!" says he to me.[4]

It wasn't long before they were out on the great ocean and the sails raised and Tomás's heart as light as a starling. They reached the Inis and took the pigs and the two women, Cáit and her mother, with them:

> There was no stop until they were landed in the boat, two fine yearling pigs, the woman of the house and her daughter, the daughter that Diarmaid, my uncle, had been associating me with always.
>
> Out on the great ocean with us. Up with the sails. A fine wind that brought us to the harbour and bay of the Great Blasket . . . There was no shortage of food for the pigs that night.
>
> The next morning after breakfast, everyone who had a pig or two pigs were getting ready to go to the mainland. I had a fine pig myself and my uncle Diarmaid had another in not as good a condition as her . . . They were all put aboard and another pig belonging to a man from the village, two of the Inis pigs, the Inis woman and her daughter. It was a big boat, and she was full to the brim with those I have accounted for.[5]

They were landed in Dunquin, and the boat set out for home again. There were a couple of other boats out with pigs, and they, too, went home. Off they set, with the pigs, up the Clasach road as the Dunquin people used all to do when they were going to Dingle. After about halfway, Diarmuid's pig gave up and refused to go any farther. The road was too long, the pig too heavy, and its feet weren't good. But Diarmaid was now among friends:

> "Stay in charge of the pigs," says he to me, "and by my word, it won't be long before I have a way that will raise them from the land of Ireland!" says he.
>
> I had to do what he said, although my own pig would have walked to Tralee. The two Inis women and their own pigs, I and the two other

pigs. We remained together until he arrived; with a fine horse; and a cart with a rail. The man with the horse was Diarmaid's uncle and, of course, my own mother's uncle as well.[6]

They put Diarmaid's pig and Tomás's pig into the cart, and the man with the cart took Tomás and the Inis woman into Dingle. Whatever about courtesy, Diarmaid and the young woman walked together into Dingle.

As regards Tomás: "When we got out the Inis woman would not let the horse go away until she had offered a drink to the horse man as well as to me."[7]

Then there was another mishap when the woman's pig made for the sea at Dingle quay after Diarmaid had given it a slap of a stick. Luckily, the hero was present:

> "God help us, the pig is drowned on the poor woman!" says he. "And is not that terrible, for a poor woman as good as she!" says he.
>
> . . . The pig's face was turned towards the quay at this time, and I grabbed the switch from my uncle's hand and ran out the quay. I stripped down my clothes from me, and swam out from the top of the quay. It wasn't long before Diarmaid spoke above me.
>
> "Don't for the life of you get involved with the pig, or she will leave you out there," says he. There was no need for him to say that to me, but the poor man was very afraid on my behalf.
>
> It wasn't long before I came up with her, and I took the switch that I had across my mouth and gave her a cut across the behind, and she went a full perch ahead with that and headed for the land. I was from one attempt to another until I had driven her in on the slip.[8]

The brave deed had been done by the warrior. What else to do but to make for a tavern up in Goat Street as soon as ever they had sold the pigs. It wasn't long before the drink was flowing freely to the accompaniment of singing:

> The old Inis woman was singing a song at this time, "*Ar Éire Ní 'Neosainn Cé hÍ*," and you wouldn't go to your food but stay to listen, and the young woman of a daughter she had better still.
>
> "The fairy music is playing," says a man to me.[9]

And she sang the sad song in the tavern in Goat Street, her favourite song about a boy who goes overseas seeking his fortune, in which he succeeds. He returns to his true love to ask her to marry him, but she has already married his own brother, and his love for her will be a secret for evermore.

They stayed overnight in Dingle, and the sport and entertainment continued on the following day. Soon the songs were in full voice again. Diarmaid caught Tomás by the hand and asked him to raise a song that would clear the clouds from his heart. Tomás obliged with *"Ré-Chnoc na Mná Duibhe,"* another sorrowful song about a fairy woman that has been granted leave from the *lios* for a short time. As Tomás says, if there were two better singers in the company there were three not as good as him. Singing and dancing were a very important part of the social life of the time, and a good singer was held in high esteem. The girls and boys thought highly of the one who could get up and sing a song.

We can imagine being present on that occasion, the golden day in the autumn of 1877, and again we can listen to the youth from the Island to the fore in the crowd in the tavern in Goat Street, his eyes closed and the company spellbound for a short while:

> *Casadh mo ghrá orm is ba náireach liom gan suí,*
> *Do leagas mo lámh ar a brághad is ar a croí,*
> *'Sé dúirt sí, 'anois fág mé is ní hábhar duit mé,*
> *Mar is bean dubhach ar fán mé a tharluigh id' linn.'*
> *'Más bean dúbhach ar an bhfán tu do ránaigh id' linn,*
> *Suigh anso láimh liom is tabhair dushlán fé gach buion,*
> *An tú Maighdean na mánla na dtáithíní mbuí,*
> *Nó an stuairín milis mánla sciob Paris ón Rí?*[10]

The Inis woman followed with another, followed by the daughter with *"An Clár Bog Déil"* ("The Soft Deal Board"), which she sang without fault:

> *Searc mo chléibh' do thugas féin duit is grá trí rún,*
> *Dá dtiocfadh sé mar chor sa tsaol go mbeinn féin agus tú*
> *Ceangal cléirigh orainn araon is an fáinne dlúth,*
> *'S dá bhfeicfinn féinig mo ghrá ag éinne gheobhainn bás le cumha.*
> *Tar a chogaraigh im' fhochairse go ragham 'on ghleann,*
> *Is tabharfad foscadh ar leaba fhlocais dhuit is aer cois abhann,*
> *Beidh na srutha ag gabháil tharainn fé ghéagaibh crann,*
> *Is beidh an londubh inár bhfochair is an chéirseach dhonn.*[11]

Tomás replied with *"Ar Éire Ní 'Neosainn Cé hÍ"* once more. It was aimed especially at the girl, of course, if she understood.

78

A fine big man bought them a drink, and,

> "I wonder," says he to me, "is there anyone else here who will sing?"
>
> "There is, my boy," says I to him, and I pointed out the two Inis women to him.
>
> The Inis women did not refuse him, and what did they do but for the pair of them to go singing the song together . . . I think I had the same thought as many present, that is that I would go without food or water for two days and nights just to listen to the two of them singing.[12]
>
> But we aren't finished yet: "I sang a song and two songs, and the Inis women three and four, and when I thought it was getting close to the time to go home I was badly mistaken.[13]

The Royal Irish Constabulary were aware of these strange people visiting Dingle. Here is C.P. Crane, who was the district inspector in the area around 1880:

> When I first knew Dingle numbers of persons in the extreme west and the dwellers on the Blasquet Islands "had no English." They spoke the Celtic language only. Many a time I have listened with interest and entertainment to the quaint, guttural tones of these frieze-clad natives attending the fairs and markets of Dingle.
>
> I learned enough to "bid the time of day," as the saying goes, but never got very far in the study of the language. Some of the Blasquet Islanders had never been to the mainland, and one old woman, having been persuaded to visit Dingle, exclaimed in her native tongue, "Oh, Mother Mary! I didn't think the world was so big!"[14]

They spent three days and three nights away from home. Tomás was the sensible one trying to organise them to begin the journey home. The Inis woman answered him back on the spot. She knew that life was just from today till tomorrow and that the company would never be together again:

> "Yerra, indeed," says she to me, "it's a day in our life and it's not always we will be able to have such a day," says she.

At eight o' clock the following morning, they started out on the road home in a hired horse and cart, and none of them in great condition.

These few days of the pigs were the happiest Tomás was ever to have.

They arrived at Dunquin and a boat had come out to fetch them home to the Blaskets.

But Diarmaid wasn't finished yet:

The Inis supplies were not taken out of the boat. Diarmaid formed a plan that we would go to the Stone for a couple of days, bring hunting equipment with us and that we would get a fine bundle of rabbits.[16]

Tomás thought they had had enough, and that it was time to be in their own homes, but: "Diarmaid was married to a sister of the Inis woman, and my mother was Diarmaid's sister; that was why I went with him every day. Of late I had become reluctant, because myself and the young woman were always carrying on together. But we got ourselves ready and raised our sails, and off we went till we reached the Inis."[17]

They spent a further two days and nights on the Stone hunting rabbits. Then back to the Inis house: ". . . songs a plenty during the night until it was one o'clock, I'd say, and sleep till late then. The old uncle never stopped drawing the two of us together every night at every opportunity . . ."[18]

On the morning of the third day, they planned to go home, rather reluctantly and sadly:

> We both had a full load coming to the boat, and everyone on the Stone followed us down to the water, and there was no whistling or noise because we were leaving.
>
> I don't mind telling you that I lost my sense of fun, whoever else lost it. Small wonder, and I leaving the time of my life when happiness was with me, and as well as that, when I was turning my back on the most wonderful young woman that walked this blessed earth at that time.[19]

Tomás paid one more visit to the holy land. After a night when Tomás hadn't had much sleep, Diarmaid entered the house and ordered him out:

> "Get dressed, it's a fine day," says the voice. I knew then it was Diarmaid of the Wind.
>
> "Get something to eat and we'll head west for Inisvickillane. We'll have a few days there. We'll have seals and rabbits, and maybe some of the women will come back with us," says he, "so, hurry up."
>
> It was many's the voice that would be more peculiar for me to hear, for there would be nothing better for me than to spend a week among the young women, because one of them was the one I chose among the women of Ireland at that time. Away with me and I got ready, and I got down to the quay and they were there waiting for me. It was a grand fine day, and it didn't take us long to reach the Inis.

They set sail for the Inis and reached it without much delay.

> There was a big family in it then, all grown up, and every one of them
> came to the edge of the harbour. You would think it was Tír na nÓg
> that day. We made for the house, and everything was ready before us,
> they had seen the boat approaching. Diarmaid was as merry as though
> he was in paradise.[20]

Again there was no shortage in the Inis, along with sport, entertainment
and good company.

> When we had eaten we went out to hunt, and every young person on
> the Stone with us, boys and girls. It was a beautiful day; rabbits
> running with dogs after them, catching one and two escaping. But it
> was close to the young women that I spent the evening, and so signs
> on it, I didn't catch much.
>
> There were six of us in all in the boat, two and two together. There
> was no one in my company except the people of the Stone, both boys
> and girls, and when the boys had a dozen killed for me they said,
> "Come on home to the house. You have enough for today; we will have
> a fine pack again for you tomorrow," said they.[21]

They returned to the house and had a meal. They had just finished
when Diarmaid and his friend Kerry arrived with a fine catch of rabbits.

> "More power to your arm, uncle," says I, "to be sure you're the fine
> hunter and not me who has only a dozen since morning," and he
> turned his face to me as I spoke.
>
> "Indeed, it's well I knew you wouldn't have much when I saw you
> with the young women this morning," says he.[22]
>
> The two men sat to the table and soon were eating a fine meal of
> rabbit and mutton.
>
> You could hear him outside the door chewing the bones of sheep
> and rabbit.
>
> "Sing a song or something for me," said he, "while I am eating."
>
> "Maybe I'll do a dance for you when you have eaten," said I.
>
> "Don't be mocking me," said he, "but sing St Patrick's Day for me."
>
> . . . I commenced singing long soft and sweet, and I well fitted for
> it, sitting there on the flat of my back in dry warm ferns, with nothing
> to be seen except my head, and just as I finished, he had finished
> eating the food.[23]

Lá 'le Pádruig is mé im' shuí i dtig tábhairne,
Bhí gasra sárfhear lem' shuí ag ól,
Bhí Máire mhánla na gcuacha breátha,
A súil mar áirne is a grua mar rós.
Bhí dís dearthár ann 'na suí ar cheann cláir ann,
'Thug gean is grá don mhaighdean óg,
Fear súiste is ramhainne ann is máistir scoláirí
A shiúl a lán is a léigh go leor.
Do labhair gach éinne ina oifig féinig
Dá mholadh a thréithe leis an maighdean óg,
'Féachaint arbh fhéidir í 'mhealladh in aon chor
Le ráite béil nó le bualadh bórd.
Do labhair an spéirbhean go míntais maorga,
'Ní mhéin liomsa éinne a bhualadh im' threo,
Ach an té is túisce a dhéanfadh mo ghnó a dhéanamh,
Sin é 'bheidh liomsa mar bhuachaill óg." [24]

Diarmaid was happy: "Mhuise, fair play to you!" says he, getting up from the table and giving my hand seven shakes.

For one moment Tomás pauses and recognises his situation as he freezes it in time:

". . . there was not a mother and five daughters in any other house in Ireland that would beat them for beauty."

And he thinks:

Youth is beautiful; there is nothing to compare with it. I thought at that time there was not a lord or earl in Ireland's ground but that I was as happy as him. With not a care in the world, stretched on the flat of my back in the sort of bed that Diarmaid Ó Duibhne had when he was fleeing with Gráinne, a bench of green rushes; wonderful company on a sea island, a crowd of young women by me on the other side of the house, that you would not know was it from heaven, from the next world or this the fine voices they had, nor no knowing which was the better.[25]

And we learn a little more about the social customs of the time:

The woman of the house was smoking tobacco at this time. She filled the pipe and gave it to Diarmaid . . . When everyone had sung a song, she organised a dance.

82

"You have been silent a good while," says hero me, "jump up and do a step for me. Take out one of those lumps of girls over there. Let someone play them a tune," says the rake.

There was no use in refusing, because he would be raging and spoil the evening. The woman of the house began lilting, and there wasn't better. I jumped out to be sure, and I called on the eldest son of the house, who was grown at that time. We danced a reel.

"Good luck to your legs!" says the rake.

We stayed like that until it was close to day, and then we all went for a sleep, and it was daytime before anyone wakened.[26]

Then they had their morning meal, and it was a good one, rabbit and mutton. The man of the house went out early to change the cows to another field and hadn't arrived back yet.

The food was laid out and we took to it, yellow bread that was hard enough, but we all had good teeth to grind it. There was no tea or sugar, and it would be a long time before there was. When everybody was full, one man took to filling his pipe, another whistling, and another lilting, and no one wanting to leave the cave.

"Out you go straight away, you pack of devils!" says Diarmaid.

Out they went as though the dogs had been set after them, in the same order as they were the previous day, in ones and twos. I picked to be in the company of the young women, as I was the day before.

Before I left the house, the man of the house had arrived, the stock fixed up and the round of the Stone made. He brought six rabbits that he had caught with his own dogs.

"The devil!" says Mícheál, the oldest son he had, "leave them to Tomás Dhónaill," that is to say, me. "Diarmaid was complaining yesterday about how few rabbits he had caught; he said that it was likely that we had spent the day dancing together," says the young man.

"Oh," says the man of the house, "if that's the way it is, you can have those for a start today, and maybe you will be every bit as good as themselves," says he.[27]

Muiris Mór then had something to eat:

A plate of meat and rabbits was placed in front of him, a mug of milk and everything we had, and he commenced to eat contentedly. But it is no exaggeration for me to say that there was not another man in the whole of Munster as well intentioned, as generous, as open and as welcoming as Muiris Mór Ó Dálaigh. I was going out again when he spoke.

"Wait awhile until I have finished this bite, and I will go along with you, and I'll get another half dozen for you," said he. "I have a little dog here that takes them out of the hole," says the Dálach.[28]

So they spent the morning. When they had enough rabbits they went back to the house.

I hung up the rabbits, and I began to dance about with one of the maidens. We did a single reel with the woman of the house providing the music. I can't say if a reel was better danced in the house since then, I don't think there was, or that there will be ever again. That's how the spirit of youth was in the Blaskets at that time, something that's not there now.[29]

The sport continued on when they went outside to the top of the quay:

We went out, myself and the two boys and the five young women, right down to the edge of the pier, the finest place that a person ever stood on, the spot where everyone always ate whatever bit they brought with them for their trip.

We weren't long there when one of the girls said that it was a fine spot to do the four-handed reel. The eldest boy answered, "We'll do it, so," and told one of the sisters to play, calling her by her name, Siobhán. And if Siobhán was good at anything it was that there was no need to repeat the request, and another good thing about her, there was never a better musician than she.

Away with the four of us dancing, and we did a fine job of it, on the shoulder of land that they call Guala an Loic Bhuí. The young lad stood up to do another dance, and his brother did it with him. Then everyone in the company sang a song or two, until the day slipped away and we went back to the house.[30]

It was time for food again:

Having stopped dancing, the food was ready, and we ate enough. There was a fine fat hen on the table, the likes of which I haven't seen since or before.

"Now that your bellies are full," says the woman of the house, "before the others come," and she placed the hen on the plate for the dancers. "But, I will have a piece myself for my playing for you," says she, because she was a fine pleasurable woman.[31]

They spent the night merrily. They spent a further time hunting the following day and then sailed for home because the weather was changing and they had plenty of rabbits.

> The woman of the Stone and her two daughters were coming back to stay until the Shrove would be over. She thought that perhaps if one of her daughters were to find someone to marry, there might be someone seeking the other one, and that it would be much handier to have her rather than going into the Inis for her.[32]

Shrove was passing, and the good times were coming to an end.

Chapter VIII

Tomás and the Two Cáits

Because Tomás loved going into the Inis and being among the company and sport that was there, he came as often as he could. It is so good that he has left us such fine accounts of his visits there:

> There was no other young man following the boat but myself, and so because of that, I and them used to be throwing canteens at each other, and it wasn't long until one of them and myself used be continually playing together–a fine nice girl–the finest singer around at the time. I had paid many visits there that season, and a fine life we had as well. We had a fine year till Christmas.[1]

Tomás leaves us a fine account of Cáit, his girl, because of his love for her, in his book *The Islandman*.

Cáit was born in 1860, and was therefore three or four years younger than Tomás. They had a wonderful romance, for those times. All they wanted was the slightest excuse to leap out and break into a spontaneous dance together, one of the other girls doing the mouth music (lilting) for them. They had a fine choice of dances, "*An Samhradh Cruaidh*," "The Yalla Wattle," "*Bhfuil an Fear Mór Istigh*," "Poll Hapenny," "*An Súisín Bán*" and "*Ríl Mhór Bhaile an Chala*." The boy or girl who could sing or dance was highly esteemed by everyone then, and those who were unable to perform were not thought much of.

Tomás's accounts of the Inis are as fine a writing as can be found in any book, in English or Irish. He speaks from his heart and love is his urge, and that makes his book the wonderful work it is.

Robin Flower says truly of it: "It will be clear to every reader that from his earliest days he was keenly observant, watching and judging the people about him, eagerly alive to their tricks of character, and appreciating to the full the humours and tragedies of their life."[2]

And this was how the people who lived there conquered loneliness: people were heading there from all sides. Their courage never failed, and they succeeded remarkably well. They were clever, intelligent, self-sufficient, strong–qualities that were needed in such a spot, cut away from the rest of the world so that their surroundings moulded and trained them.

To Tomás it was Tír na nÓg, with sport and fun and company, and fine, lively, beautiful girls with big hearts. He loved visiting and just needed an excuse to arrive. The rabbits were fine and plentiful, which brought the other Blasket Islanders there often, as well as gulls' eggs and seals. Youth was there, and the whole world was in blossom.

He became very fond of Cáit, and it became his soul's desire to marry her, and bring her to his own home, or even that he should go as a *cliamhain isteach* to the Inis himself and leave the boys free to emigrate to America, which everyone was beginning to realise was sure to happen as soon as they were grown up enough to take off:

> We put down the boat, and there was never a boat went anywhere as happy as she was going to the Inis. Life was good there, as those islands were very fruitful, plenty of rabbits, sheep, birds, and everything else needed, four milk cows, butter that was never sold but eaten, all that was there; boats from all sides visiting in the summer; and the sweet and sour milk mixed together.
>
> We never stopped till we reached the quay, and the day was beautiful in November. We went to the house, and that was not the house without fire and food. We were made welcome, with every type of food and drink in the house to be had for the taking. The four young women were at that time running the house as happy a home as any four sisters in Ireland: they were well-formed, bright-skinned, with their fair and golden hair, and as regards entertainment, you would not notice the day or night as long as you would be in their company.
>
> And when we had eaten enough, the girl that I was friendly with went out the door and, as she went out waved me out too that I might follow her. It didn't take me long to follow her, not pretending anything, and she hadn't gone far from the house.[3]

It was this event that made Tomás sure that she was the girl for him, and not only for him, but for the old couple back at home, something very important then, before there was any thought of old-age pension:

> There were hunting dogs in the Stone and they always killing rabbits. The two of us went a little from the house, and she bent under a stone and drew out two rabbits, and they really were two fine ones. She had chosen them the previous day from a couple of dozen as being the best.

"Here," she says: "bring those home to your mother, and tell them when we go in that the dogs just caught them now"–a good plan.

Although the two of us had an affection for each other before this, my love for her was greater than ever after I had seen this kind deed. It occurred to me as well, that she would make a fine friend for the old woman [at home], that she had given her the rabbits . . . [4]

The best ally Tomás had was his own uncle, Diarmaid Ó Sé, his mother's brother.

When I arrived home at bed time one night, fairly late, who would be there only Diarmaid of the Wind, and, if ever he had a tune to his voice he had it now as he mocked the old couple, how difficult it would be for them to spend another year without assistance or help, "and maybe even two years," says he. "And I have a message for you from the finest girl that walks, and is best and finest in every way," says Diarmaid. And then the rake went out, and an egg wouldn't break under his foot; he thought it had been sealed.

. . . but the days were passing, and Shrove near at hand, and the rake thought that he would have the word any time, but he is still waiting for the word.[5]

It wasn't to be, and life would never be the same.

What went wrong that his life took this turn? It was the eldest sister that was looking out for him, keeping always in mind the old couple and their needs:

My sister Máire had been in America and had returned, and had remarried. She heard what Diarmaid the rake had been up to in our house, arranging a marriage, and she arrived to see if it was true. She was told how things were, but she didn't think much of the arrangement, and she spelt it out to the old couple the obligation that the person who would be associated with them on a sea island entailed, and that whatever person would refuse them would not be a *cliamhain* to them.

She herself had a good, well-meaning girl in mind for them, who had her people near by in the village who could help us in time of need, and she began to lay it down for us, just like a woman reading the litany, that she left us all as meek as a cat . . . A sister to him who is the King of the Blaskets now, except that he hadn't the title "King" at that time nor for a long time afterwards . . .

> A week from that day the two of us were married–Tomás Ó
> Criomhthain and Máire Ní Chatháin–the last week of Shrove 1878.[6]

That was how quick it happened. They were married in Ballyferriter on Shrove Tuesday, 5 February 1878. There were many other weddings that day, a day on which it was customary to get married. When the ceremony was over, they congregated into the public house in the village. The big room was full, with music, dance and singing everywhere. Having stayed there a few hours, they all headed home for the Blasket in the evening, where the wedding feast continued on until morning. All the neighbours gathered into the house, young and old, among them the Inis people, and poor Cáit among them. They had crossed the Sound from the Inis to be there at the festivities.

Tomás sang a song, *"Caisleán Uí Néill"* ("O'Neill's Castle"), or "The Dark Woman from the Mountain," a sad, lonely song, full of sorrow from a girl whom her boy had forsaken, and that her heart was broken because of it. Was Tomás trying to portray his own feelings through his choice of song? He had not remained faithful to his own love, the Inis girl, the girl meant for him; that they should have gone hand in hand together into life in that year of 1878, a good year for fish, potatoes and turf: "Away out into the glens or to a little island in the sunset." No one knows Tomás's feelings on that occasion except himself, but at the appropriate time the company fell into a hush, and Tomás sang his long, soft, sweet song.

> Farewell to last night; such a pity it is not tonight,
> For my sweet boy that used tease me once on his knee;
> Were I to tell you my story, unlikely you could keep my secret;
> That my true love has forsaken me, and bright God and Mary isn't it pitiful!
> You promised me you would lull my baby at first,
> And then you promised that you and I would share our lives,
> Two promises you made me daily, till I entrusted my secret to you,
> But, alas, the great life is coming between me and you . . .[7]

Tomás remembered: "This is the song I sang at my own wedding, the only one I sang. I well knew how to deliver it, and had the air well off as well. You would think that there was no other voice in the house, loud or soft, until I had finished it.[8]

The reason for him picking this song has been much debated. Did it have a special meaning for him? Or was it just another song to fulfill what was expected of him at his own wedding?

An Seabhac left out the song in the first edition of *The Islandman*. He thought it too personal and too delicate for inclusion, as it described the way Tomás had forsaken Cáit. But it has been included in both Pádraig Ua Maoileoin's and Ó Coileáin's edition. Dealing with the story, Máire Mhac an tSaoi (Máire Cruise O'Brien) states in a very interesting article:

> It is as if all the regrets for what might have been are compressed into one allusion, for the song is one that belongs in the mouth of a girl lamenting her faithless lover. We today would hardly have attached much importance to it, but to *An Seabhac*, who was himself the product of the song culture, its meaning was so clear a betrayal that he felt it could not be allowed to stand.[9]

An Seabhac thought that Tomás might have some more to say about the song, and that it might have added a further interesting chapter to the book.

> I was thinking that I might get explanatory chapters from him that would illustrate his concealed opinion on the most basic and discreet philosophy that is in the heart of humans–be he gentle or simple.

But Tomás had given the last word: "Like the old Gaeltacht people–and in the rural areas of Ireland in general–he had no desire to expose the discreet feelings of his soul."[10]

We can see the same attitude from another writer of Tomás's age, Edward O'Toole (1860–1943), who wrote in his autobiography concerning his own marriage:

> I do not believe and never have believed in married people putting on paper their most intimate feelings and will content myself by saying that I had promised Nora's mother that I would do everything in my power to make Nora's life a happy one. I can conscientiously say that I never intentionally broke that promise.[11]

The debate continues. Máire Mhac an tSaoi again states:

> . . . Thomas' first love for the girl who lived on the even lonelier sister island, Inis Mhic Fhaoláin, is told almost entirely in terms of songs sung when they met at fair or fireside, songs with names like these: Ar Éirinn ní neosfainn cé hí, Ré-chnoc Mná Duibhe, An Clár Bog Déil, Aitheanta Bháb na gCraobh. All of them are intensely passionate and basically unhappy songs, as was the fashion.[12]

Tomás was only twenty-one on the day of his wedding. He had left school a mere three years. But from that day on, there was an end to the sport and dancing on top of the cliff on Inisvickillane. The trials and cares of life would now take over. Máire and Tomás lived peacefully and lovingly together. They had a large family, between boys and girls, ten in all, falling and rising. Their firstborn was only seven or eight when he was killed as a result of falling over a cliff. Two others were taken by the measles, and another son, Dónal, was drowned on 13 August 1909 on the White Strand on the island in a vain attempt to save a Dublin girl, Eibhlín Nic Niocaill, from drowning. Still another son was drowned in an accident involving a boat, and then Máire herself, the mother of his family, died in June 1904, in childbirth.

> All those sad events took their toll on the poor mother, and she was
> taken from me. It was then that I was really left blind. God spare us
> from it.[13]

It wasn't without good reason that Peats Mhicí Ó Catháin (Keane) was given the title the King of the Island. The Ó Catháins were on the Island for many generations, and may have been the first family to have settled there, and it was they who had the most land in the early days. Peats Mhicí was a fine strong man who was very progressive. He had been on the famous Blasket crew that won the *naomhóg* race in Ventry about 1880. It was said of him that he was the best oarsman in the Blaskets during his time. As well as that, he had a working knowledge of English, and so was able to speak up at official gatherings on behalf of the Blasket people and to deal with police and landlords in matters such as dog licenses and arrears of rent. His home was the first to keep visitors, and he even built an extension to the house, which acted as an extra bedroom cum classroom and had a fine view over the sea to Dunquin and a fireplace for rainy days. People like Carl Marstrander, John Millington Synge and Robin Flower would stay in this room and attend informal classes during the day held by the King's brother-in-law, Tomás Dhomhnaill Ó Criomhthain. It was these same scholars who, lavish in their praise of Tomás, in time persuaded him to take up the pen, which resulted in masterpieces of Irish literature such as *The Islandman, Allagar na hInise, Dinnsheanchas na mBlascaodaí agus Seanchas ón Oileán Tiar*.

Such was life at the time. There was necessity for help and support for the father and mother when they were falling into old age, and it would be far better for Tomás to be married to the more influential Ó Catháins than to the Inis girl, a girl of small means, regardless of how good she would be as a wife. In time the choice would pay back, and Tomás would get a job teaching the scholars who had come to learn the language. And then there were his books. Would he have written them had he married the Inis girl? Máire, the sister, was the sensible one.

As for Cáit Ní Dhálaigh, she didn't remain on very much longer on the Inis, but like most of her brothers and sisters, left and headed for America. Was it the result of heartbreak and that she had to escape from the eyes of the neighbours?

Like many who left, she was not one of the lucky ones. She didn't make her fortune. She spent four or five years there.

> A while after this the daughter of Dálaigh Mór, the shepherd of Inisvickillane, returned from America. This was the girl that the rake Diarmaid had set aside for me since we were young. She spent a few years there, but her health failed just like a hundred others.

Muiris and Cáit thought they had seen the last of their eldest child the day she left home. But now she had returned, and this time there would be no going away again, a coming that they would prefer had not happened. Still with the clean air and good food and close attention she would get from her own family, she would surely be fine again in a short time. But it wasn't to be, she was declining further always as the short days gave way to the longer ones and the sun went down more to the west each evening.

> She did not improve when she returned, but was getting worse, even though she had come to the healthiest island in Ireland. Finally she died on the Stone, and it was the season of the year [i.e. the summer].[14]

The cause of her death was TB, a common destroyer of young lives at that time and for a long time afterwards. Her own father and brothers spent the night making her coffin from timber that had been washed in on the tide. She was waked in her own home, in her own bedroom. Twelve candles were lit, one for each of the apostles. Then one was quenched: Judas, who had betrayed Jesus. The rosary was said again and again for the repose of her soul. They stayed in her company till morning, speaking in hushed low tones of the beautiful girl who had left. When the time arrived, the crude, yet solid coffin was taken out of the house, and the chairs were taken away and placed backwards to the ground to keep further death from the afflicted. The coffin was then placed on four chairs, and then the women raised their long, sweet, soft lament as they bent over it. The coffin was then raised on the shoulders of the men and taken down to the cliff followed by the neighbours who had made the sea-crossing from the Blasket, Dunquin or Uíbh Ráthach. There was a coil of hemp rope there, something that was always in good supply on the islands, and often needed. The rope was tied to the coffin, and it was lowered by four men holding the rope, while four men carried and manouvered it carefully, in case it would slip at any stage and smash against the rocks.

Again we notice the detailed account of the funeral Tomás gives us on that long day back in June 1885, memories that would remain fresh and ripe with him to the end:

> There were fishermen from Uíbh Ráthach staying on the Stone with them [the Ó Dálaighs] at the same time and, when they heard that she had died, everyone who could possibly manage it was trying to get to the Stone so as to be at the wake. These were the best people that ever stood on the Stone, the most generous, and on that account everyone was trying to get to them in their time of need, and there was a good crowd gathered there that night. *Naomhógs* were still landing on the Inis at ten o' clock.[15]

According to him, it was the biggest funeral ever on the Blaskets. Everyone knew the Ó Dálaighs, and everyone was grateful to them:

> Many gathered there during the night, and many others crossed over the bay west in the morning, as it was a beautiful day with the sea fine and calm . . .
>
> The day of this funeral was one of the finest days that I ever remember, and the hottest, and at the time that everyone was gathered on top of the quay, it was a wonder the number of people there. It was a *naomhóg* from Uíbh Ráthach that bore the coffin, with three fine men rowing–four cannot row in such a *naomhóg*. And when they were ready, they turned their backs to the Stone and commenced to shorten the journey across the bay from the west.
>
> There was a big red man to the fore in the Uíbh Ráthach *naomhóg*, and he was very heavy and fat. The heat was getting to him, and the sweat pouring off him. But if so, he didn't give up his efforts till he reached the Great Island and from there to Dunquin. Everyone thought from time to time that he would have to give up sometime,

but he didn't. This was the most energetic deed I think I saw in my time, the journey being so long.

When the funeral reached the Island quay, there were more *naomhógs* waiting there for us, and we still had to go a further three miles or more across the sea. I took a long look, and I don't think I ever saw as many *naomhógs* gathered together. I tried to count them, and I counted eighteen of them. I have never seen as many at a sea funeral since or before, even to the present day. Sixteen and fourteen was the greatest number I have seen since.

May God save them all that I have had to awaken, and may He give no bad position to any member of the human race either. Although the man on the Stone had a full household, three of that family are all there are left today; some of them in America, others in the grave, and more scattered east-west like so many more.[16]

Every time Tomás mentions the Ó Dálaighs, he breaks forth into glorious terms of praise and appreciation. It is as though the glorious days of his youth return and he is there with the Ó Dálaigh boys and girls, hunting, singing and dancing in those days we all think will last for ever but are, even as we live them, fast fleeing from us. In that short passage of writing he lauds:

The Inis–it is the healthiest island in Ireland;

The Ó Dálaighs–they are the best people who ever stood on the Stone, and the most generous;

The day of the funeral–it was the finest day he ever remembers, and the hottest;

The size of the funeral–he had never seen since or before as many *naomhógs* together in one place;

The brave deed the man from Uíbh Ráthach in rowing from the Inis to the Blasket and from there to Dunquin–he was a heavy man on a hot day and his deed has never been surpassed fo such a long journey.

Even many years later as death drew closer, Tomás had still vivid memories of the Inis. One of the Island girls, Eibhlís Ní Shúilleabháin, wrote to a friend in London, George Chambers, in 1932, referring to his book, *The Islandman:*

You know he is talking of my grandfather and grandmother and all the old plants and also, all about himself and his family and how they all went away from him, died, you know. They are all dead only his

94

two sons, one here, his name is John, he is an unmarried man [he afterwards married Eibhlís who writes this letter], the other is in America and he is married, Tomás is his name. Poor Uncle he had a big family once and they were the loveliest family here, so may they all rest in peace Amen. He also talks about himself in the book and how he was in love with a very nice girl once. I think she was living in Inishvickillane, you know that island where we had tea the day we were in Tiaracht.[17]

It was a very nice touch that it was the Uíbh Ráthach people who took Cáit's body to the graveyard in Dunquin, where her relations, including Nóra de Lóndra, were buried awaiting her arrival. There had been a firm friendship between the Uíbh Ráthach and the Inis people for years, with respect and affection for each other born from a common cause.

Tomás remembered that day and was able to write about it again as he watched and mused at another funeral, that of Cooney, leaving the Island in 1921, when he remembered not as accurately as to the number of *naomhógs* present:

> There were many *naomhógs* at the funeral and it is a grand sight to see them when the weather is fine. If the wind is favourable, they raise the sail. The *naomhóg* in which the coffin rests has only three men—there's no room for the fourth to row on account of the coffin.
>
> There were sixteen *naomhógs* came from Inisvickillane one year on a bright summer's day. They stayed together, cutting through the sea in one long line. I never saw so many at a funeral before. I thought that day I had never seen such a fine sight at sea. I was in one of the *naomhógs* myself. It was a year we had lobsters and the Uíbh Ráthach people were fishing on the Stone, and it was one of their *naomhógs* that took the body, and they did a fine job.
>
> May everyone who is gone from us be in a place better than this, and may we too join them in a short time.
>
> Amen.[18]

It was to be the last funeral on the Inis.

Chapter IX

Inis Life

We don't know if Muiris Mór's family ever got to spend any time at school. There is a family tradition from the States that some of them at least spent some time at Dunquin School, where a relation of their own, Seán Ó Dálaigh–*"the Common Noun,"* as he called himself in his writings–was the principal teacher. According to the same tradition, the same teacher was strict enough on them with the rod, and they would have preferred by far to be back at home running wild on the Inis. Still, it was important that they receive their First Communion and get the ticket for Confirmation.

It was customary for the Ó Dálaigh family to come together at the oratory every Sunday and holy day and spend some time in prayer. Even Tom and Paddy, Muiris's grandsons, used do it when they were in the Inis years later, and could not come out to mass.[1] These are some of their prayers:

> Help and grace and assistance from God to us,
> Help every day and we are seeking it,
> The Sacrament of Penance may God strengthen us,
> And the sorrow of my soul on you, O Mary, our Lady,
> She is our good friend to put us on the road,
> The God of Heaven and Mary of Glories,
> St Michael and his two great shields,
> Protecting our soul in the City of the Trinity,
> Death at the head of the bed and four apostles lamenting,
> Bríd and Peter and the apostles to lighten us,
> Jesus, faithful King and mighty Father,
> Keeping us light during the night and watching at day,
> Help us to go to the country we haven't yet been,
> May we have space there and a way to the glorious life.
>
> *A Prayer before Communion*
> Father of the son who made sun and sea,
> This sin is tying me always till today,
> Give to us your blessing and may it remain with us,
> And with joy I receive my Lord today.

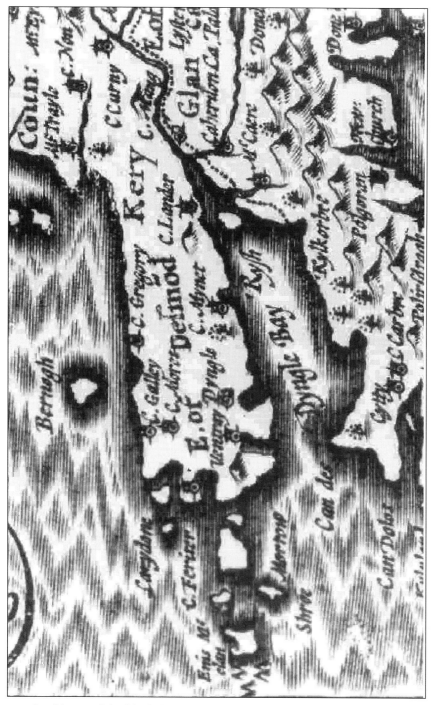

An old map of the Dingle Peninsula (note the old spelling of Inisvickillane)

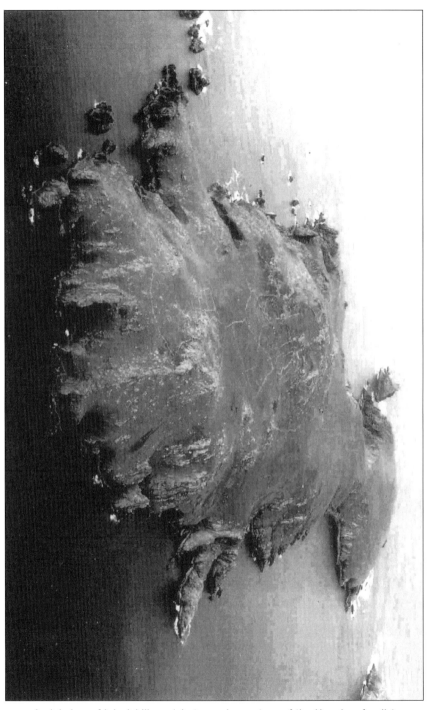

Aerial view of Inisvickillane (photograph courtesy of the Haughey family)

The tigín on the Inis with Inis na Bró and the Tiaracht in the background
(thanks to the Blasket Centre, Dunquin)

Two men talking outside the tigín at Log na bhFiolar with smoke billowing from
the chimney (photograph by George Chambers,
thanks to the Blasket Centre, Dunquin)

The tigín at Log na bhFiolar (photograph by Maria Simonds-Gooding)

A ruin on Inisvickillane (photograph by George Chambers,
thanks to the Blasket Centre, Dunquin)

The oratory on the Inis with the graveyard cross in the background
(photograph by Maria Simonds-Gooding)

Peaidí Mharas na hInise, Pádraig Ó Dálaigh
(photograph by George Chambers, thanks to the Blasket Centre, Dunquin)

Peaidí Mharas na hInise and friend
(photograph by George Chambers, thanks to the Blasket Centre, Dunquin)

Peaidí Beag na hInise drawing water from the well
(thanks to Máire Ní Dhálaigh)

Tom na hInise (Tomás Ó Dálaigh), son of Peaidí Mharas na hInise, holding a boat he built himself (photograph by George Chambers, thanks to the Blasket Centre, Dunquin)

A boat etched on stone by Tom na hInise. This stone forms part of Charles Haughey's new house on the Inis (thanks to Lís Uí Chéileachair)

Peaidí na hInise's two sons: Tom na hInise (Tomás Ó Dálaigh)
and Peaidí Beag (Pádraig Ó Dálaigh) outside tigín na hInise
(photograph by Maria Simonds-Gooding)

Tom na hInise (Tomás Ó Dálaigh), son of Peaidí Mharas na hInise

Tom na hInise (Tomás Ó Dálaigh) working on the roof of the house they built on the Great Blasket, August 1972 (photograph courtesy of Stan Reeves, thanks to the Blasket Centre, Dunquin)

Deálaí (Muiris Ó Dálaigh), son of Peaidí Mharas na hInise, with his accordion
(thanks to Lís Uí Chéileachair)

Naomhóga on the Inis (photograph by George Chambers,
thanks to the Blasket centre, Dunquin)

Tigh na hInise at Log na bhFiolar, Inisvickillane. A visit by Eibhlís Ní Shúilleabháin in 1931. From left: Tomás na hInise Ó Dálaigh, Eibhlís Ní Shúilleabháin, Nóra Ní Shé, Eoghan Sheáin Eoghain, Séamus Mhéiní, Pádraig na hInise Ó Dálaigh and two others

Tigín na hInise and a new shed built in the old-fashioned style by Charles Haughey with the Great Blasket and the mainland in the background (photograph courtesy of the Haughey family)

Outside Kruger's pub, Dunquin, July 1982: Uberfeldwebel Hans Biegel, Tom na hInise, Bridie Fitzgerald, Feldwebel Willi Krupp, Maria Simonds Gooding, Stan Gebler Davis (photograph courtesy of Maria Simonds-Gooding)

A crew from Baldonnell collecting a propeller for the Museum in Baldonnel with Inisvickillane in the background, 4 October 2005: Captain Paul Colleran, Colonel Paul Fry, Maria Simonds-Gooding (thanks to Maria Simonds-Gooding)

An etching of tigín na hInise by Maria Simonds-Gooding

An etching by Maria Simonds-Gooding of the kitchen in tigín na hInise.

Dan Bric and Charles Haughey working on the new house on the Inis
(photograph courtesy of the Haughey family)

Some of the workers involved in the building of Charles Haughey's house on
Inisvickillane in 1975. From left: Joe Kavanagh, Siney Crotty, County Clare,
Jimmy Shea, Killorglin, Maria Simonds-Gooding, Paudie Connor (Baile Dháith),
Tom Grumail, Dan Bric, and Steve Fahy (photograph courtesy of
Maria Simonds-Gooding)

Conor Haughey working on the new house on the Inis in the summer of 1977; Inis na Bró and the Great Blasket in the background (thanks to Máire Ní Dhálaigh)

The crew of the *naomhóg* An Fiach Dubh with Charles Haughey on Dingle pier 14 August 1974, from left: Gary Heffernan, Cormac O'Connor and Conor Haughey (thanks to Máire Ní Dhálaigh)

Maurice Mhaidhc Léan Ó Guithín, the last of the Guiheens
(photograph by Steve MacDonogh)

An anonymous person holding a puffin outside tigín na hInise
(photograph courtesy of Maria Simonds-Gooding)

Deer on the Inis (photograph courtesy of the Haughey family)

Deer on the Inis (photograph courtesy of the Haughey family)

Máire Ní Dhálaigh, Lís Uí Chéileachair and Nóra Murphy – grand-daughters of
Peaidí na hInise with the Great Blasket and Inisvickillane in the background
(photograph by Steve MacDonogh)

Róisín and Dónal Ó Céileachair, grandchildren of Muiris Ó Dálaigh (Deálaí) outside
the house on the Great Blasket built by their great-grandfather Peaidí na hInise

An aerial view of the Blaskets: Beginis in the foreground on the right, the Great Blasket in the middle, and Inis na Bró and Inisvickillane in the background (thanks to Kerry County Council and to Gráinne Kavanagh)

Mícheál Ó Dubhshláine

A Prayer for New Year's Day
A prayer that was taught me when I was a child,
To wake up with devotion in the garden of birds,
My knee to bend under me, beseeching God,
Asking the New Son who was exhausted hanging from the Cross.
Jesus of the Angels, the Apostles and of Mary,
Who was born without sin and is many years,
My heritage I throw on you, O Son of the Father be generous,
Give me your mercy and forgive me all I have ever done.[2]

Their distance from a school may have led to the belief that they were unable to read and write, but that was not so. They were all very bright and intelligent and had a natural gift for learning. It is likely, also, that Muiris Mór had the writing and reading. In his youth, a travelling teacher, or *scoláire bocht*, used to visit Dunquin and conduct a hedge school there before the National School was opened in 1841. Reading and writing, both in Irish and English, were taught at that school, as Seán Ó Dálaigh, the future teacher in Dunquin school, tells:

> My father told me about the Hedge School Master who used to spend a while in Dunquin when he was a child. The youth of the parish used to be gathered around him. He would stay in one home for a week and then change to another house. The people of the parish were very grateful to him because he was so good at teaching them reading and writing. He had Irish books as well and used tell the Fenian stories. He was never wanting food or a bed as long as he was in the parish of Dún Chaoin.[3]

Muiris Mór had some English also, as noted by Tomás Ó Criomhthain. He tells a story of all the Ó Dálaigh family in bed one night when there was a knock on the door that awakened everybody. Cáit and the younger ones were terrified.

> "Open the door please," says the voice. . . .
> "Who is there?"
> "A friend," says the voice outside.
> The Dálach jumped out. He lit a candle. He went to the door and let in five men, all that were outside, and spoke the one word to them:
> "Welcome!"
> Each man turned and shook his hand. Muiris had a good smattering of English, even though he couldn't tell A from B. He

went to the fire, and it wasn't too long before the full table was ready, and that wasn't bare. Fresh rabbits, bread and milk. He sat everyone of them to table, and nobody spoke until they were satisfied. They were fasting a day and a night. Then they explained to him where they had left the boat . . . As the day broke, they went to where the boat was, and the Dálach went with them. The Dálach then told them the proper way to Dingle, and they bade farewell and goodbye to each other.

And there was the happy ending:

> Two months from that day, Muiris Mór saw a boat approaching the slip and he went to meet them. They were coastguards from Dingle, and they had five pounds for him, a pound from every man that he had helped.[4]

It would seem to be the case that Muiris and Cáit taught them the rudiments of reading and writing in Irish and English during the long winter nights on the Inis, and that Cáit used to bring home little books from her trips to Dingle. They would need as much English as possible when they would go to America.

Now and again we get a recorded indication of the life of the Ó Dálaighs on the Inis. One of them is from Long's Book of Accounts, from that shop at the top of the quay in Dingle. Long's was a public house and grocery, where the Ó Dálaighs often did their shopping. Long's also bought the catches, particularly lobsters, and were willing to extend credit until such time as the pennies were plentiful again when the fishing improved in the summer.

It is well worth having a look at the accounts, as it gives us an indication of the lifestyle of the family.

Sugar, tea, porter, whiskey and tobacco were the usual purchases. It was seldom they visited Dingle, but they had their own delivery system. If any boatman was going in the direction of the Inis, he would be asked by the shopkeeper to drop off the supplies. Among those who were willing to help in the deliveries was the agent Collier himself, or one of his boatmen, which would explain the *"per"* that is often mentioned. Peats Tom Ó Cearnaigh (Kearney) says:

> Collier used to have a bull on Inisvickillane, because he had the in-calf heifers in Beginis. A boat from Dingle–a trawler or hooker–used to

bring this stock there and back. The Sheehys had a boat, as had the Flahertys, and they were fine sailors.[5]

Every boat going in the direction of the Inis would be racing in their effort to bring supplies in. "In each other's shade we live," was an old saying, and everyone knew that they would be made very welcome on the Inis any time, and in particular a time of shortage.

> . . . It is often they would bring in potatoes and other supplies that were needed from the man in the west. When they had fat pigs to sell, they used to go and fetch them, and the cow ready for market, they'd go and fetch her out.[6]

As well, the Ó Dálaighs had a couple of houses at the top of the cliff in Dunquin where they could store supplies until they would get the opportunity to come out and fetch them. There were carriers back and forth from Dingle with horses and carts carrying fish to Dingle and other supplies back. The Dingle shopkeepers would send the goods to the west, as Peats Tom tells again, about a trip he and other boatmen made from the Blasket to Dunquin to fetch flour when it was badly needed:

> We went to fetch the flour. The flour was kept that time for us in Plate's house (Guiheen) on the top of the cliff. We were dealing that time in Curran's, and the flour would be sent back to us by John Curran's wife–and it would be in Plate's house or in Pead Sheehy's house that was beside it . . .
>
> There was a bag of bread, too, for the school. We took the half-sacks of flour on our backs and the bag of bread down to the *naomhóg*. Plate brought them down as well with a donkey and cart from his own house.[7]

Flour was one of the basic necessities to make bread. Still, having examined the accounts, there is no mention of flour. Either there was no flour in Long's, or perhaps they got their flour in some other shop, or, of course, they may have made their own flour from oats on the Inis . . .

Maurice Daly Blaskets Inish

1897 Frd	*1.0.2.*
Aug 28 4lbs tea @ 2/8	*10.8*
1 st sugar	*2.4*
1 Bt whs 3/- small bottle 1/8	*4.8*
1 lb tobacco	*4.8*

2. 2. 6.

Sept 27th By Two Shares of Lobsters 13/- 1. 6. 0

Sept 27th By Two Shares of Lobsters 13/- 1. 6. 0　　　　16.6
3 lbs tea @ 2/8 1 st sugar @ 2/4　　　　10.4
3lbs tobacco @ 4/8　　　　14.0
1 Bt whs 3/4　　　　3.4
Cash to Paddy　　　　6.0

29th

Cash to Mrs Daly　　　　5.0
16 [?] per Maurice Moriarty
½ lb tea 4lbs Sug　　　　1.10
½ lb Tobacco　　　　2.4
2.19.4

Dec 15th By Cash　　　　2.19.4
1898.

April 5th 3 lbs tea 8/- 1 st Sug 1/9　　　　9.9
1 lb Tobacco　　　　4.8
½ gl whs 9/6　　　　9.6
cask porter　　　　17.0
2. 0.11

May 9
2 lbs tea 1 st Sug　　　　7.1
1 lb tea　　　　2.8
Drink　　　　1.0
Bt whs　　　　3.0
Cash lent per Kevane　　　　1. 2.6.
3.17.2.
Cash to Tom Connor　　　　5.0
　　　　4.2.2

June 13 by cash　　　　3.0.0
1.2.2
14
4lbs tea 1 st Sug　　　　12.5
1 pt & Bottle Whiskey　　　　6.0
1 lb tobacco　　　　4.4
2. 4.11
16.0
3.0.11

Dec 15 Balance of Groceries   9.6
1899

March 2nd 2 lbs tobacco @2/4   4.8
5 lbs tea @2/8 1 st Sug @ 1/9   15.9
4.10.10.
(Written sideways at edge of page): April 8th Cash received for Lobsters 3 3. 10.8
clear.
Next page. 142
Fwd Maurice Daly, Blaskets.

1899
£ s d
March 2nd Brt Frd   4.10.10
April 27th 4 lbs tea 2/6 1 st sug 1/9   11.9
3 lbs tobacco @ 4/-   12.0
Drink   1.6
1 Bottle whs   3.4
5 19 5

May 8th By Cash the share of Lobsters   10.8
5 8 9.

June 10th 2 lbs tea 1 st Sug per young Cain   5.6½
28th 4 lbs tea @ 2/4 1 st Sug 1/9   11.1
6 5. 4 ½
½ gal porter   8
6 6 0½
By 2 shares Lobster   1.12.0
4 14 0 ½
1900
March 26th 1 lb tea 1 st Sug 3/2 ½ 11b tobacco 4/8   7.10½
Per Cavane Lobster carrier.
Feb 8th (sic) 2 lbs tea 2/6 1 lb tobacco 4/8   9.4
Cash for twigs for Lobster pots 2/-   2.0
5 13 2 ½
Cash lent to Paddy   18.0
6 11 2 ½

April 20th by Cash per Maurice   2.13.4
3 17 10½

10th Cash lent to Paddy	*18.0*
2 lbs tobacco 4/4	*8.8*
4lbs Sug	*8*
5 5 2 ½	
1 8 8	
3 16 6 ½	
1 lb tea 4 lb Sug	*3.0*
1902	

May 8th

1 lb tobacco	*4.4*
2lbs tea 4/8 2 st Sug 4/8 per Sheehy	*9.4*
Apl 8th Cash lent to Mrs.	*10.0*
5 3 2½	
off	*16.6½*
4 6 8	
Drink	*1.0*
4 7 8	

May 21 By Cash / part of Lobster return	*1.11.0*
2 16 8	
21 3 lbs tea 7–2 st Sug 4/8	*11.8*
½ lb tobacco 2/2 1 Bt Whs 3/4	*5.6*
3 13 10	

New page
Mrs Maurice Daly Inishakelane

Brought Forward	*3.13.10*
1902	
May 9 21bs tea 16 lbs Sug per Sheehy	*7.4*
4 1 2	

Sep 13th By Cash	*4.1.2*
1903	
Feb 7th 1 Bt = Whiskey	*3.4*
1 pipe	*9*

1904	
Feb 6th. 1 lb tobacco per mother for Paddy	*4.8*
1 quart whiskey per mother for Paddy	*5*
1 Bt why for old Maurice per wife	*3.0* [8]

And then there were the plans designed specially to fit their needs. This, an example of an unusual food, is the recipe for making a tart, out of sorrel, which grows wild on the Inis.

My aunt, Máire Ní Ghuithín, who was born and reared on Inisvickillane, used to make a pie out of green sorrel, and no one else before made such a pie as that. This is how she made it: she put a fairly large mug of flour into a big clay bowl and added half a teaspoon of soda; she mixed the flour and soda and she blended a little pat of butter through it with her fingers. Then she moistened it with sour milk. She then gathered it together with her hands. Then she made a small cake of it and kneaded it. She then made two halves of the cake; she levelled each half on the table. Then she hung the pot oven over the fire, she let it heat, during which time she was putting the green sorrels into one of the little cakes, she shook brown sugar on them, and put the other little cake down on them, she turned the edge of the little cake down on the plate that the green sorrel and the brown sugar was on. She turned the edge of the little cake on the bottom over and in on the little cake that was down on them and one would think that it was a seam that was around the pie. The pot-oven that was hanging over the fire was good and hot by this time; she brought it over to the table where the pie was, rubbed a little butter around the bottom of the oven and shook a little grain of flour down on it. Then she put the pie deftly into it. She hung the pot-oven on the fire again. She placed the cover down on it. She placed red embers from the fire down on the edge of the cover with the tongs and the odd ember in the centre. She let it bake until she thought it was properly baked. Then she skillfully removed the cover from the pot-oven with the tongs and placed it on its edge with the right hand covered by a wet cloth to protect it from the edge of the hot oven; then she had a large wide plate in her left hand and gave a little jerk to the oven out against the plate and the pie fell from the oven on to the plate. The green sorrel pie was now ready. They used a lot of sugar in an effort to sweeten it. "As sour as the green sorrels," they say. The sorrel has many little green leaves all growing together in one little bush. They taste very sour entirely.[9]

Something else that served as a rich source of food and finance on the Inis was the rabbit (*Oryctoglagus cuniculus*). Not only were the rabbits plentiful, but they were fine and fat, heavier than those on the mainland, with a very high quality of meat, as well as being very tasty. Rabbits are vegetarian, mostly eating grass, which is of a very high quality on the Inis. It helps a lot that they are happy there and are not under threat from foxes, stoats, dogs, cats or even rats, as they are on the mainland. Their only enemies are bad weather and disease. The rabbits, however, are not indigenous to the islands, but were introduced by the Normans who reared them for food. They even provided boxes or burrows for them to inhabit, in the same manner as they provided fish ponds to farm fresh trout for the table. The rabbits were there in the time of Dandno, and we can be sure he received a handsome revenue from them. With the passing years, they became wild and were very successful on the Inis, although there are no place names in the Inis called after the rabbits.

Lockley speaks about the rabbits on Skockholm, his own island on the coast of Wales. He had made a close study of the little animals and later, in 1965, published a book on them, *The Private Life of the Rabbit:*

> They [the Normans] were finding the islands too valuable to part with, and this value was—quite evidently—due to the rabbits which abounded there.
>
> History is silent as to how they reached the islands, but they evidently throve in the salt air, and sloping ground, and dry soil, and there were no stoats or weasels to trouble them.[10]

As we have seen in Chapter IV, Lord Orrery mentioned the Blasket rabbits when he came around in 1735: ". . . during the time I was looking at the island some poor creatures ventured into a boat with rabbits for sale."[11] And the hunting of rabbits features prominently in the Blasket literature, as we have seen in Tomás's descriptions of the Inis.

The islanders used to go a long distance from home by *naomhóg* selling the rabbits, to Dingle, Caherciveen, Valentia Island or even, on the odd occasion, to County Clare. It was an adventure for them to travel so far from home. Then they would go from door to door selling: "*A Mhadam in airde,* will you buy a *coinín?*"

They would be made welcome, and the rabbits sold well as they had the name of being good for the table.

Rabbits formed an important part of the Island economy and were hunted at the quiet time of the year, the winter, when there was no fishing, field work or turf cutting.

Ó Criomhthain tells us: "From November to St Brigid's Day [is] the rabbit season. After that they are carrying their young and the meat has not a nice taste."[12]

I remember Seán Mhaurice Mhuiris telling me:

> My father, Maurice Mhuiris, Paddy na hInse and Eoghan Sheáin
> Eoghain, they went to the Inis for a week. When they had finished,
> they had twenty dozen rabbits. They decided to go to Uíbh Ráthach
> with them. Eoghan wasn't happy to go, but my father and Paddy
> went. They left the Inneoin [Blasket quay] at two in the morning and
> rowed away until they came to Caherciveen and drew up to the quay
> there. Then they went from house to house selling the rabbits at half
> a crown a pair. They sold them all and bought a half sack of flour
> each, half a pound of tea and other little things and then brought
> them home.[13]

Dogs and snares, and later on, ferrets were used to catch the rabbits,
and finally the gun. The skins could be used, too, for fur, and there was a
good market for them. They were salted and sent to Dublin by post.

Around the year 1954, *myxamatosis cuniculi*, a rabbit disease, was
introduced into Ireland. It was present in a flea that lived in the rabbit's
fur. It destroyed the rabbit population all over the country. Farmers who
were anxious to get rid of the rabbits on their farms put infected rabbits
out in their fields, so spreading the disease. It did not appear in the Blaskets
for some time, but did eventually get in. C.J. Haughey was of the opinion
that it was not introduced to the Inis by humans, but rather by
contaminated birds flying in from the mainland. It has appeared on the
Inis from time to time, and is there at the time of writing. The rabbit
population then revives until the next onslaught of the disease. That same
disease put an end to the rabbit industry, as people stopped eating them
and they have never become popular as a food again.

It is worth noting here that there is neither mouse, rat, badger,
hedgehog, dog or cat on the Inis. This is very important for the ecological
balance of the environment, particularly, for example, in the case of the
storm petrel. They breed in the rabbit burrows, but if there were rats or
even hedgehogs on the Inis, they would enter the burrows and devour the
eggs or the young, which would put an end to that species of bird.

Chapter X

We Live in Each Other's Shadows

A dhuine na páirte,
Nach í an t-ór leachta ar Leamhain í.
My dear man,
Was it not the melted gold we found on Leamhain.[1]

Those were the joyous words that Maurice Mór na hInse uttered when he came upon a barrel of rum stuck between two stones on Oileán na Leamhan, a barren rock islet west of the Inis–poetic words, the importance of which come down to us even to the present day. The island people very much enjoyed the drop, no matter whether it was black, white or yellow, and it would be the mean man who would blame them.

A well-known publican and fisherman in Ballyferriter, Jim Keane, was known to go on annual holidays at a time when the term was scarcely known. He used to take a week's holidays every year overseas in Inisvickillane. He would go in from Cuas na nAo, rowing alone in his own *naomhóg*, well stocked up with a plentiful supply of drink from his own premises: a barrel of porter and a couple of bottles of crimson whiskey. Jim always enjoyed the week's holiday away from the fuss and responsibility of his business. He stayed with the Ó Dálaighs and was always given a mighty welcome, and why wouldn't he? He would generously share all the drink he brought in with everybody. The Keanes came originally from the village of Clogher, and Jim was related to Seán de hÓra from Clogher, who was married to Narraí na hInise Ní Dhálaigh, a further cause for celebration.

Drink, strangely, was rarely in short supply on the Inis. They had their ways around the difficulties of distance and transport. Brendan O'Keeffe, a fish merchant from Valentia Island, remembers meeting the Inis people:

> When I was a young boy I used to go with my father to collect the Lobsters from the Blaskets, Dunquin and Ballydavid. The first salute after crossing the bay was, "An bhfuil an pórtar agaibh?" The price for the lobsters was a secondary consideration. I used to go ashore with Paddy Daly on the island of Inisvickillane. They used to be shearing the sheep and sometimes we would tow them in their "currach" to the Big Island.[2]

106

The drop was always welcome, no matter how it made its way to the Inis, and it wouldn't go long without being tasted and enjoyed to the full:

"There are two barrels of porter in the village since last night," says Mícheál, "and to be sure, it won't be long before they are bottoms up."

"Is not one of them that the Dálach laid out empty in the yard already, my good man," says Seán, "and the bung has been knocked out of the other by now."[3]

Maurice Mór, and after him Paddy na hInise, could also communicate in semaphore, probably learned from shipwrecked sailors who sought shelter on the Inis with vessels sailing the Sound. The system is based on the alphabet and the patterns made by two flags. This could be done for entertainment, but there was also a serious side. They could barter. A dozen fresh rabbits, fresh Inis vegetables, or lobster and fish could be swapped for drink, tobacco and sweets. A fair exchange: fresh food for sailors who were accustomed to dried and tinned foods, and the drop that cheers for the people of the Inis. They had to be inventive, and they excelled at it.

For anyone who would make his way to the Inis, the bottle was opened, first thing, and it was shared out generously with all present. And it was the same when they were leaving. As Tomás remembered about the day he and the crew came to fetch the two pigs for the market:

As we were leaving the house with the pigs, the woman of the house handed the bottle in her fist to the man of the house to fill out a drink for us. She was the woman who was famous for generosity during her time, although I wouldn't praise her any more than her husband in view of my own knowledge of them. The man struck up "Cáit Ní Dhuibhir" while he was pouring from the bottle. Out we went when we had drunk it.[4]

One day when the Ó Dálaighs were returning from drawing lobster pots, they came across the famous barrel on the Leamhain caught between the rocks. They freed it, tied a rope on to it and towed it home. When they brought it on to the land, dried it out and took the top off, it was rum–a great drink, fit for a king or a taoiseach.

Tomás says: ". . . it would have been difficult that day to find anyone happier than them, and another thing, you would not find in County Kerry any three who liked their drop more than them."[5]

They didn't let on a word to anyone, in case the Dunquin people might get the wind of it and descend on the Inis and the barrel would be finished off in double-quick time. At the same time though, they were sharing it out as usual. The Uíbh Ráthach people always brought a couple of bottles any time they landed. So the Ó Dálaighs filled up every empty bottle and vessel they could find and hid them in convenient spots all around the Inis.

That was also the best season for lobster that had ever come, as remembered by the old people, except that the Ó Dálaighs didn't do all that well on lobster fishing that year. They thought, of course, they were doing great, but they were often reeling drunk. They wouldn't put to sea without first having a good drop, and they'd also bring a liberal supply with them in the *naomhóg*, and all they ever needed was the slightest excuse to reach for the jug to quench the thirst. That's how it was as long as the rum lasted, so that they would have been far better off if they had never seen it in the first place.

Because they were not in the habit of having drink regularly, one or two was usually enough to set them off. The publicans all around the area used to be on the watch out for them, whether in Dingle, Ballyferriter or even in Valentia Island. Seán Ó hAo (1861–1946) from Leam, County Cork, leaves us an account of seeing them one summer's day in Valentia Island, and, I think, he liked what he saw:

> I saw a boat with six men in it that had come from the Blaskets to Valentia Island. They had rowed thirteen or fourteen miles. Six men rowing, strong, fine men. Blue shirts on them. Big broad hats on them. And they walked around the island and they went into the public house. They would be only allowed two pints each, and they would get no spirits at all from them. But someone asked the people in the pub why it was they would not give them more porter or whiskey. Ah, they said, they would go mad, because it is seldom they drink,–"and they would lose the head, and maybe they would get drowned on their way home because the place is so far away. The island is too far from this place, and we would be greatly to blame if we were to give them much drink."
>
> But I thought that they were the finest looking men that I had ever seen, both in dress and flesh and bone and all. And I hear they are all fishermen.[6]

Narraí Ní Mhurchú from Fahan, who was married to Seán Ó Dálaigh, "the Common Noun" and teacher in Dunquin School, had the same thoughts as the Valentia publicans. The teacher, who was something of an entrepreneur, planned to open a tavern in his new house in Dunquin, and had everything ready except the all-important official permission. But Narraí wasn't so happy and was working away behind his back. She went to Dingle and spoke to the attorney who was dealing with the question of the permission:

> "You know yourself the kind he is. He would give out a bottle of whiskey on loan tomorrow, and who would pay for it? I have enough bills to pay, and may God reward you, don't let them give him the permission. And then there's the Island people coming out here to Mass on Sunday mornings, and what would happen, a few boatloads of them and they drunk? They would be cursing me for ever."
>
> "Look," says the attorney, "you are right."
>
> He never got the license. And she was happy, though she didn't let on to anyone.[7]

The Ó Dálaigh family on the Inis grew up. Little by little a truth was dawning on them: there was no future on the Inis for them. There was no one who would marry them and settle on an island without a school, church or even people. Sooner or later the day would come that they would have to leave their beautiful home and the glorious life they had there, and that then their family would fall apart. It is certain that both Cáit and Muiris knew that the Inis adventure was but a temporary one. If their children could have stayed in Kerry, or even in their own country, it would not have been so bad, but it was America they wanted. Emigrants returning on holidays had the fair stories and accounts, as described by the Spailpín, Séamus Ó Muircheartaigh (Moriarty), from Smerwick, who left for America in 1898:

> We hear stories from Ireland of visitors who go there and return. I wonder if such are of any benefit to the country at all? They tell me that these Yanks who go home return with the pick of the young people. They go back home to Ireland loaded down with jewels, rings on their fingers and golden tips on their walking-sticks. Even the cat is a source of wonder to them on their return. They paint fine pictures of America, gold flowing in streams, and everyone in charge of some type of a machine.
>
> They never open their mouths about how deep in the mines they must go to get their hands on a couple of dollars, or how they were

sweeping the streets, risking life and limb from automobiles or lining up at the docks waiting to see if they will be hired.[8]

One after the other they left and headed for America or the mainland. The Inis was a lonely, forsaken spot, and it was very difficult for any young person to put up with it and have life pass them by. It was time for the boys to get to know girls and vice versa. They used to meet people in Dingle and in Dunquin at mass and meeting, and all the talk was of going to America. They knew there was another life besides that of being confined to a small sea island.

It seems it was the girls who left first, something that happened all over Ireland, unlike other countries in Europe from where there was also emigration. Every week there were hordes of them leaving the country, in bands of up to a dozen travelling together. It was the same in the Blaskets. If there was anything to keep them at home so as they would not have to travel overseas to a foreign country where their culture or tongue would be unknown, they may have been willing to stay–but it wasn't like that, as Fionán MacColuim writes in a letter to the *Kerry Evening Post*, 11 April 1903:

> Judging from my own experience, it would be a point of supreme importance gained, could these people be convinced that their knowledge of Irish will help them along materially in life. How is this to be done? There is practically but one way, and that is to find employment for the Irish-speaking men and women. At this moment there are in the district hundreds of hardy, honest, active and intelligent young men and warm hearted and winsome colleens all preparing to cross the seas, as so many of their people have done before them. When they are told of the evils of emigration and how much better off they could be at home, they have a ready answer on their tongues.
>
> "Will you get us something to do in Ireland?"

Whatever chance they had, the girls had to get away while they were still young, so that they might meet a man and marry. The mother and father understood this, and even brought them out of the Inis as often as they could so as they could meet other people at weddings and fairs.

Maurice Mhuiris Ó Catháin tells us, for example, about his own wedding: "Our relations came to us during the night: Tomás Criothain and Tom Cearnaí and Peats Tom; Muiris Ó Dálaigh from Inisvickillane and two of his daughters were there too; the King was there and a great number of people coming and going."[9]

If there was sport and fun and contentment on the Inis, there was loneliness and sorrow also, and the feeling that it would all have to end soon and that the day was approaching when they would bid farewell on the clifftop.

> The man on the Stone was, from then on, himself and his two sons, fishing regularly until one of them went to America, and a while after that another went, and when they saw what was happening in the end, that there was the twelve of them, between sons and daughters, slipping away one after the other, until there was only one son left . . .[10]

Fr Egan was parish priest of Ferriter from 1870 to 1890. In the year 1889, he appears to have understood that there was no one left on the Inis and that the situation was anything but good on the Great Blasket.

As he reported: "Only the Great Blasket is inhabited. It contains about eighteen families, all miserably poor and in extreme want. About half of these have been recently put out of possession by Mr Sam Hussey for non-payment of rent."[11]

It is clear that Fr Egan didn't know about the Inis. There could be a simple reason for that. They would not often be present at mass, and perhaps the subscriptions from them would be absent accordingly. Perhaps also he was under the impression that they had left the Inis. But they were there still, and held on to their grip. They understood that they had a better life than ever they would have on the Blasket, where they had no land or house.

Sometime in the early 1890s, Seán, or John Mór, left for America.

At the time of the Census of 1901, all the girls had left the Inis, and also Mícheál, another of the sons. The three younger sons were still there, but two of them were getting ready to sail. This is how the Census shows them:

Maurice Daly, aged 72 Shepherd, Irish and English.
Catherine Daly, aged 58.
Patrick Daly, aged 24.
John Daly, aged 21.
Maurice Daly, aged 19.
Thomas Kevane, aged 19, nephew, Fisherman, Irish English.[12]

It was clear from those figures that the life on the Inis was coming to an end for the Ó Dálaighs.

We sailed away from Queenstown, that is the Cove of Cork,
A very pleasant voyage we had and landed in New York . . .

Little by little the family scattered. Lís na Beannaí left for the States in 1893. She was only nineteen, and she went in the company of two other local girls, one from the Blasket, Peig Eoghain Bháin Uí Chonchubhair (O'Connor), and the other from the top of the cliff in Dunquin, Méiní Shea, better known as Méiní Chéitinn. Leslie Matson in his extensive study of the Blasket people is able to fill us in on their journey from the account he got from Méiní herself many years later:

> The news reached the Keating house in Ballykeen that Lís, the daughter of Maurice Daly from the Inish had been sent the passage-money from America and was gathering herself to go along with Peg O'Connor from the main island. Peg was a daughter of Eoghan Bán O'Connor, the Island weaver . . . Hearing this, Méiní saw her opportunity and determined to set out with Lís and Peg whom she would have known from Mass or dances in Dunquin.[13]

The Island girls were delighted to have Méiní coming with them. They booked tickets for the *Majestic,* a ship of the White Star Line, from Tim Galvin's shipping agency in Dingle. The master of the *Majestic* was E.J. Smith, who was afterwards captain of the ill-fated liner the *Titanic* when she sailed for her first and only voyage in the year 1912. The *Majestic* would be sailing from Liverpool via Queenstown (now Cobh) to New York.

We can only imagine the mixture of grief, loneliness and excitement they had as they prepared for the voyage as their lives on the islands and Dunquin were drawing to a close. A donkey and cart took their few belongings into Dingle; they walking alongside with their family. They stopped for a while at the top of the Clasach, at the spot called Leacht an Chlasaigh, and stopped to have a long last look at their native places. All the parish of Dunquin and the islands, including the Inis, can be seen from that spot. It was customary for the neighbours to accompany the travellers as far as this. Goodbyes were exchanged and tears fell, but then their journey continued, accompanied by the relations and close friends who would see them off at the train.

Then came the journey from Dingle to Tralee on the new train, with stops at the various stations to pick up more boys and girls, also on their way to the States. A similar sorrowful journey was remembered many years afterwards by a man from Gorta Dubha, Thomas Brick (1881–1979), who travelled that way in 1902:

> The first stop out from Dingle to Tralee is Lispole, where a number of other emigrants both boys and girls awaited there at the depot platform to board that train to Tralee. There was some weeping and wailing and tears dropping there at the station by the parents, relatives and friends of the emigrant boys and girls boarding the train at Lispole that day for America . . . No need to mention the situation at Annascaul Station when the train stopped there. It was the same as Lispole with tears and wailing and "goodbye Pat" and "goodbye Mike," and "goodbye Kate and Mary."[14]

They probably stayed overnight in Tralee, and then in the morning, another, bigger and faster train to Cork, and then the last train journey to Queenstown (now Cobh). They probably stayed there another night in one of the cheap hotels. After breakfast the following morning, they would have had to register at the White Star offices before boarding the tender to join the *Majestic* at anchor out at Roche's Point.

Matson writes: "One can only speculate on the feelings of the girls as the tender brought them in under the lee of the massive ship . . . The scale of what they were witnessing must have driven at least temporarily from the minds of the girls the islands and the cliffs at Dunquin."[15]

They went on board to see the coast of Ireland fading from view, and to see the Fastnet Rock to the west, and strained to see if they could get any view of Inisvickillane or the Tiaracht. They were steerage passengers, down in bunks below deck, and were restricted as to the parts of the ship they could visit. First and second class passengers were all on the upper deck.

Peig and Méiní spent the next four or five days in bed suffering from seasickness, but not Lís. Lís was a good sailor, with plenty of experience of sailing in her father's *naomhóg* to the Blasket and even to Dunquin and Dingle. She had no problem with seasickness, as many of the other passengers had.

It took seven or eight days for them to reach New York and Ellis Island, where each of them had to be closely examined. Anyone failing the medical examination was sent home on the return voyage. Our girls passed fine and then were brought to the dock and allowed on land.

Their eyes opened wide with the wonder of New York, the huge buildings, the rush, the strange speech. They were heading for Chicopee

Falls, Massachusetts, and they would have to get to another station to board a train for there. They did succeed in getting there, through the help of strangers, and approached the platform. As they were preparing to board, Méiní was unable to find her train ticket to Chicopee Falls, which she had already purchased. She was not allowed to get on the train in spite of her efforts to explain that she had lost the ticket. Peig and Lís took the train, while Méiní stayed on the platform and waved them goodbye as the train pulled out of the station. It was the last Méiní ever saw of either of the two girls; they never met again. Méiní gives us also our last contact with Lís, and we have no further account of her. She melted into the thousands of emigrants spread all over the States, some who got on well, others who fell by the wayside. We sincerely hope she was among the former.

Méiní remained in the States for three years but was forced to return home on account of ill health. She later married a widower from the Blasket, Seán Eoghain Ó Duinnshléibhe (Dunleavy), and spent a long and happy life on the Island before returning in her old age to Dunquin, where she is buried.

The last of the Ó Dálaighs to leave for the States was Maurice, in the year 1901, at just twenty years of age. It was a severe blow to the old couple for their youngest to leave when he gathered his few belongings into a trunk, took two special mementos with him: a bit of fishing net to remind him of his youth on the Inis and the fiddle that he had made himself, with a cloth folded carefully around it.

He went to Hartford, Connecticut, and got work on the railroad. We have two of his employment forms for the year 1905 when he was leaving that job. According to that form, he had worked there for three months. He was twenty-four, unmarried, and had three addresses during that three month period: 11592 Front Street; 11152 Schiltz Avenue; and 41052 115th Street. The form is signed by himself in good, clear handwriting, "Maurice Daly."

He went from there to Burnside, Pullman, close to Chicago, on the Rock Island Railroad line where he got work at the Pullman Company, manufacturing railway coaches, called Pullman cars. Working in the furnace department at first, he soon got a position as a carpenter, although he had no formal training as one. Of course, he had natural skill and experience from his work on the Inis, and there was no need for certificates at that time. If you were able to produce the goods, you got the job. According to the family tradition, he also continued making the violins.

When he started out with Pullman's, his pay was just 17 cents an hour but inside a year that had risen to 27 cents an hour. He was getting on as well as could be expected.

Pullman was a very unusual town, built specially for his workers by the industrialist George Pullman, the factory owner, in the year 1881. Comfortable houses were provided for the workers, each one very well laid out with running water, something that was very much the exception in those early industrial days in the USA when many of the labouring class were eking out an existence in ghettoes in back streets. By 1882 there was a population of 3,500 persons living in the new town, and by 1885 that had risen to almost 9,000. In 1896 it won the prestigious award of "The World's Most Perfect Town" at the International Hygienic and Pharmaceutical Exposition in Prague.

Still, Maurice was very lonely. The change had been very difficult for him. He was a seabird from one of the farthest out and wildest sea islands on the western coast of Ireland. There was no respect for the Irish language here; you were supposed to forget it as quick as you could, and even pretend you didn't have it at all. If Irish was spoken among a crowd, it caused a laugh: "The poor fool." The immigrants were trying to be more American than the Americans themselves:

> This systematic replacement of an indigenous language with that of an outside, dominant group is usually a consequence of both internal and external factors. Internal causes of language shift are primarily psychological–arising from a desire within the individual to integrate and conform. External causes tend, by contrast, to be community-centered–the result of economic, political, historical and socio-cultural determinants.
>
> Since it is the dominant group that holds ultimate power within a community, the only means by which an outsider can advance is by adopting the norms and mores of the elite, and in certain circumstances this will entail acquiring their language.[16]

Seán Ó Dubhda, the schoolmaster in Murreagh School, and collector of folklore, remembers his father telling him about the letters that arrived home from America at the beginning of the twentieth century advising the people to leave the children in school to learn English: "In God's name, teach English to the children and let them not be ignorant like the donkeys when they come out here."[17]

And so it was in the schools back home. Thomas Brick remembers the school in Ballyferriter: "The assistant teacher, Wm. Long, telling and encouraging us boys to study American history and American geography for 'that's where the most of ye are going.'"[18]

The immigrants even took away the "Ó" from their names and sent letters telling them do the same at home. Maurice wasn't Ó Dálaigh or even O'Daly any more, but Daly.

There are many stories that illustrate the turning away from their own language by the new settlers, and the manner in which those who tried to preserve and speak it were mocked and laughed at:

> One of the things I set out to do as soon as I arrived in America was to sing a fine song in Irish at a night gathering. The girls who were present on that occasion were laughing at me. They had it in their heads that if there was any way they were to succeed and get ahead in this country that they would have to forget their Irish as soon as they possibly could.
>
> One woman asked me if I had any English at all.
>
> "No," said I, "but I can read and write Irish."
>
> When they heard that I intended to teach Irish in America, they were completely in the stitches. One man told me that anyone who would do such a thing as to teach Irish in America should be shot. And he was a man by the name of Moriarty.[19]

Some of the Blasket Islanders lacked self-confidence and hence they turned their backs on the language and on the music. The letter on the next page from Kay Crohan, the daughter of Tomás Óg, and the granddaughter of Tomás Ó Criomhthain, is a good example of this. Tomás senior sent a copy of his book, *The Islandman*, to his son on its publication in September 1929, which is on display in the Blasket Centre in Dunquin:

> *From the Blasket.*
> *Tomás of the songs,*
> *I send you this book,*
> *That your father has written about his life.*
> *Every father may not be able to write*
> *Such a book even if he had lived on the Blasket.*
> *Tomás Ó Criomhthain.*
> *September 16, 1929.*

On the twentieth anniversary of his death, in March 1957, a stamp was issued to commemorate Tomás and his work. As a result of this, it was decided to erect a headstone on his grave. Letters were sent out to various people requesting monies to clear the debts, and one such letter was sent to Kay or Catherine Crohan, Tomás's granddaughter, in Springfield, Massachusetts. Her reply tells its own sorry story:

March 9, 1957.
Kay Crohan, 24 Mystic St., Springfield, Mass.
Dear Sir,
Received your leaflet with my Grandfather's picture and also the letter. The letter being written in Gaelic makes it impossible for me to know what it is all about.

I have an idea that something is about to take place in honor of my very well-known Grandfather. I have been told that plans are being made to put a headstone on my Grandfather's grave in the near future. By any chance is this information in the letter? I also believe that donations are accepted.

If this information that I have is correct I would like to know if a future date has been arranged for the affair in honor of my Grandfather. No doubt it will take place some time in this year. The reason that I am interested in the date is the fact that I am planning a trip back to Ireland next year, with the help of God. I have already booked passage for the end of June or the first of July. Traveling this year is impossible for me due to the fact that I am still recuperating from a very serious operation. However if the arrangements are made for this year then it will be my great loss not to be present at this affair.

I would like to ask a favor. Would it be possible to send me another copy of the leaflet and also to translate it into English for me?
Thank you very much,
I remain,
Catherine M. Crohan.

This letter and the following one sent in August 1957 are very interesting:

August 22, 1957. Mystic St. Springfield.
Dear Sirs,
Enclosed are two checks sent as a donation for the fund for the Memorial in honor of our very well-known Grandfather.

The two checks are both from myself and my brother and his wife, Mr and Mrs Thomas Crohan, Jr.

130 Greenbelt Lane,

Leviltown,

L.I. N.Y.

My brother and I are very proud of our Grandfather and the wonderful book he wrote. It was also a thrill for us to see his picture on the stamp, which we shall treasure.

We only wish that our Dad was alive so he too could be as thrilled as we are. . . .[20]

March 9 1957.

Kay Crohan, 24 Mystic St., Springfield, Mass.[21]

Despite his difficulties with the language, Maurice Ó Dálaigh managed to make a living in Chicago. He married Josie Fitzgerald on 9 February 1907, Shrove Tuesday, according to the old custom. While we have no written evidence as to where Josie was from, it would seem that she hailed from Gleann Loic in Dunquin. The newly married couple settled down in Pullman and got on well for a number of years. They had five children: John (1907), Mary (1909), Genevieve (1910), Anna (1913) and Josephine (1916). Then tragedy struck in the form of breast and neck cancer which Josie developed after the birth of her youngest, Josephine. She was very ill for two years before dying on 11 June 1918 at just thirty-six years of age. Muiris, left with a young family of five, aged from eleven years to two, was broken-hearted. The music on the fiddle ended and all the sport and fun, and he fell into depression. It became so bad that he was unable to adequately care for his children.

Then, very fortunately, Josie's sister Nora, who lived in Chicago, stepped in. She was married to Mike Kearney, and they had no children of their own. Nora had been working in an orphanage and was well experienced in taking care of children, so Nora and Mike came to Muiris's assistance. Mike was from the Blasket himself, a son of Cáit Shilvie Mitchell from Ceathrú, Dunquin. They took over the care of the five children and brought them to their own home at 6414 South Hermitage, where they reared them as their own. Muiris rented rooms close by to be near them. Josephine (Jo), Muiris's youngest, remembered her father visiting them at weekends, bringing a basket of fruit and sometimes a lobster, at a time when lobster was very expensive. The children never understood why he brought a lobster until later in life. John, his son, remembered that he arrived one evening with a handsome woman. Was he thinking of marriage again? If so, it wasn't to be, as the family was struck by tragedy once again. On 19 October 1920, two years after the death of Josie, Maurice was found dead in his room at 5136 Wentworth Avenue, Chicago, far from the sound of the Inis, the screech of the seabirds and the incessant groaning of the wind. A gas pipe outside the window had burst, and the gas had seeped into the room. Muiris was only forty years of age.

As his granddaughter, Patty Haimerl, who has helped much with the research, says: "They had a tragic, tragic life. It wasn't always greener on the other side of the hill. I'll bet there were many a day that Maurice wished he had never left the Inis."

Mike and Nora Kearney continued to take care of the children. They were very impoverished and often hungry; but they were tough and had hope and trust in God and a sense of humour and loved storytelling. John was a great storyteller, and often had his sisters in stitches of laughter as they sat outside the house on summer evenings. John gave them a family history lesson, too, which his daughter Patty remembers:

> My father, John, moved to Des Moines, Iowa in 1948, where he and his wife, Mary Baldwin, raised their six children. Both of my parents were "narrowbacks" and raised us to be sure to learn the names of their people and to know exactly where they came from in the old country.
>
> Our Dad's lesson went like this.
> "My father was Maurice Daly, and he was born on In-a-shity-lawn." (Laughter).
> "Where the heck is that?"
> His younger sister, Jo, was more exact.
> "It's on the Blasted Islands!" (Laughter).
> "Where the heck is that?"[21]

But besides that they had no account of the people from whom they had descended nor the place from where they had originated. It is unlikely even that they kept up any contact with the old place. Even the brothers and sisters who were in the States do not seem to have kept in contact with each other. It would be left to the next generation to try and fit the pieces together.

Muiris's daughters finished up from California to Wisconsin, and only one daughter remained in Chicago. They had eighteen children between them, and by now they have many grandchildren. The descendants of Maurice and Josie include the following family names: Abshire, Artner, Bailey, Baldwin, Baysden, Bornmann, Bowman, Conway, Daly,

Dillenbeck, Dixon, Ejma, Faloona, Fitzgerald, Fuchsen, Hahn, Haimerl, Halpin, Harnisch, Jarnigan, Klauseger, Knox, Kornhandler, Kreitzer, McMahon, Metricks, Mitchel, Niggermann, O'Brien, Ott, Palisaitis, Peterson, Puccini, Quinn, Rinchiuso, Sammon, Son, Stence, Szeweczuk, Toebes, Walsh, Wilson and Zack.[22]

They became part of the great melting pot that is America.

Now and again stories would reach home from America about the Ó Dálaighs. A newspaper cutting might arrive, like the following from 1945:

Honour for US Marine Son of Blasket Islander

Marine Col. James M. Daly, son of Mr. and Mrs. Michael Daly, Hartford, Connecticut, has been awarded the Legion of Merit for outstanding performance of service as commanding officer of a Marine Aircraft Group operating against the Japanese in the Marshall Islands.

The award was accompanied by a citation signed by Admiral C. W. Nimitz and was presented by Gen. L. C. Merritt, Commanding General of Marine air bases.

Col. Daly came from a great seafaring family–the Dalys of Innisvickillane, Blasket Islands. His father was born at Innis, on the Blaskets, and his uncle Paddy Maurice still lives there and is always consulted by the Islanders about the weather. His mother was also one of a seafaring family.

Col. Daly graduated from the U.S. Naval Academy in 1930. He received flight training in Pensacola, Fla., and in 1933 was awarded his wings. He is the brother of Lt. Col. Maurice P. Daly, now a p.o.w. in Japanese hands. Lt. C. Daly was a prominent football coach and was awarded the highest athletic honour available to a cadet in 1927.[23]

And:

"The son of Mícheál na hInise came home once. He went in on the Inis looking at the place his father had come from. He took a stone from the Inis with him when he was leaving. I remember him well," said Muiris Mhaidhc Léan.[24]

We have no account of Sean Ó Dálaigh (John Mór na hInise) except this short note from Dolores Quinn, another daughter of Muiris.

John came once (in my lifetime) to the Carney home on Hermitage. He turned up for Mike Carney's funeral in 1948 but he arrived a few days late. Mike was already in his grave. Like Mike Carney, John had lost one leg. At the time of Mike's death, John, a bachelor, was a resident of Oak Forest home for the aged. In researching this history, I received a letter from the Oak Forest facility explaining that John Daly had left the home in the early 1950's, saying that he was moving to the north side of Chicago to live with Mary, his sister. As far as the family knows, no such person existed.[25]

We do know now that Mary Daly, Máire Ní Dhálaigh, the daughter of Muiris Mór and Cáit Ní Ghuithín, did exist, lived in her later years on the north side of Chicago, probably married, and that she took in Seán, or John Mór na hInise, in his latter days. We don't know how John lost his leg. Mike lost his in an accident while working on the streetcars in Chicago. He never got any compensation.

Another worthy deed performed by Mike Kearney is worth a mention. When the Irish Free State was being established in the year 1922, Éamon de Valera paid a visit to the United States and travelled from city to city where there was a strong Irish presence, collecting subscriptions to finance its running. The Kearneys were very poor, yet Mike purchased a $10 dollar share to help the cause.

It does seem strange that when the Kearneys tried to cash that share in the thirties they were refused. The time limit had elapsed and the share was worthless. So much for the thanks they got from the newly formed state for helping in its hour of need. The Kearneys still have the share, framed and hanging on the wall in the house.

Nóra Fitzgerald Kearney, or Auntie Annie, as Muiris's children called her, died on 16 February 1948. Mike had already died on 25 June 1942.[26]

Chapter XI

Farewell to the Inis

The only member of the family to stay behind on the Inis to take care of the old pair was Pádraig, or Paddy, and even he was not happy until he had got out and left for the Great Blasket, taking the father and mother with him.

Paddy had a good pair of hands and was able to make much, and that well. He became well-known as a carpenter and was in great demand to make *naomhógs*, coffins and furniture, and even the fiddles.

They were doing well in the Inis till the end: "The year they left it they had four milk cows, and at a count the dry stock numbered sixteen altogether. They sold them, left the Stone, and came to live on the Great Blasket. They left the house just as it was, and put the lock on it."[1]

Robin Flower says:

> The last to live on the Inis were two of the Dalys, father and mother of the Daly who still has the house. Their children left them one by one, and at last they, too, had to come to the great Island; and at length, the woman first and then the man, they sickened, and, going to the Workhouse hospital in Dingle, died there out of the sound of the sea.[2]

Paddy himself tells us:

> He [my father] had four sons, Mícheál and Pádruig, [*sic*] Seán and Muiris. We used to be sowing potatoes and oats and turnips and every sort of crop there. That's how we spent the time contented until the brothers had grown into men and were thinking of making do for themselves. Mícheál and Seán went to America, and it wasn't long till Maurice followed soon after.[3]

You can be sure that the mother and father were heartbroken when they left. They knew they would never see them again. That's how emigration was then. The old life when the whole family was gathered together, loving and peaceful, was over for ever. There was little left in life for them. The brother, Paddy, who was left, missed them, not alone their company, but the work they did. "When they were gone the work became too hard for me my father was old and my mother not too well."[4]

Still, the sport and fun continued on bravely till the end, though at a quieter pace than before. Cáit Ní Mhuircheartaigh (Moriarty) from Baile Icín, Dunquin, a relation of Cáit, Muiris's wife, spent six months there in 1900 before she married. She mentioned to Méiní Shea (Céitinn, who went to the States with Lís) that she had enjoyed her stay there very much. That impressed Méiní so much that she said she would love to spend a while there herself. She never got the chance, however, because the Ó Dálaighs left the Inis shortly after.

Paddy understood well that there was only the one way out.

> I had to bring all the stock back to the Blasket and to sell it at the fair of Dingle. And then there was my father getting very old and my mother fearful of death and they asking me to bring them close to a priest somewhere.[5]

They had neither house nor hut on the Great Blasket, but an old friend came to their assistance: Mr Grey, an Englishman who used to spend regular holidays on the Inis. It is strange that foreigners, and English, in particular, were often there to help the Islanders when needed. Mr Grey got to know the Ó Dálaighs well, and there is a good chance that *Poll Ghrae* on the Inis in named after him:

> You will remember Poll na Ré, so called, according to Maurice, because the full moon shines straight through it. (p. 62). But there was another version according to Tomás, son of Pádraig Ó Dála, the name was not Poll na Ré, but Poll Ghrey, referring to Mr. Grey, an Englishman who once visited the Inis.[6]

Whatever else, Mr Grey did the decent thing, as Paddy relates:

> There was a hut owned by a gentleman from England in the Inis at the same time and he gave us the hut when he was leaving. My father told me to bring the hut east to the Blasket and that it would do me until he himself had passed away. I brought the hut from the Inis and set it up in the Blasket. My father and mother lived in it with me, but I would go back to the house every Summer. The hut that I took with me is still my home.[7]

So, sometime in the year 1903 or 1904, they gathered their worldly belongings, turned the key in the door, bade farewell to the Inis and transferred over to the Great Blasket. It was a heavy blow to part from the place they had spent the last thirty years, the best part of their lives, and to leave everything they knew and loved so well. They knew every rock, every high and low, every blade of grass on the Inis. They had the use of up to 200 acres, valuation of £20.5.0, the finest farm in the parish of Dunquin. All that they would lose. All they would have on the Blasket would be the site of the hut, or the Shed, as it came to be known, and not even a title to that much. In a field that belonged to the Protestant minister long ago, they would sow a few drills of potatoes. It was a great fall for Muiris Mór Ó Dálaigh and his wife, who had been so independent in mind and personality.

Were they made welcome on the Blasket? It would seem so. They were no threat to anyone. They had been good neighbours while living on the Inis. They would add to the life on the Blasket with the skills they had and, perhaps the most important accomplishment, music to add to the colour of the place. Paddy would marry Eilís Ní Ghuithín from the Island in 1907, and the children would be welcome in the school.

John Millington Synge, the famous playwright, visited the Island in the summer of 1905, to learn Irish and pick up local lore to enrich his plays. He stayed in the King's house and heard all the stories and history of the place. He heard the story of the Ó Dálaighs and saw the wooden hut where they had settled. He heard also that old Muiris was not happy and missed the Inis so much that he was going back to spend the winter there. Two statements Synge leaves us, but they contain a great amount of information. He could have composed a play about their lives. The subject matter was there, but Synge's health was already failing, even as he wrote:

> Then they told me about an old man of eighty years, who is going to spend the winter alone on Inishvickillaun, an island six miles from this village. His son is making canoes and doing other carpenter's jobs on this island, and the other children have scattered also; but the old man refuses to leave the island he has spent his life on, so they have left him with a goat, and a bag of flour and a stack of turf.[8]

Paddy would leave him the basic necessities. Muiris Mór could do a little fishing from the rocks himself and could kill a sheep if everything else failed–or light the fire on Cnocán na Tine. He would be independent again and have the freedom of the Inis. It could be said of him that he was returning, not alone to his old style of life, but to the style of the early monks who had settled there more than a thousand years earlier. He would be a true hermit, with nobody on the Inis but himself and almighty God.

Synge mentions that Muiris had spent his life on the Inis, but we know that was not so. He was not eighty years old either, but about seventy-five at the time.

We don't know if Cáit accompanied him that winter, and we don't know how he fared. However, it is certain that he survived, because he is included in the 1911 Census. Muiris is listed there, alive still, with his wife; his son Paddy and Paddy's wife, Eilís; and their children, Tomás, Paddy and Muiris.

Muiris Mór thought that he would die and be buried long before Cáit. Wasn't there fourteen years between them? When the old age pension was introduced in 1908, he had no difficulty in proving his age; Cáit got the pension shortly after, too. They were both delighted, as was every old person in the country–and they would have double. There would be no further need for them to be struggling with life. They would be independent. Muiris often mentioned, jokingly, to the neighbours that Cáit would have no bother in getting another man when he would be gone because of the vast amount of cash she was getting from the state.

But it was not Muiris who went first but Cáit. She seems to have lost the will to live, especially with her family scattered all over the world.

It wasn't long before the old woman was complaining of not feeling well, and she made her way to the hospital in Dingle, and after a short time she died there. The Dálach was eighty-two when he got the old age pension. A year after his wife, he too complained of not being the best, and he felt that if he was in the hospital like his wife that he might improve and get a while longer out of life. He was brought there and lived for a term, but he died there, just as his wife did before him. Both of them died in the hospital in Dingle, they who had spent so long on the islands, although it was neither shortage nor want at home that sent them there but looking for health. They were buried in their family graveyard, carried there on the shoulders of the people.[9]

That was the year 1912.

See Appendix IV for an account of Muiris and Cáit's family.

Chapter XII

Paddy na hInise

Muiris Mór's son, Paddy Mhaurice or Paddy na hInise, settled on the Great Blasket in the wooden hut (the "Shed") on a site just on the edge of the village at Barr an Bhaile (the Top of the Village). All around the walls of the shed were photographs of the relatives who had settled in the States. A pity we haven't them today. His house became a great centre for *bothántaíocht*, or visiting homes at night-time. With his craft skills, as well as being an experienced fisherman and *naomhóg* builder, he soon became a valued member of the community.

About 1910, he began to build a proper stone house attached to the Shed, a small, one-storeyed house at first, which later on he raised to two storeys. The chimney bears the date 1929, testifying to when it was constructed. The house is still there in good condition. Although the wooden hut has long gone, the site where it stood is partly built up in stone to give a veranda effect. The house was strong, steady and well-built, partly with dressed stones which, it is thought, came from the watch tower on top of the hill. One of the windows is built of this cut stone. The house is an example of his craftsmanship. Tomás, himself no mean craftsman, admired greatly its construction:

> His father was the last shepherd in the Little Blaskets, Inisvickillane and Inis na Bró. He held on to the Island after the death of his own father. He was continually sowing and reaping there, with a fine house, hunting to be had around him, and three fine men as family.
>
> They built another house on the Great Blasket. A fine wonderful lump of a house. They spend the winter here and the summer in their Western Isles where they have plenty of lobsters and crawfish.
>
> They have turf west and east. Enough for a half-year in each place. They have a fine ass and when they move from place to place the ass is also always on the move.[1]

Paddy's deftness and skill of hand extended as far as even making coffins when need demanded:

> Yesterday an old pensioner died. It was impossible to go on the sea to

bring the coffin home. We have a carpenter, Páidín Ó Dálaigh. He started cutting the material out from a piece of an old beam. He had a big saw; they began to saw and finished it.

They spent the night making the box, and had it finished at ten o'clock in the morning.[2]

When the Island teacher's Nora Ní Shé's (O'Shea) father died, it was Paddy who made his headstone and rowed and carted it to Kilmalkedar. Made from cement, it has a cross moulded into it, with the name inscribed artistically.

> Anyone who would go to Kilmalkedar cemetery today would notice a newly-made grave at the bottom of a tree. In that grave lies my father, in the same grave I will be laid. Look at the cross–it has no appearance of silver or marble–it was made in the Island; it was Pádraig Ó Dálaigh who wonderfully made it.[3]

Another example of his handiwork can be seen on the hill of the Blasket where he built a *clochán*, or a rectangular stone structure, without roof, to shelter the turf from the rain. Usually these structures are built very roughly, but in the case of Paddy na hInise's, it is perfectly and neatly built, with good corner stones and steps to give access when the clamp got high. He even included a trench around the edge to take away the water. It is a highly skilled piece of craftsmanship that is a credit to the man who built it.[4]

There are other houses around the Island that show signs of Paddy's work. It is certain that he worked on the new houses at the Slinneán Bán built by the Congested Districts Board. He also was employed to keep up the roads on the Island.

Then he could make the fiddles. They were made from timber, often wrack washed in by the sea and dried. He would spend the long winter nights working on them. Lockley thinks he was the first on the Island to make them:

> Pat Daly is a remarkable man. Born in Inishvicillaun with ten or eleven brothers and sisters, he is the only one of the family who has remained to care for the island . . . [He] built the first Blasket violin, and started almost an industry in consequence. He builds his houses and his canoes.[5]

Ríonach Uí Ógáin says: "It was a sign of the independence of the Islanders that they could make their own violins."[6]

127

Thomas F. O'Sullivan in *Romantic Hidden Kerry* mentions the fiddles about 1930: "On the Island the visitor is surprised to find a number of fiddles. At present there are four purchased in shops and an equal number of home-made instruments."[7]

It was also said that a happy visitor had sent a present of two fiddles to the Blasket, one to Paddy na hInise and one to Ceaist Ó Catháin (Keane), to add to their own collection, on which they raised wonderful sound at all times of the day and night. It came as a great, and not entirely a pleasant, surprise to the Dunquin people when the Island people moved out to live among them in later years, that music could emanate from one of their homes at noon. The hard-working Dunquin folk would never dream of starting up until after evening tea, with the cows milked and all the other duties completed. It was the difference between the life of a fisherman and that of a farmer, as well as that of a mainlander as opposed to that of an islander. The fisherman might spend the night fishing, depending on wind and tides, and then rest and play music when it best suited him.

The craft of making fiddles continued on till the forties. Other islanders, particularly the Ó Súilleabháins (the O'Sullivans) also made them. Seáinín Mhicil Ó Súilleabháin told Séamus Firtéar about it in a videotape made by the Folklore Commission in the 1980s, when Seáinín was living in Baile na Rátha, Dunquin. Seáinín is showing Séamus his fiddle:

> Séamus: Is that the same violin that you always had, Seáinín?
> Seáinín: No, it's a new one. That's a new one.
> Séamus: Did you buy it?
> Seáinín: I did. A person was going around.
> Séamus: Did you ever make one yourself?
> Seáinín: I did, indeed, and two of them.
> Séamus: And you didn't keep it?
> Seáinín: I did, but it fell and got broken.
> Séamus: And how used you make them?
> Seáinín: Out of a block of wood. Get a chisel and leave two tops on it, and have the pattern of another violin and paper and take down the pattern and leave it a couple of inches high–bore out then with the chisel–you would spend a few days or three at it, and, by gor, you would have to leave a belly on it then.
> Séamus: Would it be as big as any fiddle?
> Seáinín: It would, very close to it, except that it would be heavy.

Séamus: And did anyone ever teach you how to make it?

Seáinín: No one ever taught me, except myself to try it. I had a great interest in it.[8]

Seáinín's music studio was the donkey shed, as it would have been for many of his likes–a place to go in and close the door and scrape away without any interference. The rest of the family would drive him out of the kitchen, because the constant scraping and squealing would drive them out of their minds.

Mícheál Ó Cruadhlaoich from Cork remembers being on his holidays in Corca Dhuibhne back in the early seventies and meeting with Seáinín on top of the cliff in Dunquin one summer's evening that he will never forget:

> He was sitting there with some other men on the clifftop looking in at the Blasket. We began to chat, he with his rich Irish and I with limited amount. He asked me what did I work at. I told him that I had a music shop in Cork. The two eyes lit up in his head. He said he was a musician himself from the Island and that he used to play the fiddle. We spoke for a good while and then I asked him would he play a tune for me. At first he refused, saying he was out of practice and played very seldom now. In the end he agreed, and we walked together to his home beside the school. When we arrived at the house, he showed me the shed and told me to go in there and wait and that he would be with me presently. Inside in the shed was the donkey and cart. He appeared after a while with the fiddle and tuned her up. Then he played me a few tunes among which was *"Port na bPúcaí,"* a tune, he said, that had come from the fairies of Inisvickillane.[9]
>
> There was only Seáinín, myself and the donkey listening to this fine music. He held the fiddle against his chest, the old style. One of the strings was broken, and when I got back to Cork I sent him a new one. I never met him again, but that day remains on in my memory, and will always. It was magical.

Paddy na hInise was a fine musician on the fiddle, a talent that he got from his mother, Cáit Ní Ghuithín, and he would be welcome to any dance or ball night, such as this one where Tomás himself was present:

> The two sides of the house were full as could be of people and the middle of the house right for dancing. There were people standing at this time ready to do a bout–two eight-hand reels they were to be. The

harp [fiddle] was ready by the Dálach, and away they went. The likes of the noise you would only hear on a battlefield.[10]

It was thought for some time that the mention of "*cruit*", a harp, meant that Paddy had taken to playing the harp, but that is purely Tomás's imagination, that he compares his music to that of the harp. At the same time, it is worth mentioning that Paddy was also able to play the whistle or flute, which he could manufacture himself from copper pipes washed in on the strand, and that he could make sweet music on them:

His musical partner was Ceaist, or Pádraig Ó Catháin (Keane), and they could often be heard playing together. The musical tradition continues on in that family, with Áine Ní Chatháin, Pádraig's granddaughter, being a *sean nós* singer and box player and her son Seán, in turn, an accomplished guitar player.

Synge mentions the Island fiddles on his visit to the Blasket in 1905. He himself was a good fiddle player. He makes no mention of the melodeon or accordion being there at that time, though he does mention the dancing of what must have been *the set:*

> A little later, when the talk was beginning to flag, I turned to a young man near me–the best fiddler, I was told, on the Island–and asked him to play us a dance. He made excuses, and would not get his fiddle; but two of the girls slipped off and brought it. The young man tuned it and offered it to me, but I insisted that he should take it first. Then he played one or two tunes, without tone, but with good intonation and rhythm. . . . Then he played a polka and four couples danced. The women, as usual, were in their naked feet, and whenever there was a figure for women only there was a curious hush and patter of bare feet, till the heavy pounding and shuffling of the men's boots broke in again. The whirl of music and dancing in this little kitchen stirred me with an extraordinary effect. The kindliness and merry-making of these islanders, who, one knows, are full of riot and severity and daring, has a quality and attractiveness that is absent altogether from the life of the towns, and makes one think of the life that is shown in the ballads of Scotland.[11]

Paddy loved playing the fiddle and just needed an excuse to pick it up:

> We were going to have a night in Ulick's house because Meáig Neaic [Kruger's sister] from Baile na Rátha and Lizzie Keane from Bhaile an Ghleanna were off to America. We had everything ready, except,

no music. Paddy Mhaurice on the Island had a fiddle and we knew that if we were to go in to fetch him that he would come out with the fiddle. We had no *naomhóg*, but Maidhc Keane gave us his. I myself and a couple of others rowed in. The sea was rough enough, and we were all drowned wet. Paddy came out with us and spent the whole night playing till morning. It was great. We gave an invitation to the priest, but he never came. That was a trick we had to make sure that he would not come and scatter us. We had the eight-hand reel, the "Walls of Limerick," the four-hand reel, the *Rince Fada* (Long Dance), the "*Madra Rua*" and the "Stack of Barley." We had no sets. It was the year 1924.[12]

Paddy was also a fine fisherman and recognised as such by the Island people: "The Dálach is as much a sailor on the sea as the cat is on a tree."[13]

As well as that, he had trained the family to be very steady and athletic on the clifftop with ropes, from their practice in saving sheep who had been clifted, from hunting seals in their caves, catching seabirds and collecting seabirds' eggs on the cliffs. They would be sent for when anyone would be in cliff-trouble. In 1913, when one of the lighthouse men on the Tiaracht fell over a cliff, Paddy came to the rescue and brought him up safe and sound.

Paddy was one of the four Islanders who had a gun for rabbits and seabirds. Séamus Touy Ó Ciobháin, from Gleann Loic, leaves us an account of the Irish Volunteers pressing some of the local people to take them into the Blasket to collect guns for the cause.

Paddy, like his father Maurice, never lost his love for the Inis. It was his native spot, the place from where he originated and the place to which he would always return. All he wanted was an excuse to go there–rabbits, gulls' eggs, sheep or lobsters. In November 1922, when talks between the Irish and British on the question of independence were at a crucial stage, Paddy na hInise headed for his own kingdom:

> The Dálach has gone back to his own rock [Inisvickillane] with hunting gear. They'll have loads of rabbits when they return. Five went in the *naomhóg* and ten dogs and snares as well. They'll be there three days; they took food with them.
>
> The Dálach would prefer to spend a week in this stone than in the City of Rome; it was there he was put in the cradle. It is always deep in his nature, whatever kind he is.[14]

Referring to the period before the First World War, Seán Criomhthain tells us: ". . . when May comes each year, the Dálach raises his sails and sets out for the Inis, and spends half the year there, except to come back every Saturday. He spends the week fishing lobsters there, and they are plentiful to be had."

It would even seem that, at one stage, he had it in mind to return and settle down there permanently with his three sons and another neighbour. Tomás mentions in April 1921 that they had sown onions there, as they were thinking strongly of going back and setting up home again there:

> The Dálach is gone to the Inis since early morning, himself and another man, a son of Seán an Ghrinn . . . They went there to water the onions that they had sown some days before. The week was too dry and they were afraid the seed would die.
>
> They watered them and fertilised them as well, black seaweed that they brought a long distance, up the cliff and the height on their backs. It is said that they have a whole field of them sown, enough to do the whole Island.
>
> They have done a lot of work on the garden trying to keep out the rabbits. They spent three days sowing and two days fertilising them, and if they can keep the rabbits from reaching them, they'll do well. Every seed grows well there, even tobacco, it is a rich island in every way. These two [Seán an Ghrinn and his wife] and the Ó Dálaigh family are going to live there, it is said.[16]

They tried it for a time, but they were unfortunate with the weather, and the hunger made them flee back to the Island again. They barely made it back. Paddy seems then to have decided that going back to live there permanently was out of the question, but he could still go there in the summer months or any other time the weather would favour the trip.

Eibhlís Ní Shúilleabháin tells, in a letter to George Chambers in London, that Paddy na hInse, Eoghan Sheáin Eoghain Ó Súilleabháin, Seán Mhaidhc Léan Ó Guithín and her own brother, Paddy Mhicil Ó Súilleabháin, went into the Inis in the month of December 1940:

> . . . to stay for one night killing rabbits and such a storm came they stayed a week there. We were all afraid because they had not much flour nor tea nor groceries, but they had plenty potatoes and eat flour only once a day–that was breakfast time. They killed plenty rabbits and eat them with the potatoes twice a day they hadn't any pinch of

salt either. The two older were very disgusted with the storm and high wind, they slept together in their clothes (as there is not any beds there at present) near a very large fire with their oil coats thrown down on them. So one of the men said he was so deaf from the wind that he could not stand it any other day and if it wasn't calm tomorrow to dig him a hole in the ground opposite the house so that he would go down there and would have a rest from the wind.[17]

In 1910, when she was still just twenty-eight years old, Paddy's wife became very ill. Paddy had very strong faith, and he went to the priest and asked him to intercede with the Almighty to leave him his wife. But it was not to be, and she died shortly afterwards. Paddy was heartbroken, and as often happens in such cases, he turned completely against religion and lost his hope and trust in God for some time. He was left with a young family, particularly Muiris, the youngest one, who had been born shortly before her death. He had to send Muiris to Clogher to his own sister, Nóra, Mrs de hÓra (Hoare). This is where Muiris spent his youth, in Clogher, far from the Blasket. Nóra herself did not live to be old, but her husband Seán (*An Seanduine*–the Old Person) took good care of the boy.

Paddy was always well dressed. The Tailor Lynch from Dingle knew Paddy well and had a great liking for him. The time he went into the Inis with a suit of clothes that he had made for him, Paddy brought him home to Dingle afterwards in his *naomhóg*. On the way, a monster of some type approached the *naomhóg*, and they were in great danger that it would capsize the boat and that they would either drown or be killed. Paddy told the Tailor that all they could do was to pray. Paddy chanted a special prayer in Irish very fervently a couple of times, and the monster turned away, just as he had come, without interfering or molesting them in any way. The Tailor was very glad when he felt the ground under his feet again at Dingle quay.

Paddy and Lís Ní Ghuithín's family consisted of Tomás (Tom na hInise, or Tom Phaddy Mhaurice), born 1907; Pádraig (Peaidí Beag), 1908; and Muiris (Deálaí), 1910.

It was a great personal tragedy for Paddy to lose his wife so young. But he still had to endure another tragedy in which he was closely involved:

> There was a man of the O'Sheas in the village, and there was nobody living in the house but himself, and he about forty years of age. He never did anything else since he became a man except fishing. Paddy went talking to him to see if they could think up some plan that would

help them to make a livelihood. They discussed much and they came to the conclusion that the Dálach would go to the Parish of Ferriter, sow a few beds of potatoes that would do them for the winter, and that Seán O'Shea would make the lobster pots to go to the Inis when the Dálach would return.[18]

But first the Dálach had to sow the potatoes, a difficult task as he had no land on the Island:

The Dálach went to Clogher or to Baile Eaglaise, the two places in the Parish of Ferriter where he had two sisters married, and he sowed a few potatoes for the winter. While he was away Seán O'Shea (Seán Mhail) was making the lobster pots. When the Dálach came home they were made. The potatoes were sown and the pots made.

The fine day came and the two headed for Inisvickillane in the *naomhóg*. They would stay there till Saturday when they would be expected home at the Blasket quay about six o'clock.

Saturday came and everyone expected them. The day was calm on the sea, although the previous Friday was so fierce that no boat could go out. Six o'clock arrived, but if it did the Inis two did not arrive.

When they didn't arrive on Sunday, men went up on the hill, because the Inis house could be seen from there. They wanted to see if there was smoke from the chimney or not. There was no smoke. They were there for a while when they saw smoke rising from Cnocán na Tine, and then they knew that something was wrong. "Fire of Death," they used to call that fire, and it was never lit except when in great need.

It was clear that one of them lived. The men came home, and the news spread all over the village that the death fire was on the Inis. Everyone was very upset, particularly the relations of the two, one alive and one dead.

The sea was too rough to go to the assistance of the one that survived, but on Monday morning there was a little calming, and four strong men set out for the Inis. They reached the Inis without harm, but if they did, the story wasn't a good one. The Dálach was alive and Shea was missing.

On Friday morning previous, there was a strong gale of wind from the north-east, except that it was very calm close to the Inis. They were going to return home on the Saturday, and if they were, they wanted a couple of bags of mussels to use as fertiliser on the potatoes that had been sown in the Parish of Ferriter. With that they said it would be a good idea to collect the mussels on the Friday that they would be ready to throw them into the boat on Saturday. It was calm and quiet on the side of Inis na Bró except that a stiff breeze of wind would blow up now and then . . .

Paddy himself tells the rest of the story:

We put down the *naomhóg* then and we went to Inis na Bró. The place was as calm as a river pool, except that now and then a good breeze would blow in there. I went out to collect the musssels and Seán stayed in the *naomhóg*. He was talking in to me and I talking back to him as well. I had a bag full and it was I was so hot and sweaty at that time, that it seemed to me that there wasn't the slightest breeze from the sky, and that it was peculiar that the gust would rise now and then.

"Are you nearly finished?" I heard Seán say one time, and I understood from his talk that he was a sort of afraid.

"I just have this bag to fill," I said, "and we will head off as early as we can."

I no sooner had the words out of my mouth when I saw a bright whirl of wind approaching, turning as though it was a mill-wheel, sea spray being thrown to the clouds by it. I didn't get the chance to say, "God save us" when it hit me between the two eyes and knocked the sense out of my head. When it eased off a little, I recovered and looked over to where the *naomhóg* and Seán were, and what did I see but my *naomhóg* with her mouth down and her bottom up, and Seán out in the water and he with a grip on it. I didn't know what I could do then. I lost my senses altogether, I made an effort to jump out to him, but remembered that I could not swim and that I wouldn't do him any good.

"You're fine Seán, my boy, keep up your courage."

I said that much to give him heart. He caught one of the oars and I thought that he was right, because he was only four yards from the stone.

"If you could manage the oar now," I says, "you would be fine."

"I'm afraid I'm not going to make it."

That's all he said, and just as you would quench a candle, he was gone to the bottom from me, never to be seen again. I fell down where I was and remained there for an hour at least crying and lamenting, my friend, my faithful partner that I would never see again.

Paddy was now in a bad way:

> I was now on an island without shelter, without food and without a person within nine miles of me. I gave myself up to the God of Glory to send me help or if it were his will to give me the same ending as he had given to the other man, I would be happy. In a while I looked down and what should I see but my *naomhóg* at the edge of the stone. I moved down to her and caught on to her, and with the excitement that was on me, I looked to see if Seán was underneath, I succeeded in turning her over, but my sorrow, I had no success in trying to find him. Whatever foostering I did, I didn't notice that she had gone away from me again. But whatever look I gave, what should I see but a short length of rope that was in and out at the edge of the water. I made a snap at it and caught it quickly, and as luck would have it, wasn't it fixed to the *naomhóg*. I had no oar, except the cup. I got into her, I took the cup and went pulling the water towards me always until I succeeded in catching an oar that was a little distance away, and I worked the same plan till I got the other one. Now I had two oars, and it was certain that I would be able to get to the other Inis, and if I did, I thought I would be saved. But all the time I was on the lookout in case I might see Seán . . .
>
> Night was approaching on me and I didn't know what I could do. I said I would light the fire of death then.
>
> I did, but was very doubtful if anyone on the Blasket would see it. I was in and out all night without anyone to speak a word to, but all the time talking to myself, like someone half out of his mind.
>
> But in the morning when I saw the *naomhóg* at Ceann Cnoic, that is when I recovered.
>
> The Dálach came home in the boat that had gone to help, and Shea's body was searched for days afterwards, but that was all the good there was in it.
>
> May God grant the Paradise of the Saints to his soul.[19]

The story of Paddy and Seán Mhail captured the popular imagination and spread far and wide. Leslie Thomas, who visited the area in the early sixties, made inquiries as to how to get into the Blasket:

> At Dunquin, where the Blasket people now live, I asked for Maurice Daly. A man at Annascaul, in a bar there, had told me that Maurice Daly's father had once righted a capsized curragh, a giant's feat, in a

torn sea, and had sat on a stormy rock all night looking into the waves for the body of his drowned companion.[20]

Paddy Curran, the grandson of Máire, sister of Peig Sayers and an old Dingle fisherman, himself spoke to me on 5 March 2005. His head was full of stories of Paddy na hInise:

I knew Paddy na hInise very well. He was a fine strong man, a gentleman out and out, the finest person that I ever got to know. I used to bring out sheep for him from Inisvickillane to Dingle, twenty a time in the Nobby I had at the time. He was always great with the money. There was never any need to approach him or say anything about it. He'd come to you and put the money in your pocket, £3, good money at that time. He used always be dressed out finely, more like an Englishman than anyone else. He was a fine worker, too. He developed the lobster fishing very much on the Blasket. He used to make fine big pots that couldn't be beaten.

He had a launch for some time, but it was smashed on the rocks one year during the winter. He was great on the sea. I used to see him and his two sons heading off for the Inis with a sack of flour, and he had great understanding of the wind and the tides.

He had a sister, Nell Ní Dhálaigh, married to a Mitchell from Dingle, and they lived up in Goat Street. I remember her well. She was often in our house because she knew my grandmother, Máire Sayers. She was the mother of the Fiagach, who lived on the Blasket. He had returned from America. He was wild out and out; a person all to himself. He used go out fishing alone in his *naomhóg* and maybe he wouldn't be seen for a week, and people wouldn't know whether he was dead or alive. The Ó Dálaighs used be terrified that he'd be drowned. They would always be looking out for him, and they often had to go out on the sea searching for him. In the end they cut out the bottom out of the boat so that he would have to stay on dry land. (See Appendix II).

I also knew Guiheen from Goat Street. He was from the Inis as well. He had a son, Silvie, who worked in Latchford's. He had a Nobby called the *Molly*. He had a family of sons who were good at rugby, big hardy lads. All the Inis people were like that.

The Frenchman who came around had a great liking for Paddy na hInise and trusted him completely. He used to leave the buying of the lobsters to Paddy, and he would deal with him on behalf of the Islanders. It was he who showed Paddy how to make the special pot that was very much more suitable for catching the lobsters. Paddy made a great job of it and passed on the skill to the other Islanders. The Frenchman used to be collecting the lobsters from the fishermen from Cork to Galway and had a well in his boat for keeping the lobsters and crayfish fresh. He brought Paddy to Crookhaven in Cork once to mass and came into the Blasket himself to attend mass on one or two occasions when there was a priest there on holidays.

"Caith Chugam" ("Throw To Me") was the name they had for the Frenchman, because that was the Irish he used when he was working with them on the lobsters and they throwing them into the boat. There was a time when the Blasket Islanders could count in French, but it was counting in twos–two, four, six, eight, and so on–because that's how the Frenchman counted the fish, in pairs.[21]

Synge actually mentions the Islanders counting in French on his visit there in 1905:

> I told them that I had often been in France, and one of the boys began counting up the numerals in French to show what he had learnt from their buyers.[22]

The Frenchman had only one foot, having lost the other in the First World War, and so was also known as *Captaen na Leathchoise* (the One-footed Captain).

Pierre Treathu, the Frenchman, was very great with Paddy na hInise. He used leave it to Paddy to collect the money that was going to him from the Island people. He had only one leg. He was very religious and had an altar down in the cabin.

One time he brought the Ó Dálaighs with him to Crookhaven for mass on Sunday.[23]

The Frenchman gave Paddy a dog once, which lived on the Island and was bilingual, understanding Irish and French. The Islandmen gave a dog to the Frenchman as well, and he used to always have it in the boat with him. Any time the boat would be passing the Island, the dog would stand on the deck with his paws on the rails, looking in and barking until they passed out of sight.

Although Paddy had one foot in the old life, he was very go-ahead and loved to try out new plans and ideas. He was the first of the Islanders to have a motor boat, although it wasn't a great success. As Lockley was told when he arrived in 1935 on his visit:

God save us, we had come seventy miles up from the south in darkness and storm to the desolate Blaskets! Had we not feared the motor would die on us in the boat? Did I understand motors in boats? Padrig of the Inish would want to see me then–his motor, the first in Blasket, was for ever dying on him.[24]

Lockley tells us more about Paddy, whom he got to know on his stay:

He had begun to find the seven-mile [*sic*] pull in a canoe to Inishvicillaun harder, since he is now near his span of "twenty years declining." So he has bought a motor-boat from the French trader who collects Blasket lobsters. Pat Daly built the first Blasket violin, and started almost an industry in consequence. He builds his houses and his canoes. And now he is owner of the first motor-boat in the Blaskets. The other fishermen watch his progress with it keenly. They watched too for any magic I might perform on this strange machine. The engine was too old-fashioned and far too heavy for the clumsy Camaret dinghy into which it had been bolted; the whole was too heavy to be pulled up on any beach. It must perforce be moored off in the insecure Blasket harbourages.

A good cleaning of the fuel-jets set the ponderous engine away with a roar which shook every timber in the boat, warming Pat Daly's heart, and earning me a free pass to his island.[25]

Paddy always had the best sheep in the place, and John Moore, who had a butcher's shop in Dingle, always bought his sheep from him. John would say that it didn't matter: whether on land or sea, there were no other sheep in any place that could compare to Paddy na hInise's. They were that big that it took two men to lift them into the boat from the Inis to bring them to Dingle.

It was also agreed that Paddy na hInise was a wonderful worker–too good, perhaps. One day he took twenty dozen lobster to the top of the cliff in Dunquin, carrying them all on his back up the narrow twisty way. Everyone noticed it, a wonderful feat. Shortly afterwards, Neoden (Mícheál Ó Catháin, a Dunquin man from the Muileann), went up the same way with a dozen and a half in one bag and brought them to the top in one go.

"And," said one wise man from the Island who was watching the two, "does not Neoden live every bit as well as Paddy na hInise?"

And everyone agreed.[26]

Another example is that of Eoghan Sheáin Eoghain Uí Dhuinnshléibhe (Dunleavy). One day himself and Paddy na hInise were fishing lobsters at the Ceann Dubh at the back of the island when the wind arose.

"We'll head for the Inis," says Paddy, "it's our best chance."

On their way in they saw a great deal of wrecked timber on the rocks, but it was too rough to do anything about it. They came safe into the Inis.

That night they were in bed, but Eoghan could sense that Paddy was not asleep but very agitated.

"What's wrong, Paddy, that you're not asleep?"

"Do you not notice the wind has died down?"

"I did."

"What about the timber?"

They rose in the middle of the night and spent the rest of it hauling in the timber and piling it on the strand above the high water. They were very happy with themselves.

But what was the use? The next time they came into the Inis, wasn't all the timber burned by the parish of Ferriter people.[27]

Paddy would always be to the forefront with new ideas of how to make life easier and more interesting. A good example was the making of the tunnel at Cuas na Finnise. Cuas na Finnise was a fine cove for collecting seaweed and wrack. The only problem was that it was landlocked and had to be approached by sea, and even that was very difficult. It was a pity, because right beside it was Tráigh Earraí, easy to descend to, with only a slender rock-cliff separating them. At one point you could actually see through a fissure from one beach to the other. Paddy and Ceaist Ó Catháin got the idea of boring a tunnel between them with sledge and hammer and a *gearrthóir* (cutter). (The exact type of "cutter" they used I have been unable to establish.) This caused a great deal of merriment among the islanders, most believing that they were only wasting their time. Nevertheless, they began the work and found that the tunnel was easily bored, much of the soft stone fragmenting and falling away itself. The result was the tunnel which made it accessible for wrack and seaweed, a great boon to the islanders.[28]

On one occasion Séamus Touí Ó Ciobháin (Kavanagh), William Neaic Ó Cíobháin, Seán Fitzgerald and Billy Bhailt Ó Catháin from Dunquin rowed Monsignor Pádraig de Brún into Inisvickillane. Although they brought sandwiches, they were starving by the time they reached the Inis.

When they got there, they found Paddy na hInise there with his two sons, Tom and Paddy Beag. It wasn't long before Paddy had a fine meal ready for them, fresh boiled fish and his own home-baked bread. The monsignor said afterwards that it was one of the finest meals he had ever tasted. Needless to say, the old proverb applied: hunger is good sauce.

The monsignor loved to go to the Inis and to the Great Blasket. He went in on a few occasions with Canon McClean, a Protestant minister who lived in Ard na Caithne. Both enjoyed each other's company. The minister loved going in as well and often spent a week's holidays there.

"Let everyone keep a grip on his hat!" the monsignor would announce to everyone. He always gave this good advice because his hat had blown into the sea once and he had lost it.

And this could be called fishing:

> The Dálach and Seán an Rí [the King's son] went fishing with spillers during the day but caught nothing. They left them during the night till morning. In the morning there were forty ling, forty eels, and forty ray, and many other types of fish, the fill of the *naomhóg*. It was late when they arrived home. They kept the ling and went to Dunquin with the rest for the market.[29]

And it wasn't at fishing alone that he excelled:

> Páidín Ó Dálaigh went to Inisvickillane with a few sheep. When he was drawing close to the Stone he saw a flock of geese on the sea–a huge flock of them. He started at his best to try and overtake them. He picked up a good few of them–filling the *naomhóg*–but quite a few of them he left because the goose can swim very well when she is in her health.[30]

And then there were the seals; they weren't safe from his hunting either, even when he had a close shave with them:

> The Dálach and two others went west to Inisvickillane fishing pollock. There was a full tide. They went into a seal cave where there was a good number of them. They had no stick or anything as they went just to look at them. There were sixteen fine seals there and the same number of small ones. My brave Dálach went up to them, and because they have their own sense and they always comparing themselves to the human in many ways, what do you think but didn't they notice that the Dálach didn't have any weapon to kill them or even to defend himself, and with that away with them after him around the strand. The other two had drawn in the *naomhóg* at this

141

time and they had to take to running to come to the assistance of the Dálach–one with the mast of the *naomhóg* and the other with an oar.

Then the grown seals made it into the cave and more of them took to the water. The men took the three best of the young ones, but not for their own use, but to swap them for potatoes or oats with the people over on the mainland.[31]

Chapter XIII

Ghost Stories and Fairy Music

Robin Flower had his own ideas about the Inis ghosts:

> There is an old church on Inisicileáin, and this island too (like the
> Skelligs), was once a dwelling of the religious. The old manuscripts
> tell us nothing of these settlements, and it is only in a fourteenth-
> century chronicle of Ratisbon that the legend of the early days of the
> Great Skellig is to be found. Here it was, says the story, that St.
> Patrick drove the evil things and venomous serpents out of Ireland
> into the Western Sea . . .

He thought that perhaps that when those serpents were fleeing out into
the great ocean that some of them succeeded in stopping off on
Inisvickillane and still exist there among the cliffs and rocks.[1]

Here are some of the ghost stories from the Inis from various sources.
They merit examination, both for their qualities as stories and for the
further incidental information they give us on the Inis and its people.

The Woman of the Inis

> There was a family in Inisvickillane. They were very poor and
> depending on the sea for a livelihood. They used to eat a meal of
> yellow porridge every night before going to sleep. She never cleaned
> or washed any of the vessels, but left them to mount up as they were.
> Every night when the woman of the house went to bed, she used to
> hear someone coming to the table, and she would hear the stool being
> drawn to the table. That was all right, but she lost patience in the end,
> and she said in her own mind that she had to find out who was there.
> She said she would remain up spinning that night, and she did. In the
> dead of night, she heard the door open, and a woman entered with
> the end of her dress drawn over her like a shawl. She went to the table,
> she drew the stool to her and she bent down to eat, if she was eating,
> though she heard the sound of the spoon, because they were wooden
> spoons at that time. She spoke to her finally and asked her who she
> was or where she was from, or what brought her to the house, and said

143

that if she had known that she was hungry, she would have left her something, even though they hadn't much to spare.

"I am very grateful to you," says the strange woman to her, "because you leave much on the table every night."

"Who are you?" says the woman of the house again, "if you don't mind me asking."

"I am your godmother," says she, "and I am coming here for seven years and I will be coming for another seven years and for that seven years leave me plenty."

"How will I know when the seven years are up that I may leave plenty for you?" says the woman of the house.

"I will let you know," says she, "and another thing, one of the family will get a bout of sickness, but you need not be anxious. He will be bad and it will be hard on him, but he will get over it. And when he does get over it you will not be in any want any day from then out. The skillet that you have, keep it and take care of it. Any time you need food you need only fill it with water and put it on the fire, and you will have plenty, but don't tell this to any one because if you do you will destroy all the benefit." Then she left.

The child became sick shortly afterwards, and if he did, the mother didn't pay any attention at all. The father would be on to her every day to take care of the child and that he was worse than she thought, but she would say to him not to worry, that he would be fine, so that in the end he was becoming suspicious about her.

The woman came to her again, and she told her that she had almost let her husband in on the secret, but in God's name not to tell on her, and that the child would continue on sick for twenty one weeks, but not to be afraid, that there wouldn't be anything on him and that she would have enough and plenty from then on.

The child remained sick for a week and twenty, and then was getting over it. She always had the skillet boiling and enough to keep them going. One day a boat was wrecked down below the house on the cliff, and there were no other people in the place except themselves. She was collecting up as much as she could until she found a small chest that she wasn't able to open. It was then that she really wanted to open it, and she left everything else and took it with her. When she went to the top of the cliff, she was tired and exhausted because the chest was very heavy, and she said that she would leave it there until she would get somebody to take it home for her, and hid it in the ferns. She was going along exhausted when she saw a huge big hare coming towards her, and he stopped.

"Oh," says the hare to her, "what are you doing? Bring home that chest; it has all the riches of the world in it. There is no lock on it, but take off the cover and you will see what is in it."

The hare disappeared then and when he had gone she returned to the box and took the top off it, and it was how it was full to the brim with gold. She brought the chest home, and from that day till the day she died she had no want, nor did anyone that was connected with her.[2]

The Sea Monster

There were three from Inisvickillane out hunting rabbits once. They stayed west in a little underground hut to take care of themselves. One of the nights they were inside telling stories and relating about the old times. Something came around the hut. It was pushing in the door fiercely. They were terrified that it would break down the door. One of them was brave. He rose and said that he would go out and find out what was outside. He went out and got stuck in something outside, whatever it was. It spirited away the man, and they never saw him again.[3]

The Woman Who Confused the Good People

A girl went once to Inisvickillane for a week inquiring after her relations. One evening she was sent to the stack to bring back a stook of oats, because the men were at sea.

When she raised her head, having pulled the stook, wasn't there a woman behind her. Whatever spell the woman put on her, she had to follow her always, and she led her so that she lost her bearings. She could not find her way back to the house, because the woman was with her always, and every time the girl came to a certain well on the Stone, Tobar na Maighdine, they called it, she would recognise it. But she would fail to recognise anywhere else.

Then she became afraid, and she said to herself that the woman was out to do her harm, and that she would never find her way back to the house, as long as the woman was following her. Then she thought that if she was to turn her gown inside out that perhaps it would confuse the woman, because that was the custom long ago to

145

drive away the good people from you. That's what the girl did, and as soon as she did she found her way back to the house.[4]

A Story from Paddy na hInise

Myself and my people were living in the Inis long ago, and we used to see lots of ghosts.

We were in bed, myself and another man, and the light wasn't very good. I thought, on my soul, that I saw a person putting down his head, and I thought it was the biggest head I had ever seen.

He had every scrape on his face, and I tucked the clothes around myself and the light was quenched. Then when the light was out, he drew into himself again. By Gor, it was then I felt him coming again and he in a hurry, and he came directly over me in the bed, and he rubbed his palm down outside on the bedclothes on my face.

I can tell you that I stayed beneath the clothes until bright morning, and I bathed in sweat. Sure, and let it be known to you that I was terrified.

'Tis often since that the people of the village have heard me telling about the man with the big face.

There were crowds of ghosts in the Inis that time.[5]

Another Story from Paddy

My father was setting snares one day, and he went to check them when the night came and he drew them. I don't know for sure whether he had a rabbit or not.

He had just come home and the door shut when the door was knocked by three bangs of a fist. Everyone was inside in the house at this time, and no one else on the Inis but themselves, and no one to knock on it but someone from the other life.

My father told the story to the priest. The priest said that it was a man that had been with him for the night, and that it was for his own good that he knocked on the door, to let him know not to go out any other night.[6]

The Ghosts' Naomhóg

Another day didn't I and two others see a *naomhóg* coming from the Island, her sail hoisted up, a man steering, and she following behind

146

a *naomhóg* coming from the western Island. We were in a *naomhóg* following them. When we caught up with her on the Bealach Mór we asked them where the other *naomhóg* that was following them had gone to, because we had seen it close up to them. They said to us that they hadn't seen any *naomhóg*, or if there was one following them it was a ghost *naomhóg*. And, on my soul, it was.[7]

Paddy's Sisters Milking

I had two sisters and they used to be milking the cows every night in a shed. My father and my mother, Lord have mercy on them, were in the house. The girls who were milking used be singing every evening and nobody would notice them.

They were one night screaming and shouting, and my mother said to my father that they were not singing tonight. He said they were, but they were not, and my mother was right, because shortly the girls ran in home and terror in their hearts.

And they said that when they were in the shed that a woman came and that she put her back to the door and would not leave it. That's why they were screaming and shouting. One of them caught the door with the terror as the woman was there. And then, by my word, there was nothing there, because the door opened in with her. And it was no daze that was put on them, but that she was there.[8]

A Story that Maurice Mhuiris Ó Catháin Heard

The Inis always had a great name for ghosts. According to the old people, if they are to be believed, the place was alive with them. I used to often be there, but for all that I never met one. It belonged to the Ó Dálaighs, Paddy's people. Paddy was a great friend of mine. I used to hear the old people saying that his grandmother was in the house one day alone when eight men came into the kitchen. They sat down and were saying nothing. She filled out a mug of milk for each one of them, but not one of them would drink it. She thought that strange, and she asked them where they were from or what it was that brought them.

"We are from the Port," said one of them.

"Indeed you are not," says she, "I know everyone on the quay of Dingle, but I don't recognise any of you."

"From Portmagee, we are," says the man who spoke.

"Where did you leave your boat?" says she.

"We left it down on the Léithligh," says he.

It was strange that they had not left it on the strand. They all rose then and left. Shortly afterwards her husband came in, and she related to him the whole story.

He left immediately to see if he could catch up with the eight men or would he see the boat leaving the Léithligh. But there was no boat or sign of one on the Léithligh at that time or ever again.

It used to be believed that the eight men were people from the other life, but I think myself that they were robbers or criminals of some sort. There used to be the likes in those days.[9]

The Black Calf

In 1968, Maria Simonds-Gooding and her cousin, Marie Claire, were staying alone on the Inis:

Each night a terrible noise arose at 11 on the dot without fail. It was the storm petrels arriving home to feed their young. They made these high-pitched noises that racked the whole island. I said to my cousin that I had a great idea. The noise would go on through the night. I said, if I lit the lantern and she took it down the field that the birds would fly to the light and we could sleep. When she started to take the lantern down the field, I was still by the tent watching her when I heard and saw what I knew to be the pounding of a small black calf following her down. I was seized up with fear like I have never experienced before or since. I roared and roared at her to come back straightaway. My throat was raw for several days afterwards. She was very angry with me. She had seen or heard nothing. She said she could have broken her leg in any of the rabbit holes and she thought I was hallucinating. I was devastated by this experience, more because I had found the place I most wanted to be in and now found that it was haunted.

It was much later that she understood the story:

I never thought any more about the calf until the winter in Dunquin, by which time I had purchased my cottage, and living beside me was the mother figure of the Ceathrú, Lisa Mitchel, whom I got to know very well and whose mother was born on the Inis. One night as we were sitting by her fire chatting, she asked, "Have you heard the story of the calf?"

148

Lisa told her the story of the calf:

> One night in Tigh na hInise when everybody sat by the fire, a strange
> calf came to the door. They had four cows and four calves themselves
> at the time, but this was not their calf. They drove the calf from the
> house. The calf went off to the edge of the cliff, and went over, and
> their own cows and calves followed. As Lisa put it, "They were all
> cliffed." A true story.

It then made sense to Maria:

> I immediately realised that the pounding black calf that I had seen and
> heard that night that had haunted me was the same calf. The only
> other time that I have had reference to it was from Paddy and Tom
> while they and I were on the Inis. I was staying in a tent and they were
> staying in Tigh na hInise. They knew all about the haunted calf. It
> had been seen from time to time by certain people and not by others.[10]

Port na bPúcaí

I mentioned already that the song, *"Raghadsa 's mo Cheaití"* had close ties
with Inisvickillane, but the air most associated with that island left to us
by the Inis people is undoubtedly the slow air called *"Port na bPúcaí,"*
"Caoineadh na hInise," "Port na hInise," "Caoineadh na bhFairies" or
"Caoineadh na Sióg." The story of its origins is an interesting one, which
has many slightly different versions:

> Here is a story that happened on Inisvickillane about two hundred
> years ago. There was a man and his wife living there, Muiris Mór Ó
> Dálaigh and his wife, Cáit. Anyhow, Muiris was a herd there for a man
> named Collier who lived in Dingle. And when Muiris' family grew
> up, they used to be fishing. On a very bad night with a gale and rain,
> in or around November, they were asleep. It was then they heard the
> woman lamenting, fine and long and mysteriously. They were
> listening to her, and they thought it was the nicest music they had
> ever heard, although Cáit herself was a good singer. They were taking
> in every word she sang, and in the morning they had it off by heart.
> The people then had a good head to take things, and this is how it
> goes:
>> I am a woman of the fairy host that has come across the waves,
>> And I was spirited away for some time over the ocean,
>> And I am in this form under the spell of a fairy woman,

149

And will not be like this but until the cock crows.
Is bean ón slua sí mé do tháinig thar toinn
Is do goideadh san oíche mé tamall thar lear
Is go bhfuilim san ríocht fé gheasa mná sí,
Is ní bheidh mé ar an saol so ach go nglaofaidh an coileach.
Then I must make my way back to the lios,
I do not like it, but still I must go,
As everyone in this life must leave it,
But I will be under a spell as long as water is in the ocean,
And a fairy woman will be heard lamenting her man,
So don't interfere with the people of the lios.
Is caithfidh mé féin tabhairt fé'n lios thar n-ais.
Ní taithneamh liom é, ach caithfead tabhairt fé,
Is a bhfuil ar an saol so caithfear imeacht as,
Ach beadsa fé dhraíocht an fhaid bheidh uisce sa toinn,
Is cloisfear bean sí ag caoine fear,
Is ná deiníg aon ní le dream na leas.[11]

"Muiris Ó Dálaigh used to say that it was a woman under a spell, that her husband was at home, and that the good people had spirited her away with them. The Islanders have the air for this lament, and it is my opinion that nobody else has it."[12]

It was either the Guiheens or the Ó Dálaighs who first heard this tune and made it available to the people. It could have been Seán a' Mhódhraigh or even his father, Seán Mhuiris Liam, who first heard it. Tom na hInise Ó Dálaigh was of the opinion that it was the Guiheens, and Feargal Mac Amhlaoibh, an old friend of Tom, tells me that Tom always maintained that it was Seán Ó Guithín who first heard the tune, and that it passed on from him to Muiris Mór Ó Dálaigh. There are other opinions as well; for example, that it was a woman who heard it, a sister of Paddy na hInise, which one we cannot say.

Another telling still, this one from Peig Sayers herself, places the scene of the story in Dunquin, and associates it with the son of Sean Eoghain Ó Súilleabháin (Sullivan) from Coumeenole:

> . . . he was going home. He was approaching the place that is called the Coire, a big creek a short distance west from Tóin na Gualann. It was a beautiful evening, with the lonely droning of the waves among the stones of the strand. The sun was as red as a piece of old gold going down slowly in the west. The young man heard this song being

played. He looked down and he saw the fairy piper on a large flagstone on the strand and he playing. He had a great gift for music and dancing, and he took the fairy music. The Island people say that it was in Inisvickillane that the fairy music was first heard.

Not so, but on the big flagstone of an Coire close to Cuas na gColúr, where the son of Seán Eoghain heard it. It is from Dunquin that the fairy tune went to the Island. A man from Com (Coumeenole) who spent a while of his life in Inisvickillane brought it there.[13]

I think myself that Peig is mistaken here. Certainly there is an old story on O'Sullivan's hearing the piper in the Coire on his way home, but I do not think it was *"Port na bPúcaí"* that he heard.

Muiris Ó Guithín (Muiris Mhaidhc Léan) tells me:

I remember when the Island was in full bloom, and all the people, young and old there. I remember the musicians, the Ó Dálaighs, Seáinín Mhicil and the Ceaists, musicians all, and my own uncle, Maidhc, my mother's brother. He used to play the fiddle, and he had *"Port na bPúcaí."* He went to America, and he used to be playing in the dancehalls there. He could play *"Port na bPúcaí"* very well. Twice he came home. He came home the Year of the Lady, 1909. He left the fiddle in Dingle that time out of respect for the Lady who had just drowned.

Seán Cheaist, Paddy Mhaurice and Tom na hInise, they used to play the fiddle and the flute. Seán Ó Criomhthain had a fiddle as well. They all had *"Port na bPúcaí,"* but they didn't play it as it is heard today.[14]

Those early instruments consisted of, at first, the flute or whistle and then the fiddle, which became the main musical instrument of the Blaskets. The box was introduced into the Island at a later date, perhaps even as late as the early twenties, probably by islanders returning on holidays from the States, where the accordion had caught on very much because it was loud enough to be heard in crowded dancehalls.

Seán Ó Criomhthain, himself a fiddler, tells us:

There is an air or tune still to be heard here very often, and the name it is given is *"Port na bPúcaí."* It was not heard anywhere else until it was heard in Inisvickillane. One of the herds heard it one night when he was minding the stock. There are no words going with the air.[15]

151

Robin Flower, too, has a version of the story, as he heard it from the Islanders:

> In the old days, when this island was inhabited, a man sat alone one night in his house, soothing his loneliness with a fiddle. He was playing, no doubt, the favourite music of the country-side, jigs and reels and hornpipes, the hurrying tunes that would put light heels on the feet of the dead. But, as he played, he heard another music without, going over the roof in the air. It passed away to the cliffs and returned again, and so backwards and forwards again and again, a wandering air wailing in repeated phrases, till at last it had become familiar in his mind, and he took up the fallen bow, and drawing it across the strings followed note by note the lamenting voices as they passed above him. Ever since, that tune, port na bpúcaí, 'the fairy music,' has remained with his family, skilled musicians all, and, if you hear it played by a fiddler of that race, you will know the secret of Inisicíleáin.[16]

Having said all that, there is also a view that there is a simple, modern-day explanation for the composition.

On Easter Sunday 1983, *Aisling na Mara* cast out her anchor close to Inis na Bró. Charles Haughey, who was in residence, had given an invitation to Captain Eoin Ó Máille and the crew to come into Inisvickillane for a visit. They spent a pleasant evening on the Inis, and at night they returned to the ship and retired. The night was very calm. About two in the morning, the captain was awakened. A distant lamenting voice could be heard far out in the sea. He awakened one of the crew, Vivienne Breathnach, and they both heard the mysterious music. The captain had already heard that the voice of the whale was very similar to a sad song, and it occurred to him that it was this voice he was listening to now. The voice lasted about twenty minutes. It also occurred to him that the music he was now listening bore a great likeness to *"Port na bPúcaí."* He remembered seeing a whale around the coast of Inisvickillane at Easter 1980. He told Mr Haughey about it the following day, and it was this that gave rise to the idea that the tune the Inis man or woman had heard was the song of the whale.[17]

The words are something of a mystery as well. They are not often heard, and I had never heard the air with words until the occasion of the funeral of the poet Michael Davitt at Casadh na Gráige on 30 July 2005, when Marcas Mac Conghaile sang it to a new air of his own composition. There was a mystery and other-worldness about the words and song that made it very special on that occasion when the ashes of one of our best-known poets were being scattered on the patch he loved so well. It was also very suitable for that sad occasion as Davitt himself had spent some time on the Inis and a video was made of him reciting some of his poetry at various sites on the island. Unfortunately, that video is now missing.

The words of Bláithín (Robin Flower) were also very suitable for that occasion:

> The fairies, they say, are not immortal, they, too, know death, and the music that went over the house on the island that night was a lament for one of the fairy host that had died and was carried to this island for burial. How easily could one believe that, beyond this vast wall, the whole fairy race that once were dreams more real than living men had fled from sepulture, when the cold truths of reason had glared upon their fragility, and driven them even from the light of the moon. That fairy music, played upon an island fiddle, is a lament for a whole world of imaginations banished irrevocably now, but still faintly visible in the afterglow of a sunken sun.[18]

A Jesuit priest, Fr Seán de hÍde, paid a visit to the Island in 1930. He was a fiddler, and he learned the tune from Peig Ní Chatháin (Keane-Peig Bhoffer), a young girl who could play the accordion. He brought it out of the Island and played it in some other places in Corca Dhuibhne:

> This priest played "*Port na bPúcaí*" in Ballydavid and in other places around, but it is likely that it was not heard by anyone outside the Blasket people till then.[19]

"*Port na bPúcaí*," "*Caoineadh na hInise*" or "*Port na hInise*" is being played today more than ever and has become one of our national tunes. Sean Ó Riada heard the tune when he and his family were living in Clogher with Seán de hÓra, son of Narraí na hInise, in the early sixties. It is said that he heard it from Taimí Touí Ó Cíobháin, who got it from Paddy na hInise. Taimí used to fish with the Ó Dálaighs, and he played the whistle. Ó Riada spread the tune to other places and introduced it to many other traditional musicians. They accepted it gladly. Musicians like Paddy Glacken and Tommy Peoples play it on the fiddle while Tony McMahon plays it on the button accordion and Liam Óg Ó Floinn on the pipes.

Whatever about its origins, the spirit and soul of Inisvickillane can be strongly sensed from the music: the loneliness and vastness of the boundless ocean, the ceaseless whistling of the wind, the crashing of the waves and the mystery and the magic of the fairy world. It is one of our best-known tunes, thanks to the people of Inisvickillane, both Guiheens and Ó Dálaighs. That mysterious magic of the Inis has been captured beautifully by Seamus Heaney in his well-known poem:

The Given Note
On the most westerly Blasket
In a dry stone hut,
He got this air
Out of the night.
Strange noises were heard
By others who followed,
Bits of a tune
Coming in on loud weather
Though nothing like melody.
He blamed their fingers and ear
As unpracticed,
their fiddling easy
For he had gone alone
Into the island
And brought back the whole thing.
The house throbbed
Like his full violin.
So, whether he calls it
Spirit music or not,
I don't care.
He took it
Out of wind
Off mid Atlantic.
Still, he maintains,
From nowhere.
It comes off
The bow gravely,
Rephrases itself
Into the air.[20]

Chapter XIV

Occasional Visitors

Shortly after the famine, Sam Hussey held the Little Blaskets–Inis Tuaisceart, Inisvickillane, Beginis and Inis na Bró–as agent for Lord Cork, the landlord. Tomás Ó Criomhthain's father and his neighbour, Tomás Maol Ó Cearnaigh (Bald Tomás Kearney), remembered, as they spoke of him by the fireside:

> ". . . he was a very honest person," says Tomás. "He didn't take a penny more than he should, but the exact amount from the first day he got the title," says he.
>
> "That is true," says my father, "but it's often he would put great hardship on people to tend to himself . . . He brought the crew of two boats of us to shear sheep on Inisvickillane," says my father. "It took us three days to shear them. The man in charge of the Stone had wreck saved, and we had to bring that wreck to Béal Dearg," says he.[1]

(Béal Dearg is by the coast, near Annascaul, where Sam Hussey had a residence.)

But according to Hussey himself, he didn't have it all his own way with the islanders:

> On the South West coast of Kerry lie the Blasquets, a group of islands, the property of Lord Cork, one of them inhabited by island families. The old rental was £80 which was regularly paid. This was reduced by Lord Cork to £40, the Government valuation being £60. Now the island reared about 40 milch cows, besides young cattle and sheep and at the period when might meant right in Ireland the inhabitants, having some surplus stock, took possession of another island to feed them on.
>
> This island was let to another man, but he was not able to resist the tenants any more than the mouse nibbling a piece of cheese is able to fight a cat.
>
> For ten years up to 1887 those tenants paid no poor rate. They successfully resisted the payment of county cess, to the detriment of their fellow taxpayers, and they paid only one year's half rent out of six, and that not until they had been served with writs. And these

155

people in the year 1886 sent a memorial to the Government to save them from starvation.[2]

About 1870, Hussey, on behalf of Lord Cork, sold the islands to George Collier, a businessman from Dingle, and it would seem he was glad to be shut of them. Foley tells us about him in the beginning of the twentieth century:

> Inis Mhic Uibhleáin was until quite recently the abode of two families, but is now reduced to one. This is the family of Daleys, who were caretakers for the late Mr. G. Collier, of Dingle, and still remain on the island . . . this island is at present stocked with sheep and cattle from Dingle by Mr. Michael T. Moriarty, in whose name the island is held.[3]

T.J. O'Sullivan tells us a little more about Collier:

> Collier made a complaint in 1886 about boycotting by the Dingle branch of the National Land League by those who purchased from Atkins, that he had been compelled to travel miles to get his horses shod, and that he could not get a hooker from the fishermen in Dingle to remove sheep from the Blasket Islands where they were grazing.[4]

George Collier was, surprisingly, active in the Fenian movement back in the 1860s, being one of the leaders. Men carried out military training in one of his fields at Fearann, near Dingle. They had in mind to seize the Coastguard Station in Dingle, as well as a vessel that was anchored in the harbour. They also planned to seize the guns of the policemen. But then word arrived that the rising had been put back, and that finished the escapade.

George Collier was afterwards appointed high constable of the barony.

This same George Collier carried on business as a builder, his most outstanding work being St Mary's Church, in Dingle. A good deal of building stones remained over, and he built a couple of houses at the bottom of John Street with them, beginning at the Droichead Beag (Small Bridge), where he lived himself, up to and including the house which is now a restaurant called the Half Door.[5]

He also was the building contractor for Lord Ventry's stables at Burnham House, built in 1871:

> It may be here mentioned that the fine range of out-offices built by his Lordship at Burnham are now nearly completed, and when finished

will perhaps be the most complete buildings of the kind in the country. These handsome buildings can be seen from the road to Ventry, and give a pleasing civilising aspect to this part of the country.[6]

At the beginning of the twentieth century, Collier sold his interest in the little Blaskets to two other Dingle businessmen, Michael T. Moriarty (Micil Thomáis tSeancháin Uí Mhuircheartaigh, better known as Mickey T.) and John Moore, a butcher from Dingle. According to the stories of the time, the total purchase price was £260. They stocked the islands with cows, sheep, donkeys and mules. There was a demand for mules at the time, which, because they are very surefooted and stable, were needed for use in warfare in the Middle East. It seems that the venture with the mules went wrong, as one night in a storm they bunched together and retreated, backing from the storm until they fell over the cliff in Beginish.[7]

After some time Mickey T. sold his share to Moore, who became the sole owner of the little Blaskets from then on. He had no difficulty establishing ownership of Inis Tuaisceart, Inis na Bró and Beginis, but not so with Inisvickillane, because of the Ó Dálaighs living there. The result was a court case in November 1936 between Moore and Paddy na hInise Ó Dálaigh. An agreement was reached, and Paddy was granted the Inis on the payment of £125 (about €160). To everyone's surprise, he was able to acquire the money, a substantial sum at that date. John Moore, grandson of the above, still has ownership of three of the small Blaskets and some more rocks in the sea around them. The present John thinks that the court case was a mere formality to officially establish Paddy's ownership, and I would be of that opinion myself, because only the best of relationships existed between the Moore and Ó Dálaigh families then and always afterwards.

John spoke of that friendship: "I knew Paddy na hInise myself. Our family had a great affection for him. He was a real gentleman. We always bought the sheep from him."[8]

We are very lucky to have a valuable view of Inis life in the thirties when Paddy na hInise, his sons and a few of the neighbours used to still spend their summers there, from Ronald Lockley, a Welsh naturalist and ornithologist, who had a lifelong interest in islands. His account is not the usual tourist description, and it also helps fill in the gap of another half century in the life of the Inis.

In 1927, Lockley leased Skockholm, an island of 247 acres, two miles off Pembrokeshire on the coast of Wales. He spent his life researching, studying and writing more than fifty books on all aspects of island life. He visited some of the islands on the coast of Ireland and Britain, and records his impressions in *I Know an Island*. He was on the Blasket on 15 August 1936, the day the *Craoibhín Aoibhinn* prize was presented to Peig Sayers for her book *Peig*, when she was symbolically crowned "queen" of the Blasket. But our interest in Lockley's visit is in the time he spent with Paddy na hInise. He wanted to visit Inisvickillane, which was very like his own island. Paddy na hInise and his son, Paddy Beag, with two other islanders made him welcome for his few days' stay on the Inis. Lockley describes a way of life that had changed little since the Middle Ages in his book published in 1938, two years after his visit:

> We were well provisioned: a sack of flour, eggs, bacon, tea and tobacco, and a hundredweight of salt for curing the fish. We humped those up a winding cliff path for over a hundred feet to the sweet green sward at the top, rock-pipits and herring-gulls moving reluctantly from beneath our feet. Daly threw down his load with such a sigh of content as I have often uttered on reaching Skockholm after days on the mainland.[9]

Then he was given an official welcome:

> A huge blackface ram came hastily to his proffered cap–"A Government ram, two pounds without the subsidy," said Daly, "to run with my flock of eighty ewes."
> A winding path led by turf diggings to the centre of the island, to the homestead built in the shelter of a wild castle of rocks. This was a grey lichened building of two rooms with tarred roofs separated by a stone partition, but communicating inside–in many ways an island home such as I found on Skockholm.[10]

He then met an important member of the family, who had spent the winter alone on the Inis:

> From the doorstep leaped Lass the sheep-bitch, left in charge of the flock, and trusted to kill nothing but rabbits for her living while her master might be absent. Poor lonely Lass, her real hunger was for companionship. I was told it was nothing for a dog to stay for the winter on the Inish. She never left my heels as long as I trod the island.[11]

The tradition of generosity was part of Paddy's life, going back to Muiris and Nóra de Lóndra. The proverb was true: "When the food is scarcest it is then easiest to share":

158

By now I was not sorry to be invited to join in an attack upon a great big plate of thick rashers, which Daly's son had fried in the great cooking-pot. We drew some wooden forms up to the driftwood table. Food was thrust in front of me: a soda-bread loaf as a background to a five-pound slab of butter, of which, however, I noticed each man ate only a little, scraping morsels off with the back of a teaspoon. Close at hand was the glowing peat fire, a kettle of tea sitting on a crushed ember. Lass scavenged eagerly between our knees for the unwanted crumbs.

"It's a long while," said Daly, "since the cricket sang for us in Inishvickillaun; the hearth do be too cold for her to-day. The last chirrup was in the year my old mother died here."

He swallowed his mug of scalding tea, and brushed back the white moustaches which ran across his face from ear to ear.

"A cricket's chirrup is a home's heart-beat, and that will be true, for a cricket cannot live save in a good house with a turf fire day and night. Though in the Tearaght rock, where the lightkeepers burn naught but coal, the cricket sings to-day too. You wouldn't think in a desolate rock like that a cricket could live, and this is the way of it."[12]

They then did the tour of the Inis: "There was now time to stroll around the island before dark. Daly, whose hands were never idle, applied himself to fashioning a pair of oars out of some lengths of driftwood."[13]

They came as far as the old monastic settlement:

We came to a well-preserved chapel, Lass leaping ahead to chase rabbits among the stones. A new-fledged family of wrens churred noisily at our approach. The little oratory measured scarcely twelve by six feet, with a low doorway two by four feet. East of this entrance lay a huge rectangular heap of stones, the top layer of glistening white quartz. One or two primitive stone crosses stood up from the altar-like mass.

"There lie buried holy men," said Eugene, "with petrels nesting in their skulls."

A herd of wild goats led by two hirsute billies stampeded from the little burial-ground.[14]

On the following day, Lockley spent a while fishing, and paid a visit to Inis na Bró, hoping to find the rare Leach's petrel, but was unsuccessful:

We shot the trammel-net and pulled the canoe in search of the dozen willow-pots with which the Blasket man fishes . . . Blasket men have thick neck muscles, for their heads are forever twisted over their shoulders, now to the left and now to the right, in order to watch where they are going . . .[15]

Paddy wasn't happy with the sheep, the age-old complaint on the Inis:

> Back in the creek of Inishvickillaun Daly and his son were waiting for us in their canoe. Co-operation is essential in dealing with these flimsy boats. We had soon beached, emptied, and fixed them in their stands. Daly's son strode on in front of us, for he wanted to bake some bread. Eugene was carrying a bundle of fresh fish.
>
> We moved leisurely homeward, Lass gathering in the sheep. Daly found them two short.
>
> "Lifted," said he with a sorrowful nod towards the ravens above our heads. "The Inish do be a terrible place for lifting sheep–between winter and the ravens and the rocks and the wild weather we lose a third every year. They go to the difficult places in the rocks, and fail to get back. They starve until the ravens take their eyes."[16]

Time to eat again. There is a turf supply laid on. The old saying goes: "Fire is half food."

> We arrived at the door each loaded with a sack of turf, of which the tireless Daly had two years' supply stacked and netted in the diggings. His son by now had worked up a great turf fire and had a big loaf ready for baking. It was made of three parts white to one of maize flour, with some soda, the dough filling the cooking-pot three inches deep. The heavy iron lid was piled high with red embers. In an hour a huge yellow loaf was turned out to make room for a mess of roast Pollack, wrasse, and bacon.[17]

The following day Lockley bade farewell to Inisvickillane and went with one of the Ó Catháin (Keane) family to Inis Tuaisceart. Both Lockley and Paddy were sorry to be parting. They had understood each other. When the boat finally arrived to take Lockley away, there was a moment of sorrow:

> "He has come for you," said Daly, with a sigh, "and we shall be missing the chatter and the laughter in the old house of the Inish to night . . ."
>
> And so from the harbour of Inishvickillaun we moved north to the Great Sound, shouting a farewell to the Dalys and Eugene and his brother.

It was difficult to be sorry on a day like this, but I knew I had left some of my heart behind me in Inishvickillaun, in the good company of these simple and pure-hearted men, in the cottage and in its garden filled with tossing willow-spears, rioting nasturtiums, and nesting storm-petrels.[18]

Chapter XV

B.V.138

One winter's day in the middle of the Second World War, the raucous drone of a German flying boat broke the silence. The Island people noticed the plane, shaped like a shoe, as it droned heavily overhead from the north, and passed across the Island, low in the air, and out of sight. It was a rare and wonderful sight at that time, but even then was soon forgotten.

The plane was the B.V.138 of the Kustenfliegergruppe 906 stationed at Brest, then in the occupation of Germany. It was the duty of that fleet of flying boats to patrol the North Atlantic in search of British ships or US ships on their way to Europe with concealed arms. America had not yet entered the war, but the Germans were highly suspicious that they were secretly helping the British. It was not the business of these planes to attack, but to send a radio message to the U-boats, which were on standby and ready to strike.

The B.V.138 had taken off early that morning, 25 November 1940, and headed for the Atlantic over the Bay of Biscay. It was not the usual plane for the crew that flew it. Their plane was unfit for flight that morning, so they took the 138, which had been flown by another crew the previous day. What they did not know was that the B.V.138 had not been serviced and was unfit for flight.

There was a five-man crew:

> Oberleutnant Konrad Neymeyr, Captain
> Overfeldwebel Hans Biegel, Engineer,
> Unteroffizier Erwin Sack, Radio Operator,
> Obergefreiter Erns Kalkowski, Air Gunner,
> Feldwebel Willi Krupp, Pilot.

The B.V.138 was a fine big plane, with an unusual appearance which gave it the name "the Flying Clog." It had twin engines and included stations for the radio and navigational equipment, a galley, toilet and a rest compartment with three bunks, as well as the cockpit. It was diesel fuelled and could remain in the air for fifteen hours. There were ten of these planes stationed at Brest. They were popular with the crews, being very steady and stable in flight, but they had their difficulties. The engines were very difficult to work with, and the floats on which they landed on the water were prone to damage in rough seas.

The flight continued on into the Atlantic, the crew scanning every inch of the sea carefully with their binoculars and telescopes. Nothing unusual was sighted. When they were well west of Ireland, they turned north and flew to within sight of the coast of Iceland. They then turned south again and followed the west coast of Ireland, using the Great Blasket as a navigational point. As they were making for the Blaskets at a height of 1,500 feet, the engines began to give trouble. The crew immediately recognised that they had dirt in the filters and that they would have to be cleaned out. This was not unusual, and the skilled crew could carry out the work in a short time and be on their way again. The pilot, Willi Krupp, decided to land in the shelter of Inisvickillane to carry out the necessary repairs. He successfully put the plane down into the sea, but he did not realise the sea was so rough. While taxiing into the shelter of the Inis, the plane was struck by a huge wave, which damaged the starboard float. It was winter, the sea was very rough and the weather very broken. The crew realised now that they were in big trouble and that the plane would be unable to take off again. Their only option was to launch the rubber dinghies and make for the safety of the Inis. They brought the aircraft as near as they could to the shore, where they made an unsuccessful attempt to moor it. They then took to the dinghies and came ashore through the huge breakers at Tráigh na hInise (the Inis strand). They were lucky that it was shortly after three in the afternoon and still light.

When they reached the top of the cliff, they searched around the Inis carefully, their pistols at the ready. They soon knew that they were the only humans present. They broke the lock on the empty little house and entered, seeking the welcome shelter. There was some driftwood there and dry turf, as well as some flour and tins of condensed milk. They soon had a fire lighting. The sheep were very wild, and it was only with great difficulty that they shot one with an automatic machine-gun, along with some rabbits. They cooked a meal and made themselves as comfortable as possible. They pinned the sheepskin to the door, which favourably impressed the islanders afterwards, as they could use the skin.

After some time, they went out and lit a fire on Cnocán na Tine (The Hill of the Fire), where a fire had often been lit before in times of emergency, and hoped that help would arrive in due time. They knew there were people living on the big Island as they had seen them when they flew over it. Unfortunately, the weather was very bad, and with everyone indoors, the fire was not observed. Someone would have to have been on the hill above the village to have seen the fire, but no one had stirred out in that weather.

The following morning they went to see the aircraft and found her still floating. They left her that way.

Three days they remained on the Inis, and as there seemed to be no help arriving, and they were in ever increasing danger, they decided to leave and make for the Island. They launched the two rubber dinghies again from the strand and set out together in an attempt to land on the Island. Biegel and Krupp rowed in one, with Neymeyr, Sack and Kalkowski in the other. The sea continued very high and rough, and after some time the two boats became separated, Biegel and Krupp being blown out to sea while the boat with the other three succeeded in getting around the west side of the Island. When they came into the view of the Island village, they were spotted. The Islanders took to the sea in their *naomhógs* and succeeded in getting to them, throwing them a rope and towing them safely into the Island. The crew then told their story and explained how they had been separated from the two others, whom they now feared were drowned.

But not so. Biegel and Krupp had succeeded in getting the dinghy through the mountainous seas as far as Ceann Dubh (the Black Head) on the westernmost tip of the Great Blasket. They attempted to land there in very heavy seas and almost drowned. Biegel managed to scramble on to a rock and threw a rope to Krupp, and thus both got ashore. They still had to climb a steep cliff. Biegel succeeded in getting to the top, but Krupp found it much more difficult. He slipped and damaged his knee badly, while also being further injured by a falling rock. He had to use his pistol to gain a grip on the slippery surface, and it was only with the greatest difficulty that he succeeded in gaining the top. Biegel then set off to look for help, while the exhausted Krupp fell into a deep swoon in the grass. Biegel hadn't gone far when he met Tom na hInise Ó Dálaigh, in whose house, coincidentally, they had just stayed on the Inis. Biegel brought him back to where Krupp was. He looked to be badly injured. They succeeded in raising him from the ground. Tom was not a big man, but he was steadily built and very strong. They got the injured man on to Tom's back, and he started off, walking a little, resting a while, until they met six or seven men with the donkeys and ropes who were on their way to meet them and who brought them back to the safety of the village.

Eibhlín Pheats Tom Kearney, then an Island girl of twenty-two years, continues on the story as she remembers it some sixty-five years later, when she spoke to me at her home in Springfield, Massachusetts, in March 2005:

They looked to be very injured, in particular one of them who was badly torn and bruised and appeared dead by the way he was stretched on the donkey and he tied on with the rope. The other three had been brought in earlier in the naomhógs. These two were brought to our house, we had three of them, and I think Seaisí had two others.

They were put sitting by the fire with blankets and dry clothes on them, except for the badly injured man who was put lying on the floor with blankets around him. We put down a good fire and my father told me to boil water in the kettle and to wash the wounds with the boiling water and a clean cloth.

"But," says he, "don't waste the water on the man on the floor, if he is dead. Much better to use it on those who are living that it should do them some good."

"And how will I know whether he is dead or alive?" said I to him.

"Take off his boots and socks and tickle his feet, and if he is alive he will wriggle his toes."

I did as he said, and, sure, he started wriggling his toes. I knew then that he was alive. I cleaned him well with the cloth and washed his wounds in the basin of water and made him as comfortable as I could. We made tea and gave it to them. My mother cut up a sheet and made bandages and fixed up the poor man. Of course, none of them had a word of Irish, and we had no German, and 'tis little either of us had of the English. Still, we seemed to understand each other.

It was later that we heard the whole story, that they had come in from the Inis in rubber boats and that they got to the top of Ceann Dubh with a rope and a type of fishing hook tied to it to get a grip on the rock [sic]. It was in this way that they came to the top, except for the poor fellow that fell down the slope and was hit on the head by a falling stone, but he too, with the help of God, got to the cliff top.

They weren't long in the Island when the gardaí came in and made them prisoners. Someone had told them the story. I can tell you that we were not happy for them to be leaving us, because they were nice, decent people, and they were very grateful to us that saved them and looked after them.

The gardaí were very hard on them, when there was no need for it. They were shouting at them and treating them badly. My father was very unhappy with this behaviour from the gardaí and told them out straight that they had no right to be mean to them inside in his own house and that they would have to be nice to them and treat them fairly.

It was how my mother was becoming afraid that they would leave the Germans where they were and haul my father off to prison.

One of the guards that was there, didn't he tear off a gold chain that one of the Germans was wearing around his neck and throw it into the fire in a bout of rage. My father was very upset again at this. He took the tongs and drew the chain out of the fire and gave it back to the German.

"Don't do such a mean thing on the poor man," said he. "Can't you see that there is a locket on the chain, and more than likely it contains a picture of his wife or mother, and it is a very wrong thing for you to interfere with it."

Didn't the garda give heed what he was saying.

By this time it was getting dark, and there was no chance that they would leave the Island until morning. Some of the neighbours had gathered into our house. What did the Germans do, at a signal, but make for the door, and a great crowd of us young ones with them, and we scattered here and there all around the Island. One of the Germans ran out the door and cleared the fence outside with a leap.

My father was delighted.

"Look at that for training," said he.

Of course, we knew every inch of the Island, something the guards didn't, and there was no chance that the Germans would be found. So, they had to be left till morning.

But when the morning came, the guards came all around them and the Germans surrendered and were made prisoners again. They were brought down to the quay and into a trawler, and off they went to Valencia Island. They bade us all farewell, and they told us with whatever little English they had that they were very thankful and that, with God's help, they would come again to repay our generosity. Then they sang a song in German, bidding us farewell.

I heard afterwards that they were put into prison on the Curragh of Kildare and that they were treated right, even that they used to be freed to work with the local farmers and earn a little money for themselves, and that they could go out at night and have a drink and meet the people. They were sent home in a while when the war was over.

When the war was over a few years later and everything peaceful again, they came back to say thanks to the Island people for how good they had been to them. They invited them to Dingle and gave them a big meal with drink and all to express their thanks to them. I wasn't at the party as I had left the Island, but they told me that the man who was injured was inquiring for me in particular, because he was very grateful for the tending I had done on him. He told them all that it was I who had saved his life and that he really wanted to see me again. But I wasn't at home. I was in Connemara, in Lettermullen as a supervisor in a Gaeltarra Éireann knitting factory, and after that I went to America in the year 1948. I was told afterwards that the German called a few more times to my door to see me, but, of course, I wasn't there. Indeed, I was far from home at that time in Springfield, Mass. And it wouldn't have been so bad except that I heard afterwards that he was rich and well-off, that he had plenty of factories in Germany and that he was one of the most important businessmen in that country, such as Sears-Roebuck here with us. I think Krupps was his name.

But they were very nice to the Island people. They paid the Ó Dálaighs for the sheep they killed on the Inis, and they paid them well. They had to break down the door when they were there to get in out of the cold, and they paid for that as well. They bought a fine lock and key for the door.

Sometimes I watch the History Channel and Discovery Channel, and there is great account of the Germans, how terrible they were during the war, that they were right blackguards entirely. But that wasn't the way that we, the Island people, found them, but decent, honest people that will never be forgotten.

You shouldn't believe all you see on television.[1]

Willi Krupp was brought to hospital in Valencia Island and the other four to Cork. There they were plied with whiskey and porter which they greatly appreciated. It was not out of hospitality they got it, however, but in hope that it would loosen their tongues and that they would pass on valuable information to the Irish authorities. But never a word passed their lips concerning German intelligence.

When Willi Krupp got better, they asked him what he wanted. He said he would like to be reunited with his comrades, who had been brought to the Curragh on 1 December 1940. Konrad Neymeyr succeeded in escaping from the Curragh and getting on board an Irish ship bound for Portugal. The ship, however, put into Bristol for coal and the ship was searched, as was the custom during the war, and Neymeyr was recaptured. He was sent to a prisoner-of-war camp, in which he had a much harder time than he had had on the Curragh, and he had to remain there until the end of the war, whether he liked it or not. The others were allowed home at the end of the war.

The story of the German landing on the Blaskets took off, of course, and was greatly added to. Stanley Jennings remembered hearing the story some time during the middle forties:

> The story spread all around the district, and as is usual, different rumours were rife. People heard that a great squad of German soldiers had landed on the Great Blasket and that they were going to attack the country, and the story was believed. The Gardaí themselves didn't understand the account, and they sent for the army. In the end, when the *naomhóg* from the Island reached the mainland with the three poor fellows in the end, it was how there was hundreds of soldiers lined up in squadrons waiting for them.[2]

"Keep it; you might need it," is a well-known old saying on the Island. Necessity taught them to be handy and make use out of everything possible. That's how it also was with the seaplane. Máire Ní Ghuithín writes:

> Afterwards young fellows from the Island used to go back to the Inis to see the seaplane. They brought back with them some type of long pipes that were on her and they made moulds from them and I can tell you they were great moulds for making wax candles at that time.[3]

The Uíbh Ráthach people were not slow either in getting their share of the spoils. This letter is from a lobster fisherman from that side:

> I remember the engine of the Plane lying on the gravelly beach at the "landing place" of Inishvickillane.
>
> I have five unexploded shells, and as far as I can remember they were brought from the Blaskets, and were probably off the Plane that crashed. It should be possible to find out if this is correct, they are about 6 inches long. If you have any interest in these shells you can certainly have them.[4]

Charles Haughey hadn't long settled on the Inis when he heard the story of the German landing. During his first term as taoiseach, 1979–81, he became very interested in the event and investigated it further through the German Embassy and the Office of Foreign Affairs in Bonn to identify the airmen and see if they were still alive. The five were alive and well, and when they heard the story could not believe that the taoiseach of Ireland had actually built a home in the island where they had sought refuge so long ago. Some time after, Haughey was in Bonn on official business and met the five in the Irish Embassy. They told him all about their ordeal back in 1940. Haughey made personal presentations to each of them and extended to them an invitation to spend a holiday on the Inis. Willi Krupp was the only one who was in a position to avail himself of the invitation.[5]

In June 1981, more than forty years after the landing of the B.V.138 at the Inis, Willi Krupp returned and spent a holiday there. Great was the difference between the two visits: the second he enjoyed very much. He told the story over again to Ciaran Haughey and pointed out the places associated with the landing in 1940. There were great changes, the greatest being that the Great Blasket itself was now uninhabited. He remembered the islanders who had helped the strangers who had landed in dire need of assistance. He met the Ó Dálaighs and had pictures taken with them. He was happy and grateful to the taoiseach for his generosity.

He and a few of his friends paid a further visit to the Inis from 5–13 July 1982, when Maria Simonds-Gooding remembers meeting them at the bottom of the cliff at the Inis strand. She told them she had the propeller of the plane in her home in Dunquin and invited them to come and see it. On route they stopped off at Kruger's Pub. When they were leaving, a man approached Willie Krupp and said, "I saved that man's life." It was Tom na hInise Ó Dálaigh.

Maria Simonds-Gooding remembers her first visit to the Inis in the summer of 1968:

> [We] came to a small beach where there was the ruins of an aeroplane halfway up the cliff . . . Part of the plane was as perfect as if it had crashed a bare five minutes earlier–you'd swear it had happened that morning–silvery light metal.[6]

In August 2005, Maria got in touch with the Air Corps, and Colonel Paul Fry was very interested in taking the propeller and restoring it, and taking it on loan to display in their museum in Baldonnell.

The body of the plane was no longer to be seen when the Haughey family came to live there in 1974, but the two engines could be seen partly buried in the sand. Charles J. Haughey writes, in August 1979, "On

Sunday morning we dug up two of the German aircraft engines from the shingle beach and got them up on the rocks." And again in 1986: "We retrieved another section of the plane."[7]

I well remember Tomás Ó Dálaigh, or Tom an Oileáin, Paddy na hInise's son, on sunny mornings propping a brass telescope on the stone fence at his home beside the school in Dunquin where I taught, looking into the Inis and inviting me and the children over to have a look.

I admired the brass telescope.

> "It came from a German plane that had landed at the Inis," he explained, "they left it after them in the house. You know, I brought one of them down to the village on my back . . ."

But we didn't wait. He had so much to tell and just wanted someone to listen. Such a pity we didn't wait. He had the answers to so many of the questions that I now seek. And now it's too late.

There are still the remains of the two engines of the B.V.138 resting on the Inis strand, a reminder of the time when the two ends of the world rose against each other and the shadow of their war extended even as far as the Blaskets.

Far from us be a repeat.

Chapter XVI

Other Visitors

The local fishermen used to call to the Inis during the fishing season, and the Ó Dálaigh brothers, Tom and Paddy, and their friends would be constant visitors, even staying from Monday to Saturday. Otherwise, these were quiet years for the Inis from 1941 up to the sixties.

Michael Viney
In the summer of 1965, Michael Viney, an *Irish Times* journalist, spent three weeks there. It wasn't the history or the culture that he sought, but to be alone on an island for a time. As he said himself, it wasn't *Twenty Years a-Growing* that brought him in, but *Robinson Crusoe*.

He kept a diary for the duration of his stay, during which time he did not set eye on a human. His possessions included a couple of books, some music tapes, a gun and sufficient to eat and drink. He discovered Tobar na Maighdine (The Virgin's Well) on the first day, which meant that he had enough fresh water, though not the best, whatever else might happen. He describes the house, Tigh na hInise, still standing defiantly:

> In the shelter of the ridge is the island's only habitation: an old stone cabin with a latticed window, its tarred roof drooping and round, with cables to bars set deep in the walls. The last to live there were the Dalys, parents of the man who owns it still and who comes with his sons by canoe from Dunquin to sheer the sheep in summer . . . There are some 50 sheep on the island and they are already dragging their fleeces; tufts of wool lie about like spindrift. They keep their distance, at the island's eastern end, where the dry stone walls of yesterday's meadows are toppling rock by rock into a ragged map of husbandry gone by.

He lay in his tent the first night smoking his pipe, listening to Beethoven, a suitable musical background, as he gazed over to Inis na Bró and to the strange lunar pyramid of the Tiaracht.

In the morning the sun filled the sky, and the larks, the pipits and the wheatears sang their hearts out. He swam in the clear, cold water and was joined in his romp by the seals. At night the night sky was filled with the whispering and churrings of the storm petrels returning across the moon. During the day he was disturbed by the constant rough clamour of the great black-backed gulls. He succeeded, with great difficulty, in bagging one rabbit. There was one thinly leaved sapling leaning against the wall of the house, and he was more than surprised to find a chiffchaff climbing its twigs with a tree sparrow a short distance away. Both stayed just a few hours before flying away seeking more leafy surrounds.

There were days full of fog when his only company was the Tiaracht foghorn. He did not have any fuel for the fire, but discovered that dried sheep dung made good firing, slow but hot.

He went rambling around the island, lay on the soft sea pink under the sun looking at the razorbills and puffins. His usual fish catch was pollock.

On the Sunday, he retired to the ruins of the roofless oratory, entering on his knees and listened to the Mozart Great Mass in C. He wondered when such sacred music was last heard in this ancient site.

On the sixth day, a western storm-force nine gale arose, which came near to wrecking his tent. But the day after that, the sun shone again, and he had the chance to go back again studying the puffins, the razorbills and the choughs. Watching the wildlife of the Inish he came to the conclusion: "All around me the island kills and is killed, eats and is eaten."

He painted a picture of the old stone cabin, but did not go in, although it filled him with curiosity.

Viney knew about the Inis ghosts from *The Western Island,* but they didn't worry him, or did they?

"I am fairly down to earth about fairies and things that go bump in the night. But I could not really explain why I sleep with an unsheathed bowie knife near my hand."

Although he was alone, he was not lonely: "My first reaction to the thought of visitors was one almost of dismay. I am in tune with Inisivickillane and have never once felt lonely for people in general."

He had noticed the sundial outside Tigh na hInise, placed there long ago by one of the Ó Dálaighs. It seemed strange to have one here, in a place where there was no need for the rule of time. He had not worn a watch since his arrival, but could still tell the time, even on a cloudy day. The basic rule to him was, eat from hunger, sleep from tiredness, wake when rested.

Another gale raged on the fifteenth day, which he drowned out by music–Beethoven's Violin Concerto. He finished off the whiskey on the seventeenth day, another day of fog. He was beginning to understand how delicate the thread of life was on the Inis. If the weather did not improve, there was a chance that he would have to remain on, perhaps for another week or more. He tried to record the storm petrels during the night, but was not too successful. He was beginning to feel doubtful about the boat that was coming to take him. Perhaps the weather was too rough? He remained on the clifftop looking through the glasses, reluctant to pack the tent until he was sure. Then he caught the flash of sun on glass. Seán Brosnan from Dingle's boat, the *Ard Íde,* was coming to pluck him from the Inis, despite a gale warning. He had lost weight, had become brown-faced and knew a lot more about the wildlife of Inisvickillane than when he landed.[1]

Maria Simonds-Gooding

July 1968 was a very hot month. Maria Simonds-Gooding and her first cousin, Marie Claire, came on a visit to Dunquin, where they stayed in Krugers guest house. They had hoped to take a trip to the Blaskets and stay a few days, but there seemed to be a great many tents there, which could actually be seen from the mainland, and Maria was afraid she would not find the peace and quiet there to paint. They met Don Tucker one evening in Krugers. Don and his party were diving for the wreck of the *Santa Maria de la Rosa* which sank on 21 September 1588. Don told Maria and Marie Claire to be down at the Cuaisín in Dunquin at three o'clock the following day and that he would bring them in to any island they wished. There was no question of payment.

During the night they decided to go to Inisvickillane, although they knew nothing about it:

> It didn't even particularly inspire me to look at from the mainland, but seemed far enough out to be able to work there in solitude. I must have been talking to some of the locals that night, because someone introduced me to Tom and Paddy na hInise. They said they had a little house out there and that I could stay there if I wished. I'd find the key under the stone. I remember them telling me to watch out, as it was the island of the fairies. I didn't know what that meant, nor did I care, and no one explained it to me. I spent the morning with my cousin gathering up provisions in an old sack. We had tins of food and matches and soap and one bottle of Kruger's Port, and they all filled into one sack. We had a little tiny tent with no ground sheet.

The following day, good to their word, Don and the divers took Maria and Marie Claire to the Inis. None of the divers had ever been there either, and didn't even know how to land there:

We headed across the Sound the whole seven miles and came to the Inish, but there seemed to be no place to land. We went around the cliff searching for a landing place, but finally turned back and came to a small beach where there was the ruins of an aeroplane. Still there was no obvious landing place, and the tide was quite high. But we scrambled on to the cliff with a little track leading up just above the crashed plane . . . The little path up the cliff rose vertically above us. The divers said they would put a rope on our sack and hoist it up the cliff; it would be easier that way. The bag slipped and the sack fell right down the cliff, and Kruger's Port that cost the whole of 6 shillings and 6 pence could be smelt all across the island and around the cliff tops. What I will never forget, when we got to the top of the cliff, having rescued the sack, was the island that lay flat beyond us. The roof of Tigh na hInise must have just been tarred, because it glistened and shimmered so much in the sunlight that I thought it was a pool of water. The divers dropped the sack by Tigh na hInise and hurried back down the way they had come. They were anxious to get back.

From the moment they landed they were smitten by the spell of the Inis:

This island took complete hold of me. It felt as if every step and everything I looked at had never been walked on or looked at before. Every feeling and thought felt heightened by the awareness this place imposed on one. Tigh na hInise was a homely, intimate refuge, built into the ground with two little windows facing east, one a lattice window. But it was locked, and look as we might beneath all the stones, we could not find the key, but that did not matter, because beside Tigh na hInise was this sanctuary of a field with a stone wall all around it. We set up our little tent inside that field. We faced the opening towards the Tiaracht, from where we could see the light touch the end of the Inis as it turned around at night.

Maria, being an artist, looked for a place to paint:

The next morning my cousin and I went down to the spot where we had landed. The tide was out, and there was a stony beach below. I gathered my painting things and made my way up the cliff. My cousin was sunning herself in the fields stark naked. When I got to the top of the cliff I saw a yacht coming in. In no time at all my cousin spotted it and joined me. We lay down flat on the grass and observed a lone

174

yachtsman coming ashore in a dinghy from the yacht. When we got back to Tigh na hInise, we spotted the yachtsman coming up the island without a stitch on him. At one stage he looked up, and he disappeared when he saw us.

Later that evening he appeared, clothed, and asked us if there was anything we needed. We badly needed water, we could not find a drop anywhere on the Island. So he said he would leave a container of water at the bottom of the cliff before he left the next day.

The following day the boatman brought them into the Tiaracht:

The lighthouse keepers became quite friendly, and when I explained that I would be staying alone on the Inis, they said that at 11 o'clock every night they would cast a light out to the Inis, and if I was in trouble to light a fire, and in thirty seconds they could have a message over to Valencia Island for a lifeboat to come and fetch me. We bade them farewell and went back to the yacht. When the week had passed the skin divers arrived at the appointed time to take us back as my cousin had to get back to Killorglin. I asked the divers would they leave me and to come back to fetch me in another couple of weeks. They agreed.

I spent two more wonderful weeks on the Inis, leading a very free but disciplined life. Rise with the light and go to bed with the darkness. There were a lot of fishing boats coming around, and when the divers came to take me they appeared at my tent very early and unexpected while I was still in my sleeping bag. They were in a big hurry. We packed up quickly and I bade farewell to the Inis.

It was on this first trip that Maria saw the black calf. (See page 148).

She afterwards made many more trips to the Inis, usually staying in Tigh na hInise with her dachshund, but sometimes, if Tom and Paddy were there, in her tent in the walled field.

As regards food during her stays on the Inis:

There were rabbits and limpets. I had learned how to snare rabbits on the Great Blasket with Seáinín Mhicil. This was done with the greatest care and in a humane way. When the food had almost run out, it became rabbit stew for breakfast, lunch and dinner. The rabbits were much bigger than those on the Great Blasket. I'd boil the rabbit in the kettle. You must either hang a rabbit for several days or eat it immediately. It was delicious until you had too much of it. The islanders were the best cooks of all. They were experts at both rabbits and fish. They would lay the freshly caught mackerel on a tongs on low cinders and cook it on each side quite quickly.

The sheep became very important as they were amongst the few living creatures around me. I noticed that they divided into two flocks, totally separate from each other. They were very curious and had almost no fear of me, as they had hardly ever seen people. But I think they were more curious about my dog, which they would actually come up to and sniff. I had him well trained not to go after them. When I would spend hours in the same spot painting, I would build up a rapport with the sheep, and I included them in my work.

I had no contact with the mainland. The islanders used to say to me, "If you paid me a thousand pounds I wouldn't stay on that island alone." I could never understand it, nor did I ever ask why, knowing there was no answer. It seemed so natural to me, and fear never entered into it, except the fear of the black calf which I saw on my first trip reappearing, and even that fear passed away. It was a very Spartan life, and I survived usually through very bad storms, but I disciplined my day by watching the tides and going down the cliff to pick periwinkles and limpets, and if the weather permitted, my painting took up many hours of the day.

In Tigh na hInise I made a light with sheep wool and some paraffin oil I had brought, and there was a sundial there, and stray pigeons coming in off the Atlantic used come in and stop off for a rest. The light of the Tiaracht at night was another source of light and life to the island, even though it was not possible to speak to the lighthouse keepers. The richness of the grass and the field that had been built for the blind sheep: these enclosures felt very intimate in that wild and sometimes frightening sea. I think survival and the beauty of the Inis in this wild sea creates an energy that at all times brings a sharp awareness with it. To go to the south side of the island was like taking an outing to a different place. The racket of the seagulls defending their nests and whirling around told you it was completely their territory. It was in a compact space. I was fascinated that the young sea gulls are grey and the adults were very protective. There were a lot of those sea pink flowers, very spongy.

I remember Pat Hayes and Eamon de Buitléar, in fierce wind, ringing the stormy petrels. They used to catch them at night at eleven.

As they flew in they put up this net and caught them, put a ring and
a number on them and let them go again.[2]

Maria painted many scenes from the Inis. She succeeded in portraying
the wildness and loneliness of the Inis in a wonderful manner. Her work
forms part of the rich heritage of Inisvickillane.

Sheán Sheáin Í Chearnaigh

Apart from Tomás Dhónaill Ó Criomhthain, we have few written reports
about life on the Blaskets. However, Seán Sheáin Í Chearnaigh has written
a delightful account about a trip he took to the Inis in the late sixties with
his brother-in-law, and two ex-Blasket islanders, Paddy Beag Ó Dálaigh
and Paddy Mhicil Ó Súilleabháin. This account was published in his book
Iarbhlascaodach ina Dheoraí. It is an important account in that it shows life
on the Inis as seen by the Blasket islander. Seán was no stranger to the Inis
as his family had strong links with the island. His grand-uncle was
drowned along with Seán Ó Guithín and one of the Dunleavys in 1873 or
1874 while transporting lambs to Inis na Bró. His grand-aunt Léan Ní
Chearnaigh was married to Seán Ó Guithín and was left widowed after the
tragic events of that day. He was very familiar with the tales and the
folklore of the Inis. One day Seán's sister, Cáit, and her husband Pádraig
Ó Braonáin from Dublin paid him an unexpected visit to his home in
Muiríoch. After a while they ventured down to Johnny Franks' pub in
Ballydavid, and they decided there and then to visit the Blasket Island.

They headed back to Dún Chaoin and into the Daly house in Baile na
Rátha. They were met by the two Paddys, Paddy Mhicil Ó Súilleabháin
and Paddy Beag Ó Dálaigh, who were getting ready to travel to
Inisvickillane, and that they would be most welcome should they decide to
come with them. First of all they called to Krugers pub and bought a
dozen bottles of porter and some food.

They filled up the *naomhóg*. The weather was lovely and the sea like
glass. They started rowing, but did not raise the sail as there wasn't a puff
of wind. They eventually reached the beach on Inisvickillane. The beach
was covered with seals, but they scattered as soon as they saw the *naomhóg*
approaching. They weren't too happy as they wanted to kill a seal for a
meal. They sent Paddy Beag out to Leac na Roilleog, and he killed a big
fat seal and brought him in.

The night was falling on the Inis with seabirds circling and seals calling
from the cliffs, and it seemed as if it belonged to another world.[3]

They landed and brought some stuff up to Poll na Mine Buí. They lifted the *naomhóg* onto the stand and made for the house, which was nice and cosy and dry.

> We cleaned it out and lit a big fire because there is no shortage of turf there. The Dalys cut the turf in the summertime, while they are on the Inis shearing the sheep. After lighting the fire, we gathered ferns to make our beds at nightfall. This is part of our culture and we are well used to it. The evening was very nice with a fine view over the hills. We could see Macgillycuddy's Reeks to the south, Dingle Bay to the south-east and the Blasket Islands to the north-east looking forlorn.[4]

They set two dozen snares at Barr na Mionnán to catch rabbits during the night. They then headed towards the chapel.

> There is a graveyard outside with a stone cross in the middle. The chalice is still in the chapel, but it is chipped. Priests used to escape to the Inis during the Penal Laws and they used to say mass in this chapel. We are not sure who is buried in the graveyard, but the old people maintained that a saint was buried there. The graveyard is quite large, surrounded by a nice field built with stones. No one ever took a stone out of that field. A priest reading a book used to be seen wandering around the chapel. The old people used to say that it was a priest doing purgatory.[5]

Afterwards they returned to the snares, and they took three rabbits and roasted them along with the seal. When they were cooked, the Islanders enjoyed them, except for the city man, who brought along his own lunch to eat.

They lit the tin lamp, and fashioned a bed out of the fern and spent a good part of the night talking and telling stories, even though they had a small radio with them.

Around two o'clock they returned to the snares. You had to do that before daybreak as the rabbits would be taken by the seagulls and by the rooks.

Lights could be seen from all the lighthouses: Skellig Michael, Fastnet Rock, Bull Rock, Valentia as well as the Tiaracht. It was a mystical sight. They walked on with nothing underfoot only the storm petrels. They caught an extra dozen rabbits during the night. They returned to the house, ate some more rabbit and seal, with the city man eating out of his lunch box. They lay down on the fern and stayed there until 12 o'clock noon.

We were woken up by three sailors standing at the door. They needed water. They were English sailors who were fishing the previous night north at the Tiaracht. Myself and Paddy Beag brought them to Tobar na Maighdine and they filled the big barrel with water. They gave us plenty of tobacco, and promised to leave some fresh fish on the beach for us if we wanted some, but we didn't.[6]

They lifted the *naomhóg* off the stand, and they left the Inis with a dozen rabbits and the big basket of fish the sailors left behind. The beach was full of seals. They turned west towards the Narrow Sound and from there to Banc Gharraí an Bhéil towards an Tiaracht. They were welcomed by the three lighthouse men. They thought it strange that the houses were so clean inside and out. They gave them supper and invited them to stay for two or three days to enjoy their company. But the travellers were keen to return home, and they were also worried that the weather could change, forcing them to stay for a few months, because the Tiaracht is the worst place on earth. The lighthouse men were three single men. They were very interested in the Irish language and could speak it fluently. They gave them the fish which was much appreciated. They took off and raised the sail on the *naomhóg* at Speir Shéamais Uí Mhilleáin, and they had a fair wind which brought them all the way into Dunquin pier. They paid a visit to Krugers pub as Seán Ó Braonáin wanted to buy the two Paddys a few drinks. It was midnight before they reached Ballydavid.

Chapter XVII

New Islanders

In March 1936, the district court decreed that Pádraig Ó Dálaigh would have ownership of Inisvickillane for 999 years at the rent of "One peppercorn." That meant that he had complete ownership, something that was rare enough on the islands on the west coast.

It happened once that Charles J. Haughey, a young, rising politician was travelling through Donegal when he arrived at a little village named Haughey's Isle. He was impressed by the name. Although it may have been one time long ago, it wasn't a proper island any more, but now had dried out and was removed from the sea. It was this that awakened Haughey's interest in islands and gave him the idea that he would like very much to live on one himself. He first tried the coast of Mayo, the county from which his family had originally come, seeking an island that he could buy. There were many islands along the coast of that county, many of which were for sale, but there was always the one difficulty: the title was not clear, which meant that there could be legal difficulties ahead. He had to give up as far as Mayo was concerned.

It happened that he was talking to Maria Simonds-Gooding, the young artist, after he had opened her first exhibition in Dublin. Haughey was then minister for finance. During the conversation, she mentioned that she had just spent time on one of the Blasket Islands, Inisvickillane, a most beautiful island in west Kerry. Haughey remarked that he had a great interest in islands himself and was on the look-out to purchase one. Maria replied that this was the one for him, and that there was a good chance he could buy it, as the owners were growing old.

That is how Charles J. Haughey got interested in Inisvickillane. He got the chance to visit it for the first time some time later.

As he said himself: "I first landed on Inis Mhic Uibhleáin at Easter 1973. It was a lovely sunny day with a gentle breeze blowing. It had all the magical quality and breathtaking beauty I had heard and read about so often."[1]

He knew then that this was the island he wanted. He began the negotiations. Mikeen Kane from Dingle acted on Haughey's behalf. He was the son of Jim Kane, the publican from Ballyferriter who used to spend his annual holidays on the Inis years previously. The three Ó Dálaigh brothers, Tomás, Paddy and Muiris, were approached. At least he was not refused outright, and that gave him hope. When the brothers got down to thinking it out, Paddy, Tomás and Muiris realised that they were not getting any younger and that it was becoming increasingly more difficult to take the nine-mile voyage and then try to land and reach the top of the cliff.

When on his summer holidays that year, Haughey again visited the Inis. He asked the brothers to come into the Inis in the helicopter with him, and they agreed.

Haughey arrived in the helicopter on the Móinteán at the clifftop in Dunquin to meet them, but unknown to him some considerable difficulties had arisen. The Ó Dálaighs, who would not flinch at going on the highest cliff on the Inis or on the Tiaracht on a rope, or taking to the sea in a south-westerly gale, hesitated at boarding the helicopter. Paddy gave up on the idea and told his two brothers to go on in without him. The other difficulty was that of the Irish. Would they understand Charlie's English and be able to keep up a conversation with him? To be on the safe side, they brought along one of the neighbours, John Kennedy, who was well versed in the English language. Among others who went in that day were Charlie himself, Eoghan Kane, Mikeen Kane, Máirín Feirtéar (Ferriter), as well as Muiris's twelve-year-old daughter, Nóra, who was very good on the accordion.

There was no need for all the fuss. Charlie and the brothers hit it off from the start. Charlie already had a great admiration for the Ó Dálaighs from what he had heard and read about them, and as regards the Irish, he was well able to keep up with them. The evening was a great success, and Tomás and Muiris took great pleasure in showing Charlie around the Inis.

Charlie Haughey remembered the day well:

> I landed again on the Inis on the 15 August 1973. Eoghan Ó Catháin, Mike Kane, Muiris and Tomás Ó Dálaigh were with me. We went on a helicopter from Dún an Óir Hotel, and we had lunch on the Inis. The day was wonderful–warm. We spent most of the day outside the house in the sun listening to Muiris and Nóra playing the accordion.[2]

They played the old island tunes, including, "*Ó, Neilí an Fuacht,*" "*Madra Scaoilte*" and the great music of the Inis itself, "*Port na bPúcaí.*" It was a good beginning. Charlie wanted to foster a friendship with the Ó Dálaighs, the old Inis people, to have the continuation from the old times.

The negotiations continued on, and even they were not too difficult. The brothers, especially Paddy and Tom, didn't have much interest in, or experience of, money. They led very simple lives, and their needs were very frugal. The greatest difficulty was the wrench of parting with the island. The breakthrough came with the important agreement that they would have permission to keep sheep on the Inis and permission to come and go as they pleased for the duration of their lifetimes.

On 6 April 1974, a taxi arrived in Dunquin and brought the brothers over the Clasach to Dingle, and the agreement was signed to make Charles J. Haughey the owner of Inisvickillane. It was just about a hundred years since Muiris Mór Ó Dálaigh and Cáit Ní Ghuithín had first settled there, seventy years since they had left the Inis for the Great Blasket, and twenty since the Ó Dálaighs had left that island to settle in Dunquin. The money was paid over to the bank. They were asked if they would like some cash to take away. After some thought, Tom said he would be happy with, say, £2, to bring home a fine piece of bacon for the dinner. The bargain was sealed with a drink in one of the local hostelries. I don't think there was any music or song.

Charles Haughey paid his first visit there as official owner of Inisvickillane on Easter Saturday 1974. The whole Haughey family left Dingle in a fishing trawler and sailed into the Inis, but, as happens so often, the sea was too rough and they were unable to land. They had to be happy with spending the evening on the Great Blasket and then returning to Dingle. The following day, Easter Sunday, they had better luck, this time in a helicopter, and they spent a very pleasant day examining their new island, planning and imagining the new house they would build there in the near future.

They were back again in July 1974. They brought three tents this time. They also brought a two-way radio system with which they could contact the Ferriter family in Coumeenole, at six o'clock each evening, to ensure that everything was all right. The two brothers, Paddy and Tom, were there at that time shearing the sheep, and the Haugheys used to spend the evenings in their house, Tigh na hInise, with them, talking, singing and drinking. There were between eighty and ninety sheep there at that time, each of them in very good condition, as was the tradition of the Inis sheep. The weather was not too fine at the beginning, but improved later. The brothers showed them around the Inis–and explained the different spots to them–where the fishing was good, the well, the Léithreach, the rock from which they would load sheep or perhaps passengers into a *naomhóg*.

(Unloaded *naomhógs* were pulled up on the strand.) They also told them much of the lore and legend of the place.

The brothers spent a couple of days there, and when they were departing, they left the key so that the family could use the house. From then on, they went there every night.

The Haughey family came again in August, with some other relatives and friends. The sergeant paid them an official visit one day. He enjoyed it very much, as it was his first visit ever to any of the Blaskets.

The weather was very bad in the beginning, and one night the wind was so strong that one of the tents was blown down, and the occupants had to move into one of the others. But it passed and the weather improved. They spent the long sunny days swimming, fishing and exploring. Each night they came together in Tigh na hInise. A metal hut arrived for them. It was erected and served as a kitchen at first and was used for the same purpose by the builders later. Everything had to be brought in by boat from Dingle, by Mikeen Kane or Tom Fitzgerald, and above all, welcome was extended to a fine, badly needed barrel of porter. Some of the lightmen from the Tiaracht paid a visit once and left a flag, with instructions to erect the flag if ever they were in trouble. They would see it from the Tiaracht and come to their assistance. It was arranged also that the Inis people would send three flashes of light to the Tiaracht every night at nine o'clock to let them know that everything was fine. From then out, the lighthouse keepers were in daily contact with them, and they could also relay messages to and from the mainland.

The biggest adventure of that summer was the saving of the dog. He belonged to one of the neighbours in Dunquin, and the Ó Dálaighs had brought him in to help them round up the sheep for shearing, which he did admirably. But when the Ó Dálaighs were returning to the mainland, there was no way the dog would join them in the *naomhóg*. He was too scared of the sea. He escaped and hid out somewhere on the Inis and was not seen again until the night before the Haughey family were to leave at the end of August. It turned out to be a night of thunder and lightening, so bad that the dog approached the door, terrified. It was not difficult to coax him into the shelter. He was brought out the following day in the helicopter and safely delivered to his master—an adventure that put a fitting ending to the holiday.[3]

A beginning had been made to a pattern of visits that would last for many years. They would pay a visit to the Inis any time they had a few days to spare, if the weather was suitable, particularly at Christmas and the New

Year, Easter, Whit, the June public holiday weekend, the annual month's holidays in August, and a few days in late October-early November.

A wooden hut was erected beside Tigh na hInise. They got a rubber dinghy for fishing and sailing around the coast of the Inis. Their catch was mostly mackerel and pollock. A system was devised to raise up supplies to the clifftop, called "the Lift", and using it they raised some of the old German aeroplane to the top. Conor succeeded in building a windmill that provided basic power to work light, a radio and a music player. Charlie had always intended to use natural power: the wind, the sun, and when and if possible, the power of the sea waves. Although they tried a windmill three times, it failed each time, the wind being too strong and the machinery breaking down.

The boys learned how to set snares for the rabbits, how to cut and save turf, and how to sow and harvest potatoes. They continued on with the age-old tradition on the Inis of welcoming everyone. Life on the Inis was ideal.

It was that year that they tried to bring the water from Tobar na Maighdine (the Virgin's well) to the wooden hut, as they had no running water yet. The problem was the height. Was the well higher than the roof of the hut, so that the water would feed by gravity? That was the question that no one seemed to be able to answer. It happened that Tom na hInise was there at the time, and he was able to show that the well was lower than the roof. Charlie was impressed: "An astonishing demonstration of intelligence and resourcefulness and the ability to use whatever happened to be at hand to solve a problem which up to then had baffled the rest of us."

He remembered how they illustrated it: "There was a translucent plastic barrel there filled with petrol. The well could be seen from the spot, as could the hut. Tom made sure that the top of the barrel was level, making use of the petrol. He then laid a wooden beam across the top of the barrel, one end pointing towards the well and the other towards the hut. Then, with a sharp eye, Tom was able to demonstrate clearly to all that the well was lower than the roof and that they would have to think of some other plan. A wonderful demonstration from someone who had only spent very little time at school.

The intelligence of the Ó Dálaighs always impressed Charlie. On another occasion:

> Tomás and Paddy Ó Dálaigh came out on the Wednesday and went
> back to the mainland on the Friday. They took back three live sheep

184

with them in the naomhóg. It was fascinating to see them herd the sheep by the age old methods down to the Léithreach so that they could catch the three to take back with them.

The connection with Uíbh Ráthach was made again, a connection that had been very strong at one time: "An additional channel of communication was established–John Casey of Portmagee and his boat, *Ard Fionnbar.* On most days he fished for lobster around the islands and on occasions brought us out supplies of stout.[4]

The work of building the new house began in 1976.

Tom and Paddy were of the opinion that the wrong site had been chosen to build the house. The best site, according to them, was their own house, Tigh na hInise, and that it was there that the new house should be built. They had heard it from the old people about another house built at the new site at some time; that the roof had been blown off in the course of a south-western storm. Even the fire on the Inis had been quenched by the storm and had to be lit again by a quartz stone.

When Charlie chose the site in Gort an Earraigh, Paddy told him out straight: "You will find your house in America. We know. It happened before."

But Charlie chose the site he wanted, which, in his opinion, would cause the least interference to the natural surroundings and also because it had one of the finest views in Ireland. He took the same care with the building itself. Every effort was made to build it as appropriately as possible for the site and the environment.

Charlie admitted: "The spot where Tigh na hInise is built is the spot of the least wind, it is the most sheltered and calmest place on the Inis. Tom was right."

On Sunday, 12 August 1976, the plans for the house were laid out by Standish Collen and Dan Bric. Later on in the evening, the whole family came together, and Seán, the youngest member of the family, turned the first sod. The building of the house had begun.

The following morning, Dan, Joe Cavin (Kavanagh) and Larry Slattery began to lay the foundation. On 21 August, Jimmy "Curley" Murphy and Tom O'Sullivan, stonemasons, came in and began their work. The work would last three summers under the guidance of Dan Bric.

It was Tom Fitzgerald who picked Dan for the job. Tom, a great friend of Charlie's and later a senator, played an important part in the building of the house. He had much experience of building, and his brother, Páidí, had a hardware shop in Dingle. Tom often brought in the material needed in his own boat, and he often worked on the building himself and solved many problems in the building of the house in a remote island in the middle of the great ocean.

Dan was a good choice for the task that was placed on him. He had been there only a day or two when he discovered a disused quarry on the north-western side of the Inis. The stone in this quarry was the same as that from which the ogham stone was made, and it was clear that the ogham stone had come from here. He cut out fine flagstones that were later used for the mantel over the fire and for the door lintels.

They spent the summer of 1976 working, and continued right up to the month of December.

They bought one of the old-type slides from Connor in Ventry. These were used in the hilly, stony land around Slea Head by the farmers for hauling home the turf, feeding sheep and carrying stones. They slid along the ground like sleighs and could travel on terrain where a wheeled cart could not go. It worked on the Inis, but was so slow that it was soon discarded. A dumper was then taken out on hire, and it worked very well until the end.

Every one of the masons had his own distinctive style of building, which can easily be discerned from examination of the walls. Larry Slattery drew in most of the material in his boat at this time, and he was also mostly responsible for cooking the meals, and very good they were.[5]

Those who worked that first year included Pat O'Connor, Jimmy Murphy and Tom Sullivan, stonemasons; David Collen on the dumper; Joe Cavin, Larry Slattery and Ken Hamilton attending.

Pat Connor from Baile Dháith will remember the days on the Inis as long as he lives:

> We would work for three weeks without a break, even on Sunday.
> Then we would have a week free, and we would get paid for that week.
> It was fantastic. I worked for fourteen weeks there. If it wasn't for the
> salmon season, I would have stayed there till the end.[6]

Danny Sheehy from Baile Eaglaise spent the summer of 1977 working there. He remembers that they would come together at about nine o'clock on the Monday morning. They would meet Dan Bric and all would go into Dingle together. The shopping for the week would be done, and then they would have to have a few drinks to fortify themselves for the trip. Seán Brosnan from Dingle would take them there in his boat, the *Ard Íde*. Seán would have a very difficult job dragging them out of the pub. With luck they would assemble at the quay in Dingle about 2 P.M. It was a voyage of a couple of hours to the Inis, by Ventry Harbour, Slea Head, Dunmore, the Scológ and the *Gob* of the Island. There would be no hurry as the first day was always allowed for travel and settling in. When they would arrive at the Léithreach, everything would be transferred from the boat to the strand, and it was another heavy task to take everything to the top, in particular the barrels of porter.

The men Danny remembers working there included: Jimmy Curley, Muiríoch; Pat Connor, Baile Dháith; Tom [Mhic Grumail] Grumell, Cathair Scuilbín; Larry Slattery, An Gleann Mór; Dan Sullivan, An Coimín; Dan Bric, Na Gorta Dubha; Joe Cavin, Na Gorta Dubha; Siney Crotty, Kilbaha, County Clare; Ken Hamilton, An Gleann Mór and Dublin; Dave Collen, son of the house engineer and his father, Stan Collen; Timmy Shea, Killorglin; Tom Herrity; Colm Scanlon, Baile an Lochaigh; Ron Tomlinson, Fearann; and Ken Crawford.

Larry Slattery did the cooking in the beginning, in the wooden hut, and afterwards Joe Cavin took it over. Charlie had a great admiration for Joe's cooking, particularly the fry-ups he presented.

They would spend the night in Tigh na hInise. A good part of the night would be spent drinking, singing, arguing and telling stories, all gathered around the fire. Some important questions and problems were discussed, like whether there are really ghosts on the Inis, Dan's adventures in Dublin, the good points of a Kerry sheepdog, and the proper way to construct a house on an island. There was a couch in the hut, and Joe slept on that. They had also a big sponge mattress, which could roll together during the day and open out at night. It took three or four, everyone with his head to the fire, which was kept ablaze always. One or two others would sleep in the wooden hut. Exhausted and after a few drinks, there was never any difficulty in sleeping till morning.

The large oak, ash, beech and walnut beams that transverse the house were put in place. These were trees that had grown at Abbeville, Haughey's home. They had been uprooted in a storm, cut into beams and transported to the Inis, an important symbolic connection between the two houses. Everyone was happy with this achievement, a deed worthy of Fionn Mac Cumhail himself, at his best day.

Charlie wished to do everything in the old traditional way. The walls would be built without any concrete block, entirely of Inis stones drawn from the old field walls to the site. As much as possible would be from the

187

island. The stones for the fireplace and hearth were drawn from Faill na Cárthaí. The walls are three feet thick. In time lichen and moss would grow on the stones, and the house would melt into the surroundings in such a way that it would be difficult to discern. The principal room would be the sitting/dining room, with an unsurpassable view south to the Uíbh Ráthach Peninsula, Valentia Island, Puffin Island, the Cow, the Calf, the Bull and, of course, the two Skelligs, the small Skellig and Skellig Michael.[7]

The work for 1977 came to an end on 9 December, having begun on 7 June. The walls inside and outside were completed by that stage, the roof in place, the floors laid and the windows fitted. A reservoir for storing water in the ground for the house had also been completed. One small difficulty arose towards the end of the stay. The phone system broke down, and they were left without communication with the outside. Food was running low and hardship beckoned. They succeeded, however, in getting a signal over to the Tiaracht, and from there a message was flashed to Valentia Island. On 8 December the lifeboat arrived with a supply of cigarettes and biscuits. The phone was quickly repaired, and the workers remained on till the following day, when the helicopter arrived to take them off according to the plan.

The Haughey family stayed in *Tigh na Carraige* (Stone House), as they called the new house, for the first time during the summer of 1978. That year was also remembered by them as *bliain na naomhóige*, the year of the *naomhóg*. Tom and Paddy Ó Dálaigh had made them a *naomhóg* a few years earlier which was christened *An Fiach Dubh* (The Raven). It had been brought to Malahide at the end of summer 1977, and put on the stands there. During the winter, the family trained steadily in the Malahide Estuary, with the aim of being ready for the following summer's regattas. When they arrived the following year, they rowed from Dingle to the Inis, a not inconsiderable feat. They did further training around the Inis itself, and when the racing season began, they entered for the Ventry and Dingle regattas. The crew consisted of Conor Haughey, Cormac O'Connor and Garry Heffernan. Although they acquitted themselves honourably, the local boatmen proved too experienced. They discovered that their *naomhóg* was too heavy, that it was a fishing *naomhóg* rather than one designed for racing. They left an order with one of the local master boat builders, Eddie Hutch, to construct a proper racing *naomhóg*, in which they would test themselves against the Kerry boatmen again the next season.

The most popular tune to be heard in the family circle that summer was "The Lonesome Boatman."

The year 1978 was also when the wind generator was erected. But most of all it was the year when the house was completed.

Furniture from Abbeville was transported to Shannon Airport by CIÉ, and from there to Inisvickillane by Sikorski helicopter. That included a great dining table with a dozen chairs designed by Mícheál Mac Liammóir, the dramatist, made from Abbeville walnut with the Inis symbol of the cross from the Inisvickillane ogham stone inscribed on all the articles of furniture. All the furniture was made from Abbeville wood–walnut and beech. An interesting addition was a set of fire irons and candelabras designed and executed by Anthony Hedgecock, a German artist who lived in Donegal, whose work had been seen by Charlie at the trade fair in Ballsbridge. Senator Ted Kennedy took to these articles on a later visit to the Inis and wished to present a set to his mother, Rose, but the craftsman had returned to Germany and could not be contacted. However, John Hillard made exact copies of the pieces, and the senator was able to present them to his mother for her bedroom. The pottery chosen was that of Louis Mulcahy, Potadóireacht na Caolóige, Ballyferriter, which had a strong local flavour.

A sundial, made by Ken Thompson, similar to that erected in front of Tigh na hInise, was put in place in front of the new house.

The family held their first dinner together at Tigh na Carraige on Friday 18 August 1978. Charlie was very happy. The vision had come to fruition.[8]

Dan Bric and his men, Joe Cavin, Siney Crotty, Tim O'Shea, Pat O'Connor, John Dowd and Steve Fahey, finished on 12 September 1978. Before they left, Charlie commissioned Tom Roche, an artist living in Dingle, to paint a portrait of Dan, Joe, Siney and Tim, those who had been most responsible for the building. The portraits are still hanging prominently in the house on the Inis as a memorial to their craftsmanship.

The wind generator was not a success, due to the wildness of the Inis. More often than not, the mechanism was broken by the force of the wind. Then solar panels were tried in October 1978. They worked satisfactorily. Charlie also had an eye on generating power from the waves at Cuas an Éin.

Dan paid the Inis a visit on 28 December 1978 to see how everything was faring and was happy to report that, apart from the wind generator, everything was working perfectly. The two tanks were full of water and the solar panels were in full working order.

Easter 1979 saw the family back again. There were about fifty seals on the strand, and the puffins were making their nests on the cliffs having arrived back for the summer. They cut turf, set potatoes and put the running water in operation for the first time.

For the annual holidays, they left Howth on Friday, 27 July, in the yacht *Taurima* and sailed the full course along the east and south coasts, stopping at Rosslare and Kinsale before landing at the Inis a little after midnight on Sunday, 29 July.

Saturday, 4 August 1979, proved to be a special day: "We brought the first barrel of Guinness up by the *ardaitheoir* (the lift). This historic event was celebrated with much pomp and ceremony."[9]

They also had a new water source, Tobar na Cárthaí. Tom na hInise had shown the well to Charlie. It was difficult to get at from the land, because it was down a difficult cliff. It was always approached, in the old days, from the sea, and much used by the fishermen to slake their thirst in summer. The Ó Dálaighs thought highly of this water, and rightly so. The water tastes very good, never goes dry, and it has been a great success.

Now that the new house was completed, it was very evident that Tigh na hInise was beginning to fall apart and needed immediate and urgent attention. Joe Thompson, who was employed to improve the condition, began his work in 1989. Helped from time to time by his son and Brian Farrell, he was happy to stay on the Inis until the work had been completed. He stuck to the old style as far as he could, pointing the walls and putting in a flagstone floor of Liscannor stone. Joe also had a great interest in the wildlife on the Inis and, because of his long stay, was able to make many interesting observations. Two storm petrels were nesting in the walls of the Tigh at one stage, and Joe had to postpone his work until the little birds were hatched and gone. Joe sowed an herb and flower garden, sowing the flowers which had grown in the Inis in days long gone by.

Everyone who worked on the Inis had their own stories connected with their stay there. To most of them, it was just like Tomás found it so many years before: Tír na nÓg. There are stories going around still, and *ní mise a chum ná a cheap iad* (I didn't compose or invent them):

Joe's travel arrangements
The helicopter was leaving the Inis, and Joe Cavin came out on some little business. Afterwards, he was in Tigh Kruger, having a drink and waiting for the helicopter to come and bring him back. He struck up a conversation with an American drinking at the bar, who was giving Joe a full account of his life in the States. He was loud in praise of his lifestyle,

and Joe was beginning to get a little bored with the conversation. He was more than glad when he heard the noise of the helicopter approaching outside, and he explained politely to the visitor that he had to return to work.

"And how will you go there?" asked the American, looking at Joe who was a bit raggy in appearance.

"My helicopter awaits me outside," replied Joe, going out the door.

The visitor followed him out and saw Joe boarding the helicopter and taking off into the air and out across the sea. The American stayed looking after him wide-eyed.

The Wine

They ran short of drink on the Inis–a great crisis–a shortage of porter and no boat coming. There was no way that the operation could continue in such circumstances. Dan knew, however, that Charlie had stashed away a case of wine under the bed unknown to everybody. He knew that Charlie would understand their dire predicament and, being an understanding man, would have no objection if they borrowed a few bottles for a while.

And that's what they did. Dan produced the case of wine and they drank the contents and were happy, though they would have preferred it to have been a barrel of porter.

At the beginning of the next week, the usual shopping was done and the number of bottles consumed were bought in the supermarket and faithfully replaced in the case which was put back under the bed.

Some time elapsed before Charlie arrived, but he came finally, bringing with him some of his friends to spend a few days on the Inis.

When they had sat to table, Charlie produced the case of fine French wine and filled out the crystal glasses, being loud in his praise of this particular vintage.

They drank a health and raised the glasses to their lips.

Charlie drank a sip and threw it out with disgust.

It wasn't long before he understood what had happened, and it caused great laughter and jollity.

"And, it wouldn't matter as much," he used say, "except that they drank it out of mugs."

"Not so," Dan would say, when he heard the story. "We drank it out of the bottles."

And it is true. Charles Haughey always told it.[10]

191

A Good Fire

"Throw a few briquettes on the fire," says Dan one night; "it's getting a bit cold."

They were all sitting by the fire after their day's work, everyone with pipe and glass, talking and chatting.

Somebody got a bale of briquettes, and without even taking off the binding threw it into the fire, followed by two or three other bales.[11]

The Taoiseach

"And how did you get on with Charlie, Dan?" asked a neighbour of Dan's when they were talking about the golden days on the Inis.

"Wonderful," said Dan, "no problem. You see, Charlie was, at that time, the taoiseach of the country, but I was the taoiseach of Inisvickillane. We both understood this, and there was never any problem."[12]

Siney

Siney Crotty was from County Clare, a great traditional singer. An LP record was issued of some of his songs while he was on the Inis in 1977: *The Lambs in the Green Fields, Songs from the County Clare*, by Topic Records. There were three songs of his on the record, "Farewell to Lissycasey," "*An Cailín Deas*" and "Lovely Mary to the Sea Do not go." It stated on the sleeve:

> Siney Crotty, a native of Ross, near Kilbaha, has a lot of the style of decorated singing that is popularly and quite rightly often associated with singing in Irish. His songs are rare, sometimes unique, and it becomes clear that he has been the source and foundation of a number of them, in one respect or another, fashioned or altered others.

It happened that Danny Sheehy was in Dublin at the time the LP was launched, and he brought the first copy home to Siney in the Inis. Danny got great enjoyment from going over to the Inis in his own *naomhóg* and presenting the LP to Siney. They had a great night and Siney spent the night singing.[13]

Lisa

Lisa Mistéal, the daughter of Narraí na hInise and Seán de hÓra from Clogher, wasn't so lucky when she tried to visit the island where her mother had been born and reared. Lisa lived in the Ceathrú in Dunquin, beside Maria Simonds-Gooding. Lisa explained to her that she had never been on the Inis and that it was her last ambition to pay it a visit before she left this life. Maria did her best to help Lisa to achieve her wish. She spoke to Charlie, and he agreed that Lisa should be taken in at the first opportunity:

I asked Charlie a few times if he could take her out on the helicopter as she was getting on in years. One day I heard from the men who were building the house on the Inis that they were going out the next day, taking off from the Móinteán in the morning. I told Lisa that they would be going out and that we'd go down to the Móinteán and that, with a bit of luck, she'd get a lift over. She was delighted with the idea. She went to Dingle the day before and went to confession to prepare. She bought a new pair of shoes, she made a cake of bread to leave on the Inis as a present for Charlie as well as bringing along some religious object wrapped in paper that she was going to leave there, but she wouldn't tell me what it was. She also brought along a large mug in case she'd get sick. It would be her first and last journey to the Inis.

In the morning I picked her up in my Morris Minor. She was wearing a fine big overcoat and a lovely scarf. We drove down to the Móinteán. All the men were there waiting for the helicopter to arrive from Dublin. The day deteriorated quickly, with big heavy clouds and rain coming in off the sea. The men all scattered, some to Krugers and others to Dingle, leaving just Lisa and myself waiting. We held on. I thought we had it made when, about two hours later, we heard the helicopter approaching in the sky above. It circled around Krugers a few times, but nobody came out of the pub. Then it landed near Lisa and myself. I could see it was pretty full, all Charlie's men. Then Charlie stepped out with his orange lifejacket on and the huge propellers still circling overhead. It was very noisy. I roared out to Charlie, could Lisa Mitchell go to the Inish? He didn't answer but shouted back, "Where are my men? Where are my men?"

I answered that they had gone to Dingle.

Lisa says to me, "You wouldn't want to step on his corns today."

Then Charlie came over and shook hands with Lisa and said, "Mrs Mitchell, we will get you in later today."

But that never happened because the weather went from bad to worse.

Nonetheless, the pilot took Charlie and his men over to the Inis and dropped them off. They were left without any shelter in the rain and wind because Dan Brick had the keys and they couldn't get into the house. The helicopter was not allowed to turn off its engines on the Inis in case it didn't start up again. So it came straight back and waited both for the men to turn up and the weather to improve. Eventually he got all the men over, but there was no possibility of including Lisa. That was her last attempt to get over. She went home broken hearted.[14]

Farewell to Tom and Paddy

Tom na hInise and Paddy Beag Ó Dálaigh left Dunquin quay one bright evening in the summer of 1977. They brought the sail with them in the *naomhóg*, but that wasn't much use as the weather was very calm. They had an engine on the boat, but, for some reason or other, they were reluctant to use it. They both had aged and felt the strain of rowing the long trip into the Inis. They were lucky, as it happened, that Seán Brosnan from Dingle was going in as well in the *Ard Íde*. He caught up with them, threw them a line and gave them a pull into the Inis. They were very grateful, and as a token of their thanks, Tom made Seán a model *naomhóg* and presented him with it. Seán afterwards had the *naomhóg* on display in his son's shop, also Seán, in Dingle for years.

They only brought tea and sugar in with them. They would catch pollock and mackerel, and that provided all their food for the duration of their stay, although they would have been welcome to share the great store of food there for the workers. Then the weather changed, rain and fog. They were held up on the island in Tigh na hInise, a damp house and cold fireplace. Charlie felt very sorry for them with himself and his family sitting to a full table, without any shortage, while the unfortunate brothers had little or nothing. Charlie sent a chicken to them on a silver plate with all the appropriate sauces. In a short time the chicken arrived back, with profuse thanks, and the excuse that it was never their custom to eat chicken.

They were like that, particular enough in different ways. A woman in Dunquin made them a fine currant cake. They never tasted it. There were too many sheep droppings in it, they thought.

In time, the weather improved and they collected the sheep. They found it difficult, because the dogs had got out of the habit of rounding them up, the sheep themselves had gone wild around the Inis, and they themselves had slowed down. But they used the old method of the little black men, like roughly made scarecrows, one here and one there; and casting little stones

194

here and there and with the experience of the years, they succeeded in penning the sheep. They always preferred to do it themselves without help. They sheared the sheep and brought the wool down to the *naomhóg* in bags. They bade everyone farewell and rowed their *naomhóg* out the harbour. It was their last visit to the Stone. They had about eighty sheep left.

Little by little the sheep started to fail, without anyone to tend them. By summer's end 1980, there were only about 30 left; and in January 1981 the number had fallen to 18. In that summer there was only 15 left, and every one of them in extremely poor condition. On 15 August, to take them out of pain, one of the Haughey family fetched the gun and shot the remainder.[15]

Chapter XVIII

Many Memories

I do not feel lonely here at all, but it's a magic island, perhaps that's how
I would describe it. And you must remember that it is the island of
fairies as well, with "*Port na bPúcaí*" and all that . . . there is something
magic here that is not to be found in any other place on earth.[1]

Anyone who has ever visited the Inis retains fond memories of it. So it was
with the Haughey family, except for one memory that wasn't bright. Many
local people remember the same night, and their memory also is sad.

It was the soft, gentle night of 13 August 1976. It was so warm that the
Haughey family left the house and sat outside talking, singing and
drinking. Their attention was attracted by hundreds of lights back and
forth on the sea between themselves and Dunquin. They were puzzled,
but in a while they went back to talking. In the morning the reason for all
the lights was on the radio: it was a sea search for Tomás Ó Catháin from
Dunquin, who had gone missing. He had left the Blasket that evening
where he and his wife and young three-month-old child, Nelly, were
enjoying their holidays. He was going in to Dunquin for supplies. On the
return journey in the rubber dinghy late at night, he went missing.

Tomás was never found. He is buried in the Fishermen's Garden.

> Cad tá i ndán don a bhaintreach atá go cráite,
> An bheainín bheag mhánla is í fós chomh fada ó bhaile,
> Mo ghreidhn í a iníon óg an leainbhín beag ráithe,
> Mar gur imigh Tomás uainn is nár fhan fiú chun slán a fhágaint.
> Stadfadsa feasta, níl i ndán dúinn aon réiteach,
> Ó d'imigh Tomás uainn níl aon ní le déanamh,
> Ach ár dtoil a chur le chéile le Mac Rí na Glóire,
> Go bhfóire sé ar ár ndroch chás is ar a anam bocht go ndeine trócaire.[2]

And a fair memory was of one evening in August 1977 when Conor
went out to Dunquin to fetch some supplies and returned in the evening
with Eilís Ní Dhálaigh, the daughter of Muiris (Deálaí), whose father was
Paddy na hInise. C.J. was overjoyed to welcome her to her ancestral island.
She had been named after Eilís na Beannaí, the daughter of Muiris Mór.

196

Eilís still remembers the welcome she received. There was a goodly crowd present in the Big House, but C.J. announced to everybody, "Make way for Eilís Ní Dhálaigh, the queen of the Inis."

Everything was made available to her, and in the evening C.J. himself gave her the grand tour around the Inis, explaining and showing everything that had been accomplished—the deer, the generator, Tigh na hInise.

When she was leaving he asked her, "Well, what do you think of the old home of your ancestors now?"

"Had I known it was so beautiful, you wouldn't have it at all!" she said with a laugh.[3]

C.J. showed his feelings for the Inis in a programme he made with Ciarán Mac Mathúna, *Mo Cheol Thú*, which was broadcast in the summer of 1987.

> In one of the sailing books, the Inis is described as one of the loneliest anchorages in the world. We don't find that, because we always have quite a crowd of us here, our family and our friends. So loneliness is not the feeling, as far as we're concerned—but it does have that mysterious quality—I would use the word "magical" really. It has a different feel about it, a different atmosphere. It is very far out into the sea, and then it is raised up out of the sea, so that you feel that when you're out walking about the Inis you are nearly walking on the moon . . . magical, different, remote, special, the land of the fairies. You feel there could be a presence there that is something above human, but not frightening nor spooky. Everything natural, in the middle of the sea, and above the sea. There is wonderful marine life, there are seals popping their heads up and looking at you, and there is wonderful bird life there, an array of all types of birds there. It has a very friendly, compatible climate. It is not a harsh climate. There is never snow or frost. The weather can be better than on the mainland because the clouds can pass over and drop the rain when they hit the mountains on the mainland. But, of course, it can be very wild.[4]

They often wondered that the weather was so good on the Inis, even when not so fine on the mainland. They deduced that the black clouds became trapped by the mountains on the mainland, but by that time they had cleared the Inis.

One day in August 1983 it was so hot on the Inis that they almost succeeded in frying an egg on the flagstones outside the house.

C.J. loved anyone local or anyone who had any Island or Inis connections coming on a visit:

> I am sure you would like to know that even though the old way of life on the Blaskets has disappeared, there is still plenty of activity which derives from the old Island community. For instance, this year, we had a party on Inismhiceáláin, to which many of those connected with the Blaskets and Dunquin came. I think it was as near to an old-time Blasket night as possible.
>
> So all is not lost![5]

The Bottle

In December 1976 a letter arrived from Tremawr, Padstow, Cornwall, from Bernard Richards saying that he had found a bottle on the beach there on 3 December, and inside a letter from Seán Haughey. Seán had thrown the bottle into the sea at the Inis in the previous month of August. Ciaran had thrown in another bottle on 26 August 1977, and David O'Toole found it on Roonah Strand, Westport, County Mayo, on 13 October 1977.

Seán Haughey composed a fine piece of poetry one evening, 2 January 1978, while watching the sun sinking on the sea west of the Inis:

Sunset on Inis Mhic Uibhleáin

Slipping from reality to dreams
Facts immerse into imagination.
The wind pushing the fiery red air
Amber lights shining behind the clouds
Mythical lands mysteriously appear,
Reflections in silence.
A flash of green disappears into the sea,
A horizon transformed
Into the black circle of thought.
Emotions carried deep to eternity,
Visions bring messages
From beyond the universe,
Past voices whispering
On the sea and in the ferns
Minds hum from that which was and will,
Now with the very stars in the sky
Another secret of all creation discovered.

Suddenly!
A sea bird cries–
Dreams and reality combine.[6]

On another occasion Charlie made a special arrangement with the aviation authorities to contact the jet plane Aer Lingus 117 on its way to Boston as it flew over the Inis. Charlie was able to speak with the pilot through the radio system at a height of 35,000 feet. It could be heard very clearly and the conversation continued on for 200 miles.

Charlie himself remembered another mystical occurrence:

> One evening late we saw Hy Brasil, the island that rises above the sea every seventh year. It was a beautiful magical island. We spent a while looking at it in the North West by the evening light. We took photos of it also.

They also remember mushrooms on the Inis.

Great Day

One of the greatest days in the new Inis was Friday, 12 August 1988, the day the president of the French Republic, François Mitterand, came on a visit to the Inis. He had lunch with Haughey, his wife and family. He had two friends with him, the writer Paul Guimara and his wife, Benoite Grould. It was a beautiful day with the bright sun of summer beaming down on all and the Inis glorious. They arrived in a "Chamborde," the president's helicopter, a little after midday and stayed until late in the afternoon. The president fell under the spell of the Inis and expressed an opinion that there wasn't a more beautiful spot on earth. C.J. remembered his words: *'Je n'aurais pas cru qu'il existait un endroit aussi beau dans le monde.'* (I never believed that there could be such a beautiful place on the face of the earth). He walked briskly around the Inis and amazed everybody at his fitness and energy. He used the walking stick that had been presented to C.J. by the Kerry Deer Society, and when he was leaving, C.J. in turn bestowed the stick on him as a souvenir of his visit. The tricolours of Ireland and France were flying high over Inisvickillane on equal level. Everyone had a delicious lunch, oysters, lobster, salmon and drinks: a *Chateau Cheval Blanc, 1962* and *Baron De'l* and *Beaumes de Venise.* Everyone in the family had participated in this historic visit. It was a wonderful success.[7]

But some of Charlie's favourite memories were of more personal, less important–in worldly terms–days: the day his grandson Seán Patrick, age thirteen months, came on his first visit to the Inis; on the day they arrived on the Inis at the beginning of June, and Inis na Bró was covered with purple, with the sea pinks in bloom.[8]

Chapter XIX

Bird Life, Seals and Flora

There are twenty-two different types of seabirds round the coast of Ireland. They live, for the most part, on the sea and only come to land to nest and rear their young. Afterwards they leave for the sea again. Of those twenty-two types, nineteen are present to a greater or lesser extent around the Blaskets, where there is little threat to them and they have the place to themselves.

The birds that are not present include the sandwich tern and the little tern. The gannet, our finest seabird, although not on the Blaskets, is very well represented in the seas around the islands. They have their main colony on the Little Skellig, and can be frequently seen diving from a great height in suitable weather. Indeed the gannet is very present in the Blasket literature and folklore. Charles Haughey, a keen observer says, "I remember one morning a spectacular display of gannets diving off Cuas Nua."

Inisvickillane is, above all, the kingdom of the seabirds.

As far back as 1888, people were showing interest in the Blasket seabirds, and the Blasket Island Expedition carried out a survey. Such surveys are still carried out, e.g., in 1980 under Vincent Sheridan, who included a survey on the birds of Inisvickillane. Another such survey, from 1988, was done by a team of twelve under Hugh Brazier and Oscar Merne (Irish Wildbird Conservancy/Wildlife Service). This survey of Inisvickillane was carried out by Terry Carruthers (Killarney National Park), David Duggan (Glenveigh National Park, Donegal) and Tom Murphy (Irish Wildbird Conservancy). They spent four days on the Inis, 13–16 June 1988. Haughey let them have his home to stay in, and they were very grateful to be fine and comfortable during their stay, rather than having to rough it in tents.

Although such surveys provide us with valuable information, they are of course, of limited value, because of the short stay of the surveyors. A proper survey would need to be carried out for the duration of a whole year, because birds are constantly coming and going depending on season and weather. Since it is not possible for someone to be there for the whole year, especially since the lighthouses have gone automatic, any further information from interested people is valuable. Éamon de Buitléar spent long stays on the islands filming the wildlife and ringing the storm petrels. Maria Simonds-Gooding spent weeks painting on the Inis, and others like Joe Thompson, and the Haughey family, have added to our knowledge. Wonderful work is also being carried out by the Corca Dhuibhne branch of Birdwatch Ireland, with members like Jill and Ian Crosher and Michael Cleary. Another great source of information is provided by Frank King from Blennerville, one of our leading ornithologists. From those we get a good idea of the seabirds that frequent the Blaskets in general and Inisvickillane in particular.

We will here deal with the birds which have a special affinity to the Inis:

Storm Petrel, An Guardal (Hydrobates pelagius)
This is the most important bird as far as the Inis is concerned.

The storm petrel is a tiny little bird, just slightly bigger than the swallow, with a dark, sooty colour and a white behind. He spends the day hundred of miles out on the ocean, gathering plankton and tiny species from the surface of the waves. He does not return until night to avoid meeting up with his arch enemy–the greater blackbacked gull, who has retired by that stage. He is not fearful of storm or gale. When he returns to the young, he regurgitates the food which he has swallowed during the day. If you take one into your hand, he spits out a drop of foul-smelling oil, the only defence he has.

Charles Smith makes special mention of the *guardal,* or storm petrel, in his mid-eighteenth-century writing. He describes the petrel as the most interesting bird in Kerry, not found in other places.

> The only bird that I have heard of, which is peculiar to this county is a small fowl which I have already mentioned, as an inhabitant of the Blasket Islands . . .[1]

This bird is so special to Kerry that Smith does not have the English name, but gets the Irish name from someone locally:

> There is a small bird, which is said to be peculiar to these islands, called by the Irish, Gourder, the English name of which, I am at a loss for, nor do I find it mentioned by naturalists. It is somewhat larger than a sparrow, the feathers of the back are dark, and those of the belly are white, the bill is straight, short and thick, and it is web-footed. When they are first taken, the country people affirm, they cast up about a teaspoonful of a very fetid oil, out of their bills. They are

almost one lump of fat, when roasted, of a most delicious taste, and are reckoned to exceed an ortelan, for which reasons the gentry hereabouts, call them, the Irish ortelan. These birds are worthy of being transmitted a great way to market, for ortelans it is well known, are brought from France to supply the markets of London.[2]

The Island people used to eat them roasted. It wasn't worth boiling them because the meat melted so much. Fortunately, Smith's idea of marketing petrels was never taken up, or we might have no petrels today. In the summer the petrel comes to land but spends the winter on the sea, returning about St Patrick's Day. He brings the summer and takes it with him when he goes again in September or October, as noted by Joe Thompson on the Inis:

> Two young Storm Petrels at the tigín, one left early on Thursday 24th October. The other had still not left the Inis on 29th October. He had very little down and was standing all the time. I would say there were still plenty of young Petrels in the walls around the tigín. I would say that the last young birds would have left around the 4th November. Also in May we came across two nesting storm Petrels in the garden wall of the tigín and one had a ring on it. I took the number and released it back. It turned out that the bird was rung in 1971 by Cummins for the British Trust of Ornithology and was one year old when it was rung which made it about twenty years old, the oldest I think recorded on the Island.[3]

Deálaí told me about the storm petrel:

> He is terrified of the blackbacked gull, so it is only at night that he returns home. He comes home with the supply in the dark. You would find him on the Inis–a tiny little bird. I never saw him on the Blasket or on the mainland. He comes out when the gull has gone to sleep. The little ones are waiting and hungry. That's when you would hear the whispering and chattering all during the night. They bring home the food in their stomachs and they bring it up again for the little ones. If you go near him he spits at you, but he is very harmless. He leaves again before the break of day, for fear of the gulls and goes way out into the ocean again hunting.[4]

He is also called *Peadairín na Stoirme,* or Little Peter of the Storm, from St Peter's walking on the water, an impression he makes when seen at sea.

Mother Carey's chicken is another name he is known as from *Mater Caritas*, Mother of Charity, one of the titles applied to the Blessed Virgin at one time.

There are between 45,000 and 60,000 pairs of storm petrels in these islands. The Little Blaskets are an important centre for the storm petrel. Between Inisvickillane, Inis na Bró, Tiaracht and Inis Tuaisceart together, they form the greatest petrel colony in Europe and the second greatest one in the world.

According to a survey carried out in 2002, there were 27,279 pairs; the greatest collection in the world in Inis Tuaisceart, 6,394 pairs in Inisvickillane, between 1,000 and 5,000 pairs in Inis na Bró.[5]

There are two other little petrels, Leach's Petrel and Wilson's Petrel, both very rare.

The petrel young can be heard whispering in Tigh na hInise and in the stone walls around the island during the summer. It is one of eleven species that are amber-listed on Birdwatch Ireland's "traffic light" conservation system, signifying that it needs particular care and protection.

Richard Murphy, the poet, heard the whispering. He put pen to paper and wrote thus:

Stormpetrel

Gipsy of the sea,
The winter wambling over scurvy whaleroads,
Jooking in the wake of ships
A sailor hooks you
And curves his girl's name on your beak.
Guest of the storm
Who sweeps you off to party after party,
You flit in a sooty grey coat
Smelling of must
Barefoot over a sea of broken glass.
Waif of the afterglow,
On summer nights to meet your mate you jink
Over sea-cliff and graveyard,
Creeping underground
To hatch an egg in a hermit's skull.
Pulse of the rock,
You throb till daybreak on your cryptic nest

A song older than fossils
Ephemeral as thrift,
It ends with a gasp.[6]

Puffin, An tÉan Dearg (Fratercula arctica)
This bird is plentiful on the Inis and the Little Blaskets. It is also included
on Birdwatch Ireland's amber list, as the numbers are declining. It is
thought that between 20,000 and 30,000 pairs were around the islands in
the year 1968, but that the number had fallen to 4,500 pair in the year 1988.
There were 389 puffins present on Inisvickillane in the 2000 Survey.[7]
The puffin also spends the winter on the ocean. Often thought of as the
clown of the sea due to the bright colours of its parrot-like beak (red, blue,
white and yellow), which is able to grip five or six fish at the same time.
The beak is only red in summer time. They nest in the rabbit burrows.
The young bird is called the *fuipín* in the local parlance.
Seán Ó Freáilí from Bhaile Bhiocáire, Dunquin, fell to his death over a
cliff in Inisvickillane while hunting young puffins at the beginning of the
last century. He had a strap of *fuipíns* hanging from his shoulder which
pulled him over the side.[8]

Kittiwake, Faoileann Bheag na Tiarachta (Rissa tridactyla)
The Island people called them the Little Tiaracht gulls, as they are so
plentiful around that island. In the 1988 survey there were 802 pairs in
total around the Little Blaskets, and 516 pairs were around the Tiaracht.
Again, they go to sea during the winter. They are grey in colour on the
back, and their wings are black-tipped. They are to be found all around
the Irish coast, but are most plentiful around the Blaskets.
There were 150 on Inisvickillane in the 2000 survey and 186 on Inis na
Bró.[9]

Fulmar, An Chánóg Bhán (Fulmarus glacialis)
These birds have the appearance of a seagull, except that the wings, the
back and tail are grey. They were not present in Kerry at all before 1913
and in 1939 they made their appearance on the Tiaracht. In 1988 there
were about 2,000 pairs of them nesting around the Blaskets, and it is
thought that number has doubled at present. Though they are to be found
all around the coast of Kerry, they are most plentiful around the Blaskets.
The latest Seabird Survey of 2000 gives a count of 672 fulmars.[10]

Manx shearwater, An Chánóg Dhubh (Puffinus puffinus)
This bird is also on the amber list, due to diminishing numbers. If so, they are not diminishing on the Blaskets, where there are about 20,000 pairs present. On Inis Tuaisceart alone, it is estimated that there are 13,680 nests, the greatest collection in Ireland besides Puffin Island in Uíbh Ráthach where there are about 20,000 pairs.

The 2000 survey includes 643 Manx shearwaters on Inisvickillane and 5,611 on Inis na Bró.

The latest survey states Inis na Bró contains about 8,000 pairs, the Great Blasket about 5,000, and Inisvickillane 900, with about 1,000 on the Tiaracht.[11]

The bird has a black back and wings with white tips. He also spends the winter on the sea. The young is called a *fothaíoch*.

Great Black-Back Gull, An Chaobach (Larus marinus)
This is a well-known bird, which seems to be declining in numbers. In the Blasket survey of 1988, there were 464 pairs on the Great Blasket, and about 288 pairs on Inis Tuaisceart, but that number had fallen to 100 pairs in 1999 and only three pairs in 2000. There were 76 pairs on Inisvickillane in 2000 and 19 on Inis na Bró.[11] The young bird is called a *grogaire*, or a *gulaí*. The Island boys used to have them as pets.

Lesser Black-Back Gull, Faoileán Droma Duibhe (Larus fuscus)
In the 1988 survey, there were 419–429 pairs on the Great Blasket, with Beginis to the fore with around 130 pairs. According to the 2000 survey, there were 162 pairs between Beginis and Oileán na nÓg and 156 pairs on Inisvickillane.[13]

Herring gull, Faoileán (Larus argentatus)
This bird is not plentiful. In 1988 there were about 140 pairs around the Blaskets, and 58 pairs on Oileán Buí. The survey of 2000 showed 40 on Inisvickillane and 7 on Inis na Bró.[14]

Razorbill, An Crosán (Alca torda)
Formerly very plentiful, the numbers have fallen badly. They are on the amber list. In the year 1968, there were around 5,000–7,000 pairs, and by 1988 the numbers had fallen to 320 pairs.

The numbers in the 2000 survey stood at 97 on Inisvickillane and 374 on Inis na Bró, representing the entire population of the Blasket razorbill.[15]

Shag, An Seaga (Phalacrocorax aristotelis)
There were 23 present on Inisvickillane and 5 on Inis na Bró in 2000, in a count taken in poor, foggy conditions.[16]

Guillemot, Foracha (Urla aalge)
There were 97 on Inisvickillane in 2000 and 374 on Inis Tuaisceart out of a total of 471 around the Blaskets.[17]

Arctic tern, An Scréachóg (Sterna paradisaea)
They are to be seen around the little Blaskets, especially Beginis and Oileán na nÓg; 70 pairs in 2004.[18]

Chough, Préachán na gCos nDearg (Pyrrhocorax pyrrhocorax)
This is the one of the most remarkable birds we have in Corca Dhuibhne. They are also very plentiful on the Inis. Charles Haughey remembered one morning: "We saw a family of ten choughs feeding outside Tigh na Carraige."[19]

They are notable for their black plumage, red beaks and red legs, and they frequent the cliff edges. The peninsula contains the greatest concentration of choughs in north-west Europe.

Some of the birds that are on the Inis are birds of passage, seeking refuge from rough weather or a place to rest while recovering from weakness or illness. Such was the following case, as described by Joe Thompson:

> We spotted Greylag Geese on 29th Oct flying out towards the Skelligs. Some returned towards the Island and landed south of us. Other noted spottings were in May. One male Ortolan Bunting. This bird kept around the road to the Tigín for about 3 weeks also 1 male Rustic Bunting about 3 weeks.
>
> 5 Golden Plover were sighted in summer plumage towards the end of May. We also had a cuckoo for three days until it disappeared.

And again Joe noticed the following in October:

> A very strong East wind was blowing for practically one week during this migratory period and subsequently a lot of birds were blown out towards the Inis. The different types of species and numbers were very large and they remained until the wind stopped. All then moved on except the indigenous birds. Interesting to note that a few birds of

prey suddenly appeared again, Merlin, Kestrel and Peregrine probably keeping an eye on their good fortune.[20]

Grey Seal, An Rón Glas (Halichoerus grypus)

Anyone who would like to see many seals straight out of the water together let him go to Inis na Bró and sit up on the cliff there. Below him he will see Leac na Rón [Seal Flagstone]. He will see seals stretched back asleep there, fine under the sun up on the Leac. He will see many seals coming in from the sea there, and he will see many leaving to go fishing for themselves, and he will hear twenty odd bull seals all bellowing together up on Leac na Rón.[21]

So wrote "the Common Noun" early in the last century.

Tomás tells us about the seals too, from experience: "They reached Inisvickillane, a noted place for seals in caves, and there are many of them. You would need quiet weather and a fine full tide."[22]

When the Haughey family came to the Inis in 1973:

There was a very large population of seals all around the Inis but especially among the rocks and caves to the south and west, which were literally black with them. They bred there in the caves. Regretfully, when the massive slaughter of seals was committed some decades ago along the west coast, the Inis was not spared, and its seal population was wiped out completely. They are only now beginning to re-appear, but there is still a long, long way to go before they come anywhere near the numbers of those early days.[23]

It seems that there were not many seals there before the nineteenth century.[24] Although no proper seal survey has been carried out since 1989, it is estimated that there are in or about 2,000 seals around the coast of Ireland today. The grey seal can be found from Ireland to France and back to the coast of Scotland, up to the coast of Norway and from there to the coast of Greenland. The two principal places for them on the Irish coast is Iniskea on the coast of Mayo and the Blaskets. The Blaskets contain from 500–700 seals. It is clear from place names like *Cuas na Rón* (Seal Cove) and *Cuas an Éin* (Seal Calf Cove) on Inisvickillane and *Leac na Rón* on Inis na Bró that they have been long associated with these islands.

The female who is expecting birth goes on the strand from August on and gives birth any time from September to mid-November. The young are given birth to on land, and inside a fortnight they are out swimming.

They are white to begin with for sixteen to twenty days and then the dark fur grows. The mother then leaves them, and they must fend for themselves.

A bull seal is from 1.95m to 2.3m in length from nose to tail and about 240kg in weight. The females are from 1.65m to 1.95m in length and about 155kg in weight. They are grey or brownish grey in colour. They scarcely leave the sea but live in the caves and holes in the cliffs. Smith, writing in the eighteenth century, says:

> These animals live entirely upon fish; they cannot feed under water, nor remain long below the surface. When they dive for their prey they shut their mouths and eyes, and purse up their nostrils so close, that the least drop of water cannot enter. They are frequently obliged to ascend for air, but are presently down again, if they see any object that alarms them. They bite most severely, the mouths resembling that of a tiger, and they hiss with a spitting noise.[25]

Islanders thought highly of seal meat for eating, and the skin would be preserved and sold on the market on the mainland.

> The skin fetched eight pounds, a pound a man . . . They were both a great help towards living at that time, both meat and skin. A sack of meal could be had for a seal skin then. There was nowhere that you brought a piece of seal that you wouldn't get the same amount of pork if it were to be had.[26]

The oil was used for light and for cures. Every house had a bottle of seal oil, and people believed it to be great for the arthritis and for the hand or foot that was injured. Here is an account from Eilín Ní Shúilleabháin (Neilí Sheáin Lís) of her grandfather taking the oil from the seal, in the year 1923. It is clear that it was no longer regarded as a food by that time:

> He lifted off the cover from the oven, and it is how some of the seal was being boiled for light and it had a lovely smell–you would think it was pork–and there are people alive who would eat it as quick as pork, but I don't think there are any of them left, because it's often I heard my grandfather saying that they used to go back to Inisvickillane killing them, and that they would have a full boat and that they would salt it and eat is as much as any fish in the sea, and dying to eat it too, and that the people from the mainland often came in for it and that they would get a bag of potatoes for one now and

then. I stayed there watching him and he used to be stirring it always and the oil would be rising to the top of the pot, and then he took it and poured it into an old pot, and I can tell you that the oil was as clean coming out of it as any fresh water, and he spent another ten minutes boiling it when he had poured it into the old pot, and the containers were nearly burned and he hung them over the fire again and he got up to two further buckets out of it, so that in the end the vessels were as dry as your palm, and he kept the oil for himself for the winter, with God's help we will be alive.[27]

If the seals were slaughtered in November, yet the Island people were fond of them and friendly towards them, both Inis and Blasket people:

There was a man in Inisvickillane and he had a pet seal. He would give it milk when it was small. When it grew it left and returned to the sea, but one day when the men were fishing they saw a seal a distance away from them. The man recognised that it was his own pet. He called him over and stretched his cap out to him as though giving him milk. The seal came over and was playing with him.[28]

It is the human who is the seal's greatest enemy. As we have seen, in the old days they went after them for their meat, their skin and their oil. That has finished long ago. Seal hunting was a popular sport in the nineteenth century and up till the 1970s, but that has died out also. Still, many are caught up in the fishing nets, and many are wantonly slaughtered as happened in the autumn of 2004 in Beginis. The fishermen blame them for destroying their nets and destroying the fish, but the slaughter of that time made many people very disgusted, and we hope it will lead to increased vigilance on the part of the state and that the officials from the National Park and Wildlife Service pay regular visits to the islands to ensure their protection.[29]

Inisvickillane Flora

"The Island is low and bleak but yields a very rich herbage."[30]

It was a Dublin man, Richard Barrington, as far as I know, who was the first visitor to Inisvickillane in July 1880. This was his second visit, because his first visit was not too successful. He was undertaking a botanical study of the Blasket Islands with a grant he received from The Royal Irish Academy. He says himself:

210

They are interesting, in being the most westerly land in Europe, if we except the Azores. They lie west of 10°30' west longitude, and immediately north of the 52nd parallel of latitude. Counting rocks which rise little above high-water mark they number 109 islands, but six only are worthy of the name, the rest being void of vegetation, with one or two exceptions . . . A circle having a diameter of eight miles would include all the Blaskets, except a few rocks.

No botanist having ever examined this remote group with care, I made an effort to explore them in June 1879. Having reached the town of Dingle, which is nine miles from the extreme west of the promontory, the police informed me that an unsuccessful attempt had recently been made to serve processes on the Blasket Islanders, and they were hostile to strangers.[31]

A bad start you might say, and you would be right. He would be better off returning home again:

This proved to be correct, and I found considerable difficulty in landing. At Dunquin, a small village on the mainland, opposite the Great Blasket, the boatmen declined to row me across. I heard subsequently they suspected I was a policeman. All sorts of excuses were made. Finally, after four days' waiting, I procured a boat, the Rev. Father Egan, P.P., having spoken to the people on my behalf.[32]

But all was not as it seemed:

On approaching the Great Blasket, which is one mile distant from the nearest point on the mainland, the people were seen to run from the houses, and congregate on the edge of the cliff over the landing-place, shouting and gesticulating at the same time. Heaps of stones were piled, and the natives began to throw them at our boat.[33]

It didn't look too promising, but they managed to sort it out and once they realised that he was not a threat to them, they welcomed him with open arms:

Much loud conversation took place, which lasted a considerable time. In the end I was permitted to land, provided I kept at a distance from the houses. Seeing no harm was intended, the inhabitants became friendly, and many of them accompanied me during a walk of three hours, which I then took over the island. Unfavourable weather and want of time did not permit a longer visit in 1879, but I saw sufficient to make me anxious to examine the flora of the islands carefully, which could not be done without a stay of some days on the Great Blasket.[34]

That was the end of the 1879 trip. He took another trip in 1880. He got a completely different reception this time, and with reason:

I again went to Dingle in July, 1880. No difficulty was now experienced in procuring boats. On the contrary, the people received me with many expressions of welcome, as I had interested myself on their behalf during the severe distress in the spring.

I landed on July 16th. The mud cabins are of the poorest description. I slung my hammock from the rafters of a vacant one, called the schoolhouse. The curiosity of the natives was intense, and I suffered more from intruders when examining specimens, and placing them between blotting sheets.[35]

He noticed the distress of the people, the poverty, the hunger and destitution, and the amount of people made homeless after being evicted by Sam Hussey, Lord Cork's middleman. It seems that the winter of 1879–80 was a bad one, as this letter, which was printed in the *Kerry Sentinel* from the parish priest of Ballyferriter (1870–1890), shows:

It is with deep anguish I see the gloom and despair which are settling down on the vast majority of my people. For some time past, my house is daily besieged by applicants for relief, each having a tale of woe and want more harassing than the preceding, and, oh, how heartrending, it is not possible to alleviate their grief and mitigate their distress . . .

If these poor people can have potatoes and sour milk during the summer half year, and potatoes and fish, or even potatoes and salt during the winter, they consider themselves superlatively happy.

During the winter, however, the food of very many among them is Indian meal bread and porridge or Indian meal stirabout with a little milk largely, very largely, diluted with water to make it serve all round.

Their clothing has been of the cheapest and most primitive kind, corduroy and some home-spun frieze or flannel. Their houses would not be considered fit habitations for beasts by farmers in other parts of the country.

In these times of dire destitution and distress, turnips and salt are the food of many of my poor people and are considered–well, I won't

212

say a delicacy–but they are by no means despised; and those who possess a supply are esteemed lucky by some of their neighbours.

Only the Great Blasket is inhabited. It contains about eighteen families, all miserably poor and in extreme want. About half of these have been recently put out of possession by Mr. Sam Hussey for non-payment of rent.

A gunboat and a posse of police recently invaded the shores of the Island for the purpose of seeing these evictions on the part of Mr. Hussey carried into execution, and for the purpose of levying Co. Cess. . . .

Among the mountains of the extreme west of Kerry in the wilds of Ferriter are the poorest of the poor. The very hens have been carried off from one of these poor creatures under a civil bill decree . . .

Here are poor farmers who send their children to service to earn the rent. Here are others fed from day to day on the hope of getting the long-wished-for remittance from America.

In the parish of Dunquin, the people are burning the heather and bushes; and there is a great probability that some families may in consequence of inability to procure firing be forced into the workhouse . . .[36]

It was during this time that Barrington paid his first visit to the Blaskets, and little wonder that the islanders distrusted him, at least until they got to know him.

Barrington himself tells us that he stayed on the Blaskets from Friday until the following Tuesday. But according to Tomás, Barrington stayed a full two weeks. Maybe the long weekend stretched into a full week. They had great fun with him, not to mention the music, singing and dancing every night with plenty of whiskey, wine and tobacco. It seems that this was the first time that the islanders had any friendly contact with strangers, and was the beginning of many years of comings and goings on the island.

How wonderful it would be to be there to witness the islanders getting to know Barrington. That young man in the corner with the twinkling eyes, that's Tomás Dhónaill Criomhthain, and his wife Máire Mhicí holding her firstborn son, Seán, on her lap. He would later fall over a cliff trying to catch a seagull . . . And look at the man and his wife and their young kids running around: they are the Ó Dálaigh family who had travelled over from the Inis. Good to see them.

213

And the island poet, Seán Ó Duinnshléibhe, and the song he composed praising Barrington, likening the Blaskets to Paradise during the time he spent amongst them. Tomás says:

> The poet Ó Duinnshléibhe was also there and he was good at entertaining the "gentleman."
>
> He sent a lot of goods to the Blaskets after returning home, and he sent a pound of tobacco to the poet. He composed a poem praising him afterwards.[37]

Here it is:

Amhrán an Bharódaigh

> *A Bhairrit, is mór é do dhúlgas i nDuibhneach,*
> *Mar is duine uasal séimh thú go bhfuil daonacht it chroí istigh,*
> *Is tusa ár n-athair is ceanas liom an insint,*
> *Do thug bia dúinn gan ceannach, do chuir tobac im phíp chugam.*
> *San bó leo.*
>
> *A Bhairrit, ní foláir nó is d'fháidh mhaigh gur dhíobh thú,*
> *A mhic na dea-mháthar nár cáineadh a shínsear,*
> *In éirim, is t'athair ná faca riamh fíorbhocht*
> *Ná go réiteodh sé easpa go tapaidh gan maíomh as.*
> *San bó leo.*
>
> *A Bhairrit, má mhairim go dtagair arís chugainn,*
> *Is ag mo chroí bheidh an gealas duit, a mharcaigh an díograis.*
> *Beidh fáiltí go leor ag an óg 's ag an gcríon romhat,*
> *Is dófad mo leaba sa chaladh nuair a stríocfair.*
> *San bó leo.*[38]

Tomás always remembered those happy days, and here are his memories of that time:

> It has been a few years since the visit of this good man and it gives me great pleasure to write about him.
>
> One day a boat from Dunquin arrived and while boats often came it wasn't always good tidings they brought–that wasn't the case this time because on board was this gentleman with a companion armed with all sorts of good things.
>
> The school was closed for the holidays and the priest gave him permission to use it.

He invited everybody to visit him in the evenings and no one refused.

He had lots of clay pots filled with beer and he welcomed everyone young and old. Everyone who sang got a drink. They were slow arriving in the beginning due to shyness. A girl arrived and was given a glass of wine. Then another girl. He got up and gave her a glass of wine. The old women had a few drinks and six of them started singing together.

It was the best entertainment he had in his lifetime.

Eventually the men had to use a stick to stop the women from their singing. Six toothless, grey haired old women singing together every night.

During this time three of the O'Shea family from Valentia were fishing amongst us. They were fine dancers and one was an excellent lilter. They were given lots of drink as well.

He stayed two weeks with us. He was a decent man and a gentleman and these two qualities were etched on his face. That is the end of my tales of the gentleman and a gentleman he certainly was.[39]

During this time Barrington completed a good survey of the plants and herbs of the Blaskets. He tells us that 130 people were living on the Great Blasket at this time. All the other islands were deserted except for the lighthouse men on the Tiaracht and the remains of one household on Inisvickillane.

He noticed 162 different species of plants on the Great Blasket and placed Inisvickillane in the second place in importance: "Next to the Great Blasket, Innisvickillane is certainly the most fertile in species. Some cultivation exists here, and one farmer resides."

Potatoes and oats were growing there, and there were cows, sheep and plentiful goats on the Inis. He also noticed that the growth on all the islands was better on the north side, as the south side was open to the prevailing winds.[40]

He tells us that there were three types of bushes growing on the Great Blasket and the same on the Inis. What a pity he doesn't give us more details about the people and the way they put some of the plants to use. Lots of people maintained there were three types of herbs growing as well as flowers, weeds and tillage, but they didn't take much notice of the flowers because they were of no practical use to them. There were some edible flowers, some that were used to cure human and animal ailments and some that were useful for dyeing clothes. We stress the importance of

215

not using any of the flowers or herbs on our list to treat any human ailments. It is advisable to visit your doctor.

Barrington noticed some plants native to the Great Blasket that are not found on other islands on the Irish coast, such as *Cardamine sylvatica*. He also found it strange that certain plants were growing on the islands when they are more likely to be found growing inland in woods, such as *Primula vulgaris* on Inis na Bró, and on the Tiaracht he found *Lavetaria arborea, Tree Mallow, Crann Liúireach* growing, but maybe not that strange growing on the latter what with the comings and goings of the lighthouse men.

In all he collected 174 samples.

Mr Haughey was also interested in the plant population on the Inis and in 1992 compiled the following list from observation on his walks: scarlet pimpernell, bog pimpernell, tormentil, angelica, sheep bit, scabious, chamomile, self heal, yarrow, birdsfoot trefoil, eyebright, bladder campion, sorrell and different varieties of orchids.

He also mentions that the family had sown the following plants, and the mention is important as we know that these plants were introduced rather than them being native: cowslips, wild garlic, cloves, foxgloves, and twelve pots of rosemary.[41]

I already mentioned that Joe Thompson spent a good part of the years 1989 and 1990 on the Inis. He also had an interest in the plants and sowed the following seeds on 29 October 1990, very late in the year to sow: rue, thyme, fennel, rosemary, chives, mint, parsley, lovage, dill and tarragon.[42]

He also sowed nasturtiums around the Tigh Mór and Tigh na hInise in the old garden by the wall. He got the idea from Lockley's description of 1933:

> . . . While the others got food Daly showed me his garden, a stone-walled enclosure containing a bank tall with lobster-pot willow wands, their silver-green spears tossing with the light air from the south. Nasturtiums climbed rioting in and out through every hole in the wall. Potatoes looked well, set, as is the custom here, in ridges two feet across, three rows in each.[43]

Although it was late in the year, the herbs sown by Joe succeeded. All grew and he was able to say before leaving the Inis for the winter:

> The herbs are growing satisfactory to date only one plant, a Rosemary, died back and looks a bit dead. I will replace it with a new plant.

All the nasturtium seeds have struck and the young plants are about 2 inches in height and nothing has attacked them (yet) and they are growing very fast.

This completes the Herb section in Innishvickilann up to November 1990.[44]

Chapter XX

The Inis Red Deer

The red deer, *Cervus elaphus*, has been in Ireland for some 26,000 years, with records of them for some 6,000 years. The earliest record in Kerry dates back some 4,000 years to a find on Ventry Beach. Archaeological research shows that the antlers, bones and skins were in common use in the manufacture of tools, ornaments, food and clothes in prehistoric times. They are often referred to in the old literature, in particular in the Fenian Cycle stories, and they have been associated with place names in the west Kerry area such as Baile na bPoc (Town of the Buck), Páirc an Fhiaidh (Deer Field), Carraig an Fhiaidh (Deer Rock), Coimín an Fhiaidh (Deer Cove), Gleann an Fhiaidh (Deer Valley) and Sliabh an Fhiadh (Deer Mountain).

In the parish of Dunquin, of which Inisvickillane is part, St Gobnait, the patron saint, is closely associated with the deer. According to the old stories, Gobnait was the daughter of a sea captain, whose boat fled before the storm to the refuge of Ventry Harbour. The boat was duly moored and the crew given leave of absence until the storm abated. There was a wood in the area at that time, to which Gobnait made her way. There an angel appeared and spoke to her.

"It is God's will that you should remain here and spread the faith among the people. Continue to walk until you meet three white deer, and remain there," said the angel.

The angel disappeared and Gobnait was left alone. She walked westwards over the Clasach. She did not stop until she arrived at the clifftop in Dunquin where she saw the three white deer.

She remained there and established a small monastery for herself, joined by some local women.

She spent some time there until the angel appeared again and told her, "You have fulfilled your task here, and it is God's will that you should move on and stop when you meet six white deer."

Gobnait then left Dunquin and continued on south until she met the six white deer at a place named after her, Kilgobnet, between Killorglin and Killarney. Again she spent some time there until she received the order to continue on until she met nine white deer. That happened at Ballyvourney, on the borders of Kerry and Cork. She remained there and is buried at that spot.

We have another story that dates back to the seventeenth century.

Máire Feiritéar, sister to Pierce, the poet, was married to Séartha Criomhthain, one of the minor nobility of the area, who had a residence in Dunquin.

Máire and Séartha invited Pierce to dinner. On the day of the dinner, Séartha sent a boy out on the mountains with instructions to kill a deer for the dinner, and at the same time, sent another boy to Dingle to bring back a supply of wine.

The first boy spent the evening trying to catch a deer, but had to return empty handed. So also the boy who went to Dingle was unable to procure the wine and came home empty handed, and they had to kill a black sheep for dinner.

The dinner was placed before Pierce. He studied it and uttered the words:

> *Is mairg na glacann ciall,*
> *Is ná cuireann srian lena ghuth,*
> *Agus i dtaobh ná fuaireamar fíon ná fia,*
> *Is maith an bia an chaora dhubh.*

In the eighteenth and nineteenth century, a favourite sport of the nobility was the deer hunt. They came even from England to Ireland to enjoy the thrill of the hunt. Some of the landowners actually kept the deer on the mountains for that purpose, like Peter Thompson, the agent of Lord Ventry about the time of the famine. He lived in Baile an tSagairt House just east of Dingle, and had a herd of deer in a walled park. Both house and park can be still seen today. Thompson was fairly unpopular from his habit of enforcing rent collection. He died near Dublin on his way to that city. When news arrived back, some of the wall was knocked and the deer released and dispersed all over the mountains. It remained in the local speech, a mild curse: *"Imeacht fianna Thompson ort."* (May you go the way of the Thompson deer).

But by the beginning of the twentieth century, the end had arrived for the red deer in Ireland. The only place they were protected was in Muckross Estate in Killarney, and they are there today as strong as ever. There were never deer on any of the Blaskets, and it is not a natural habitat for such animals, such places being too constricted for them.

As soon as the house was completed in the Inis by Charles Haughey in

1980, he put his plan to conserve the red deer into practice. After much planning and preparation, the first stag and doe were successfully transported from the National Park in Killarney to Inisvickillane on a Sirkorski helicopter on 20 March.

When the family arrived on the Inis a few weeks later, at Easter, the deer had settled, and better still, before they left they had further reason for hope that the first fawn had been born. The stag could be seen nobly strutting around the island, a wonderful sight against the setting sun.

Haughey recalled the beginning of August 1980: "As we dined that evening the red stag appeared outside our window and made a splendid sight."[1]

As soon as the family would land on the Inis, they would go to see the deer. By Easter 1981 there were two native Inis deer, although one of the does had died.

The deer were very shy at the beginning and were rarely seen, but little by little, when they realised they were safe and unthreatened, they settled and did not flee from people so much. On the first day of the holidays in August 1982, the five does and the stag walked fine and steady by the new house, one after the other, something that cheered everyone.

On their first visit of 1983, they found a stag halfway down the cliffway with the rope that was used to grip on the way up and down wound round him. The ground around had been trampled into mud, and it was clear that he had been there for some time. He was weak both from the hunger and from the efforts to free himself. The rope was cut to free him, and he was left lying on the spot in the hope that he would shortly recover and join the herd. However, the following day, there was his body in the sea below the Step, to everybody's disappointment. And that was the end of the first Inis stag; but the other five deer were doing fine.

On 28 March, Tim Larner brought in another stag and doe to supplement the herd.

A few beautiful days were spent on the Inis by the family at Whit 1983:

> Larks sang constantly and melodiously and seemed to have taken over the Inis. Hundreds of puffins were nesting above the Tráigh. Our five deer seemed to be in excellent shape, though rabbits seemed scarce.
>
> The whole of Inis na Bró was a deep purple colour which we had never seen before.[2]

Everything carried on thriving and increasing. Now and again they would be noted.

19th August 1983: There were seven deer, one stag, four does and one fawn.

23rd August 1984: During dinner six deer were grazing quietly outside the window . . .

26th–29th October 1989: Seven deer with thirty seals on the beach, two kestrels and one hare . . .

3rd–7th July 1985: We were happy to see three fawns shortly after their birth, ten in total there now . . .

Easter 1986: A call from the Lighthouse on the Tiaracht to say that the body of a deer had been washed in at Loop Head. A good chance it was the one we lost in 1983. Sorry also to find the body of a young deer at Cuas an Éin. Cause of death is unknown . . .

15th June 1986: Tom found a fawn just a few days old asleep under a stone. He took some photos.

11th August 1986: Wonderful display by the deer outside the house at nightfall, eight altogether . . .

23rd August 1986: The members of the Kerry Deer Society visited the Inis to see the deer. They saw only seven. When they were leaving, they presented C.J. with a walking stick made of Killarney hazel and deer antlers.

In April 1987 potatoes were brought in for the deer to supplement their food.

16th April 1987: Four does and a stag were brought in on a Sikorski helicopter from Donaraile, Co. Cork. One hind died on landing.

August 1987: 2 Stags, 9 does and 5 fawns on the Inis. The big stag was not to be seen, so there must be 17 deer there altogether.

Easter 1988: 18 deer altogether and every one in good condition.

August 1988: 22 deer, 4 stags, 1 grown and 3 young.

August 1989: 25 deer in full.

Easter 1990: 7 or eight does.[3]

In 1990 Seán Ryan made a report on the deer, having paid two visits to the Inis, one in April and one in November. Ryan noticed that the does gathered together in the spot with the best feeding, but that the stags headed for the sheltered spots. It is a sign of food shortage when the deer chew cast-off antlers and even dry bones. That happens in Killarney, but has rarely been seen on the Inis, particularly in the early years, since they seemed to have all the good food that they needed. The stags' antlers were bigger and heavier than those of their Killarney brothers, perhaps because the grass is richer on the Inis. As well, the growing season is longer there than on the mountains. Even in mid-November, there was still growth of 70–80 per cent at a time when growth would have ceased in Killarney. Another advantage the Inis deer had is that they had access to every bit of the Inis and were not barred from the best grazing. There was also a chance that the salt spray contains calcium, which would contribute to antler growth. There was little evidence that they fought among themselves, a sign that they were happy and that there was enough for all. One problem that was presenting itself was the potential shortage of grass in the future if the herd became too large.

It was also obvious that they had settled down well, better than in Killarney. They accepted even the noise of the helicopter without bolting in fright. The deer in Killarney bolt at the noise of a motorbike even when two miles away. The Inis deer had also laid out pathways that they regularly used, and they had also established escape routes in case of crisis.

A danger to the deer was the proximity to the sea, which might tempt them to go out to sea to collect seaweed, which may have caused the odd drowning. They might also have approached too close to the cliff edge and fallen over to their death, something that happens in Rhum, one of the Scottish isles. A number of them had been washed up from time to time on Ventry Beach and Baile an Chaladh. However, the greatest threat to such a small herd in a confined space like the Inis was from inbreeding.

The Inis is the only island in Ireland with a deer population, which makes the herd important as a national asset. If anything, such as disease, caused the disappearance of the mainland herds, the Inis red deer would be of immense importance in preserving the species and building it up again.

Seán Ryan was unable to complete an accurate count, even in a space as small as the Inis. A team with radios would be needed. He finished the report with words of praise for the Inis itself:

> It is an incredibly beautiful island; everywhere there are superb and breath taking vistas of seascapes, landscapes and incomparable skies, all as yet unsullied. The experience of the island's wildness is perhaps its greatest asset. To possess such an island, with its rich cultural heritage and majestic scenery, is to be one of the luckiest people in the world.[4]

His count was as follows: 29 red deer counted on the Inis, but there were more likely to be 32, made up of 8 stags, 7 does and yearling fawns, 7 hinds and one other of indeterminate type.

It was his final opinion that: "The deer are now in excellent condition.

They shook with fat as they looped past. Their condition must be an indication of the richness of grazing to be found."

C.J. remembers the summer of 1991: "Five or six young stags were lying down just over the brow of the hill to the east so that a little forest of antlers appeared on the skyline."

But now and then there was bad news: "There are about 40 deer roaming all around the Inis and at least nine stags. A mature stag was brought out by helicopter in March but headed straight for the sea and was almost certainly washed up in Valentia later."[5]

By this time the deer had become part of the Inis, and little by little they are mentioned less in the Inis diary; 1992 was designated the Year of the Eagles, and they were especially focused in on. But now and then the deer are mentioned again:

August 1992: There are now about 50 deer. There is need to cull the stags to avoid excessive inbreeding.

August 1993: There are now about 60. Management is needed to cull all the stags and bring in fresh blood. Both stags and hinds need testing, dosing and injecting.[6]

That was the next problem, to see after their medical needs. In August 1993, seven of them were penned and received medical attention. Two more stags and six does were also introduced from Killarney.

That work was continued in 1994: "We penned 16 deer using the O'Dálaigh method of the *fear dubh*. It worked very well."[7]

One evening they watched a thirty-minute fight between two big stags. The old stag came away victorious, for the moment. A complete count included:

2 grown stags
2 yearling stags
28 adult does
16 hinds
48 deer in total.

36 were tagged, registered and given medical attention.

Pat Mulcahy advised that more does be brought in from Killarney as some of the Inis does were getting too old.

In 1995 the work with the deer continued. There were fifty or more there that year. Another stag got wound up in a rope. He was released but, like before, died a few days after. Seven deer were brought in from Killarney: 2 stags and 5 yearling does.

The count in November 1995 stood at 57 in total, and perhaps 59.

1996: 18 Deer received medical attention, 4 males and 14 females.

12th–15th December: Pat Mulcahy and team come in to examine the deer. There was a total of 55. 15 stags were sent to Galtee Deer Care.

20 fawns were born in 1996.

1997: C.J. is of the opinion that the deer and the hares were the two projects that succeeded the most in the 1982–1997 period.

Easter 1997: About 70 deer in total.

By the end of that year the number had grown to 91.

1998: At least 80 deer. They pass the house without noticing the people.

1999: More than100 deer present, 1 master stag that has a 12 point antler.

Easter 2000. Grass very scarce. The deer not in great condition. Seven dead around the Inis. Seems to be a shortage of food. Worse, a dead stag is found with a bullet-hole in its head. It seems clear that he was shot from a boat out at sea. Two more bodies near by also had bullet marks. New stag needed.

August 2000: C.J. walks by the deer. A small number approach and for the first time ever try to examine him. Antlers are found that have been chewed for protein.

Summer 2002: 10 huge stags with great antlers on each of them come up as far as the house.

2003: 110 deer present, all in good condition.[8]

The final question is, what does the future hold for the deer? It seems clear that the Inis cannot take an increased number.

Hares

The Irish hare is native to Ireland. There is frequent mention of him in the old stories and manuscripts and he is often given magical powers, as we have seen in the story in Chapter XIII, in which the hare advises the woman from the Inis.[9]

Still, there was no hare in residence on the Inis or on any of the Blaskets, according to Seán Ó Criomhthain:

> I never saw any hare on the Island. That was an animal that was not to be had there. But I did hear a story about a man from Dingle that brought two hares to an island near the Blasket that is called Beginis. I suppose he knew what he was doing, but they didn't do well. They did not propagate there. They were brought to Inisvickillane too, but they didn't propagate there either.[10]

When Haughey had settled down on the Inis, he also brought back the native Irish hare.

> We were delighted to see an adult hare and two young. On Friday 19th August 1983 Tim Larner spotted seven deer consisting of one young stag, 4 hinds, 2 calves as well as a number of hares . . .
>
> We stayed from Sat. Oct. 29th to Mon. 31st. The deer seemed grand and to our great delight we spotted a mature hare and two leverets. The seals were mating on the Tráigh . . .[11]

Chapter XXI

The White-Tailed Eagle

Raghadsa 's mo Cheaití 'bhailcéireacht amach ar na sléibhte ó thuaidh,
Nó ar oileáinín mara 'nár naonair mara dtéann na héin chun suain.
Ansúd a bhíonn nead ag an bhfiach dubh is an fiolar ag éamh cois cuain,
Is mise ag agairt chun Dé suas gan solas an lae do bhreith uainn.

Kathy and I will go walking out on the northern hills,
Or to a little sea island alone where the birds go to sleep,
It's there the raven has its nest and the eagle calls over the harbour,
And I asking God above not to take from us the light of day.

This is an old song much to be heard among the people of Corca
Dhuibhne. It also has a special connection with Inisvickillane and, suitably,
the eagle is given an mention.

John Windele, the Cork antiquarian, paid a visit to Corca Dhuibhne in
June 1838. He was friendly with the parish priest of Ballyferriter, Fr John
Casey, himself a noted local scholar and historian. One day Windele went
back to Dunquin with the priest, who was going to say mass for the
fishermen at Faill Cliath, the cliff at the top of the Dunquin landing place.
When mass was over, some of the fishermen took them both out for a trip
to Inis Tuaisceart.

Windele noted:

> The Great Blasket crowned with a Martello Tower this island is three
> miles long with a population of about 120.
>
> Next we coasted Inis na Bró (the island of the Quern) and
> Iniscollane at its side. This last is a great breeding locality for Eagles.
> We saw as we approached one of these birds perched on a rock
> inaccessible to man.[1]

These sea eagles were plentiful up to and after the famine and were
often seen, particularly in summertime:

> Last week an eagle was seen to drop a fresh bream on a field in the
> parish of Dunquin. The persons who saw it were astounded at seeing
> the stranger so early in the season, as it is seldom if ever seen before

June . . . and the same day was stormy. There were severe gales on May Eve and May Day and two more since, but a farmer at Coumenole, John O'Sullivan, has an early garden of potatoes with several blossoms already opened.[2]

Those eagles were to be seen during the youth of Peig Sayers (1876–1958) in Dunquin. Here's her son Maidhc (Mike), remembering a trip with his mother to visit his grandparents in Baile Bhiocáire:

"Mam," says I, "what name has that big hill over there?"

"That's Mount Eagle, for you, Love," says she. "That hill used be full of eagles when I was young, although there is none there now. There is a big lake on the top and the eagles used to be in the cliffs above it. But it's a long time now since there was any eagle's nest on it. A doctor in Dingle bought the last one from a woman in the parish of Ventry."[3]

Seán Ó Dálaigh, "the Common Noun", also remembered the eagles in the second half of the nineteenth century: "Up to about fifty years ago eagles used be plentiful around Mount Eagle. They were that plentiful that the hill was named after them. But nothing lasts forever. There is not one of them there now for many years."[4]

Then Tomás, who was born in 1856, has to say this much about them on the Blaskets: "I don't remember ever seeing an eagle either in the sky or on the ground."

We can take it from those accounts that the eagle disappeared sometime between 1860 and 1880, and that they went from the islands first.

And what happened to them? Simple. Every one of them was destroyed, particularly with guns and poison. The Common Noun tells us the reason:

They are very destructive birds are these eagles. Any place there are eagles and they nesting there they carry out great destruction on the people of the neighbourhood. They are at their worst when they have their young. As the small birds grow they demand a lot of meat and the eagle spares no effort in supplying them.

And what meat do they eat?

They say that the eagle eats no meat only the meat of birds or animals that he captures live. He wouldn't taste the corpse of any animal he would find dead, even if he was to die of the hunger. He travels far from home hunting for himself. He goes way up in the air looking

227

down beneath him, and he has amazingly sharp eyesight and there is very little that goes on without him noticing it.[5]

A lamb, a young calf, a piglet, goose, duck, hen or turkey would not be safe when the eagle is around, or, at least, that's what they believed. Small wonder that they were put an end to. The farmers with guns saw to that. Also, there was a fashion among a certain class to have them stuffed and mounted on the mantelpiece as conversation pieces for visitors. There was also a demand, around that time, for their eggs, a pound each, to be sent to various museums around the world. Tomás gives us an example of this when he is describing a stack on Inis Tuaisceart:

> Cloch i seasamh: This stone has the appearance of a castle, standing straight up from the sea and almost as slippery as a bottle. There is a patch near the top of the stone that is called "The Eagle's Nest"; where the eagle builds his nest. There's money to be made there, and a hundred men watching it. But they don't disturb it. It cannot be approached by rope, because it is on the top the nest is, and on that account the egg or the eagle has to be thrown down. There was only the one climber on the island in my time that used take them from it, another man in Dunquin and a third from the parish of Moore. Just three in these parishes. You'd get a pound for an eagle's egg or a young bird that time. But it's many's the thing you could buy for a pound that time that you couldn't get now for a long time.[6]

Foley tells us in *The Ancient and Present State of the Skelligs, Blasket Islands, Donquin and the West of Dingle* (1903): "The rocks abound with sea eagles and hawks. The sea eagle is larger than the golden but not as noble."[7] And there are the stories about them like the ferret and the eagle.

> There was a man on the Western Island and he had a ferret. One day he went out hunting rabbits on the hill with the ferret. He let the ferret into the burrow, but whatever happened, he let slip the string that was keeping him from his hand so that the ferret remained in the burrow and he had to return home without either rabbit or ferret.
>
> A while passed and the man had forgotten about the ferret. One day two boats from the Island were out fishing. They saw, some distance from them, an eagle swooping through the air. They shortly saw the reason. There was a ferret gripping him by the throat. In the end the eagle fell into the sea with a crash between the two boats. The eagle was dead on the water, and the ferret on his back fully alive.

They then noticed that there was a string hanging from his foot. They took him in and the man recognised him as his own from the bit that was taken out of his ear. He put it in against his breast and brought it home. He had been missing from the month of November to the middle of summer.

They made out that the eagle had attacked the ferret thinking it was a young lamb he had. He was mistaken.[8]

In July 1986, Dr Tony Wilde (Irish Wildbird Conservancy) conducted a survey to see if the sea eagle could be brought back. There were certain problems, one being the farmers and their custom of laying strychnine to kill vermin. A law was then passed banning the use of the poison.

In 1991, Dr Klaus Fentzloff from the German Raptor Research Centre in Burg Guttenberg, made a further study of the project. He came to the conclusion that the Inis was a very suitable site for the reintroduction of the sea eagle and that it was well worth giving it a try. He advised that the birds be brought in from a zoo, where they would be accustomed to captivity, rather than bringing in a pair from the wild.

The year 1992 came to be known as the Year of the Eagles on the Inis. After very much planning and preparation, a pair of eagles, Maedhb and Aillil, were released on 3 April. Dr Fentzloff had presented them. Another pair was presented to Fóta Island in Cork on the same occasion. It was hoped that the sea eagle would be back in its former dominion in Inisvickillane. The pair were let out in front of the Tigh Mór with a string left tied to each of them for the time being, to give them an opportunity to settle down. They also had rings with electronic tags to monitor their progress. On 8 April, the strings were cut and the eagles fully freed. They seemed very happy in their new environment as they flew out to sea.

From then everyone was watching the skies to see if they would return. On 14 April, Maedhb was sighted and seemed to be very much bothered by many blackbirds and ravens, which had gathered round and were pestering her. The very opposite had been expected, but the local birds were not happy that these strangers had come into their midst, and were letting them know as much. Worse was to come. No sign was seen of Aillil until the report arrived that his body had been found on the beach at Waterville in Uíbh Ráthach.

Maedhb continued on making small flights, being tormented continually by the other birds, even when she was landed on the ground.

Conor shot a few rabbits and tossed them to her in case she was hungry. She could be seen continually, but not without her retinue of birds.

She seemed in top form in August 1992, and the family got great delight in seeing her through the window while dining at evening, Maedhb on one side on the house, flying regally, and the red deer on the other. She gave many displays of skilled flying, in spite of the unwanted attention of the other birds. Sometimes she turned on her back while up in the air and would bare her talons threateningly to them. Everyone who saw her enjoyed the experience. As time went by, she became accustomed to the place, and she would fly out to sea, the queen of the air above and below her. Then she would disappear and rarely show herself, and in the end everyone thought she had left the place entirely. There were no sightings in 1993, '94 or '95, and she had almost been forgotten, except to hear the odd report, usually from fishermen, that she had been seen way out to sea.

On 16 August 1996, Maedhb came from the sky and landed again on the Inis. Everyone was delighted to see her, and they were especially pleased that she seemed in very good condition. It wasn't the blackbirds nor the ravens who were now crowding her, but rather the seagulls that continually harassed her.

She did show up a few times in August 1997. It was clear that she was now independent and able to take care of herself. The only problem was that she was without a mate, which really meant that she had no future. She left one day and was never seen again.

In hindsight, had a number of pairs been released, rather than one pair, perhaps the project would have achieved better success.[9]

Chapter XXII

Inis na Bró

Inisvickillane and Inis na Bró have always been associated, being so close to each other. As Tomás Ó Criomhthain notes: "There is only the length of a ship between Inis na Bró and Inisvickillane, and although they have separate names, they are almost the one island."[1]

There is no account of anyone living there in any permanent sense, though fishermen often used to live temporarily there for some time during the summer months, when it was more convenient to do so than to return home. It was also used for grazing sheep, and the shearers would often stay over for a few days. It contains 102 acres and so could easily nourish fifty or sixty sheep. Lambs used to be brought in from the Inis also to separate them from their mothers. It was to this island that Seán a' Mhúraigh and his two companions were bringing the lambs when they were drowned in 1873. (See p. 56).

According to the population Census of 1841, there was no one living there. But five lived there in 1851. They must have been fishermen living there temporarily at the time of the Census.

It is named Inis na Bró, i.e. the Quern-stone Island, from having the shape of a saddle quern, used with a quern stone for grinding grain, high on both sides and dipped in the middle.

Paddy O'Leary and Lee Snodgrass, archaeologists, paid it a visit in 1976 and carried out an archaeological search. They succeeded in discovering some archaeological clues that would give us to understand that people did, in fact, live there over an extended period in pre-historic times. The greatest problem in living there would be the difficulty in landing, except when the sea and the weather is calm. Paddy and Lee think that habitation there would have been more favourable in former times, such as the early Christian period, when the weather was warmer and kinder.

They took note, in particular, of the promontory fort named Dún Laoi, situated on the western cliff, some 350 feet high. It is in the shape of a half-circle, with a defensive ditch on the land side and the natural protection of the cliff and the sea on the other. There is no sign of the remains of any stone structure, and the *dún* has that appearance of not being completed.

231

There is also a hut site present, a few sheep hollows and a *gallán* or standing stone. There are also field fences and drill marks which show that some cultivation was carried out there some time in the distant past.[2]

Seán Tom Ó Cearnaigh could remember George Collier having sheep on Inis na Bró:

> As I was saying already, I well remember when Collier had possession of the islands and had sheep on them . . .
>
> One day a boat–a trawler–came from Dingle to take away the sheep that George Collier's wife had sold to Savage from Tralee, I and two others were fishing bream and pollock back towards Inis na Bró–and it was the sheep from there they were going to take away that day.
>
> We were fishing with lines, and however good or bad we were doing we said to ourselves that we would go into Inis na Bró to catch young birds, the razorbills and the young petrels that are very plentiful at the Autumn of the year. We had a fair bag of them. They are good and fat. They used to be salted long ago, and they used be eaten fresh as well–roasted or boiled.
>
> At this time the Dingle people had come ashore, and were gathering the sheep together to corner them and catch them and bring them out in the small boat to the big boat to bring them over to Uíbh Ráthach, where they would be put on the train at Cahersiveen to Tralee, or wherever they were wanted. They had dogs, and they set the dogs after the sheep, and the sheep were very wild with no experience of dogs, and then the dogs couldn't be stopped.
>
> The sheep took off, and I thought that lots of them would go over the cliff, and I went after them when they turned. When I reached the top of the cliff I saw one of them below swimming and trying to come into land. He would get his face as far as the rock but would be unable to get a grip and come up.
>
> I told the other two that the best thing we could do was to go and get him before he was swept away, and we went in the *naomhóg* and reached him. He was a fine Dexter ram and he was still alive. One of us caught a grip on him, but, indeed, he was unable to lift him on board. He had a big heavy fleece and two of us had to catch him by the feet and turn him on his back. As well and as fast as we did it we were still too late and he had died before we got him on board.
>
> There was a barrel of meat on him.[3]

Here's another account of fishermen staying over on Inis na Bró:

. . . We loaded on a dozen lobster pots and set out until we drew up on the western side of Inis na Bró.

There is no house or habitation of any type on Inis na Bró but what might be described as an old stone fence up on it. That was where we planned to store the supplies we had brought with us from the Blasket. We built a small four-sided stone wall and filled it up with soft sea-pink that we found growing on the cliffs. We set the sea-pink afire with a drop of paraffin and we soon had a fine fire blazing with the sea pink aflame because they were as dry as snuff. Then we got a fish, a fine conor fish, and we cleaned it and put it on the pan with a lump of butter. When this was ready we made a tin of tea for ourselves. We had no milk for the tea and so had to drink it black except that we had plenty of sugar . . .

As you might expect, the Island people had a custom of making their bed on Inis na Bró when we would be a number of days away from home fishing there. Down in a cove called Cuas na Loiche we would make our beds. It was a long neck of land away up and out from the bank and a overhanging stone that would keep out the rain. But if the wind was from the south east the rain would be in on top of you. But there was no wind nor rain on this particular evening I mention and the cave was fine and dry. We gathered more of the sea-pink and scattered it over the floor of the cave and we spread the blankets down on them.

. . . we went east then to our beds and stretched in them. It was a fine comfortable bed, I can tell you, with the blanket underneath and the sail of the *naomhóg* over you up to your mouth. Everyone got out their pipes and reddened them and were puffing away, and we were very relaxed there in cave in the dim darkness. We spent a while chatting, as you might expect, but one after another everyone of the four of us fell asleep.

. . . That's how we used spend the week from then out–going back there Monday morning and coming home every Saturday that we were able.[4]

Chapter XXIII

Old Graffiti

Unfortunately, among the natives of Coumeenoole who visit the island for devotional purposes, it has become a fashion to scratch graffiti on the exposed area of the stone and it is considerably disfigured.[1]

Mícheál Ó Guithín, Peig Sayers' son, remembers something of the Inis from his early years. The young men were fleeing there from the manhunt, as described in his book, *Is Trua ná Fanann an Óige* (Pity Youth does not Last):

"Great God," says I to my mother, "what's up with the people that they are all running down, or is it how someone has fallen over a cliff that there is so much excitement?"

"No, love," says she. "Do you not see the warship?"

"Where is she?" I asked.

"There she is coming north from the Fiach. Diarmaid Thomáis was right last night, when he said she was coming. All the boys are away escaping back to Inisvickillane."[2]

Some people who did spent time on the Inis, for whatever reason, left their mark behind them. Indeed that custom may have gone way back to the time of the pilgrimages to the Inis as described above. There are initials carved down by the cliff edge at the strand like

EC [or FC?]
1777

That goes back a long way and we don't know who carved it.

But we have a good idea who inscribed the following, the family of the Ó Dálaighs, and other relatives. It was the custom to write names in English although they spoke only Irish.

Thomas Daly
Patrick Daly
Maurice Daly
Patrick Daly

234

Michael Daly
1/4/??

John Sullivan
Probably one of the Sullivans of the Island, perhaps Muiris's (*Twenty Years a-Growing*) father, Seán Lís; or Seán Mhicil, or his son, Seáinín Mhicil.

M. Manning
This is Mike Neilí Ó Mainín from Tíorabháin, Ballyferriter, who fished lobster for thirteen seasons from the Inis in the 1920s and 1930s of the last century. His crew consisted of Mike himself, Séamus de hÓra and Dave Goggin from Baile an Éanaigh. They would stay on the Inis from Monday till Saturday in the old Ó Dálaigh home, sleeping in a heather bed. They had a sail on the naomhóg. They caught lobster and crayfish which they would sell to the Frenchman. They had their own store pot.[3]

Another friend of Paddy na hInise was Taimí Touí Ó Ciobháin from Gráig. They got to know each other from Paddy's visits to Clogher to his sister. It is part of the family tradition that Taimí and some of his friends, including Paddy na hInise, took off for the States one summer when the fishing was bad. They spent the summer there, but didn't get on very well as the States were going through the Depression at the time, the end of the 1920s.[4]

Other names

M.H.
Patrick Daly
John Kean 1909 or 1901.
Cruger X July 1931

When Kruger came home from America about the year 1929 . . . he headed for Inisvickillane the following year fishing lobster with his uncle, Séamus Sheosaimh [James Hoare] from Ballyferriter. It was some change for Kruger, who had no experience of that type, but, of course he was with the Ó Dálaighs, and they would stay there from Monday to Saturday, something else Kruger didn't like, because he was young and lively at the time and used to sport and company, something that wasn't to be had on the Inis, but seals moaning every night, without music or dance. So sign on it: Kruger spent just one season on the Inis; he had enough of the place.[5]

Kruger had returned from the States because of his health. On doctor's orders to get plenty of fresh air, he went fishing on the Inis. Whatever about the shortage of song and dance, there was plenty of fresh air, good plain food and exercise, and he recovered his health. Of course, his uncle, Seán Sheosaimh de hÓra (An Seanduine) from Clogher, was married to Narraí na hInise, the daughter of Muiris Mór and sister of Paddy na hInise.

Thomas X Daly X July 1931.

LK

T Grummell

T Grummell

1979.

John Daly

MH

Patrick

James Hoar 1890

This James Hoar or Séamus de hÓra was a fisherman who used to stay from Monday to Saturday on the Inis. He had a liking for the drink, and when he was out it is often he could be found in the tavern. He had a sister, however, who had reared him, as his mother had died young, and she would go after him in the donkey and cart to whatever pub he was in and order him out. He would always heed her and come home in the cart with her. He inscribed his name with a nail or a knife on the Inisvickillane ogham stone, and the name is still clearly visible and legible. We don't know who *Cobba* on the stone was, but we do know the identity of James Hoare, who inscribed his name on the stone in 1890.[6]

John M Keane

It seems to be Seán Mhaurice Mhuiris Ó Catháin, "Faeilí".

Seámus Ó Bric 1921

Séamus was from Gorta Dubha. He was involved in the IRA in the struggle for independence while still very young. Someone came to the house in Gorta Dubha one day and advised the father that it would be better for the young Bric to be absent from the house that night. That was enough. Himself and a few of his companions took off into Inisvickillane. It was while he was there that he inscribed his name on the cliff. One of the companions remarked that it would be as well if he was to write a letter to the Black and Tans telling them of their whereabouts. After a while word came that all was safe again and that they could return home.[7]

John J. O Sullivan
In the oratory.

P. Dunleavy
Patty Dunleavy, a son of the schoolmistress on the Island, Máire Ní Mhainín from Kilvickadownig, who was married to Muiris Mór Ó Duinnshléibhe. Patty had a great love for the Island. He became a schoolteacher himself and married a girl from another island, Cape Clear. He used to return to the Blasket every summer and stay in his old home, which is still the finest house on the Island. He loved visiting Inisvickillane, and C.J. always made him welcome.

Appendix I

There are other sites named after Mac Uibhleáin, too, such as Cnocán Ard in Baile an Reannaigh in the parish of Marhin down by the beach. *An Seabhac* says of it: "There is an old indefinite memory that in this spot is buried 'Mac an Oileáin' or 'Mac Fhaoláin,' the one who was on the most westerly of the Blaskets–that he was drowned while trying to land there. It is not clear why he wanted to land there."[1]

There is an ogham stone on top of a sand dune which was associated with the monastery. A storm at the end of the eighteenth century uncovered seven such stones, which would indicate that the site was of very considerable importance in early Christian times. Lord Ventry, the landlord, "rescued" six of them to his residence at Burnham, where they remained in a shed for many years until erected by the avenue on the right-hand side just before the house, now Coláiste Íde, where they can still be seen. Two others can be viewed at Chute Hall, another Ventry residence, outside Tralee. The seventh ogham stone can still be seen in Baile an Reannaigh (Ballinrannig), close to its original position. The local people call the area Ceallúnach Bhaile an Reannaigh (Ballinrannig church yard), because unbaptised babies were buried there. It is generally thought that no trace of the monastery remains, but that is to oversimplify the issue. The surrounding terrain consists mostly of sand dunes, which are constantly on the move, and much has been uncovered there, including a cemetery and stone buildings at the Teampall Bán (White church yard) from medieval times. There was also a later Protestant church in the vicinity until the beginning of the nineteenth century, of which nothing is known.

Another site that may have a connection with Mocheallóg is Cill Mocheallóg in Tuosist parish on the border of Kerry and Cork. Loch a' Cuínleáin (Loch 'ic Uibhleáin) is situated in the same parish, and T.F. O'Rahilly is of the opinion that it is named after Mocheallóg Mac Uíbhleáin, the patron of Corca Dhuibhne. It may be that Corca Dhuibhne extended this far at one period of time and that Mocheallóg founded a monastery at both extremes of the territory.

It may be also that Kilmallock (Cill Mocheallóg) in County Limerick gets its name from Mocheallóg.

Another indication of the influence of the saint is the naming of important people after him, one such being Giolla Mac Uíbhleáin Ó Conghaile, the king of Corca Dhuibhne, who is mentioned in the Annals of Innisfallen for the year 1040 as having died: *"Morsd Gillai Meicc Uíbhleáin Hui Chongaile, rig Corcu Duibne."*

Mentioned also is Giolla Mac Uibhleáin Ó hAnamchadha, the bishop of Ardfert, a few years before the Norman invasion. *Giolla* means "dedicated to" or "servant of" and indeed who would a bishop defer to except to someone of great importance.

Those Irish saints, Brendan, Bríd, Ciaran and Gobnait were for the most part of the noble class.

But if Mocheallóg was so important and influential, what became of him that we search to provide a few basic facts about him today?

It would seem that the Ciarraí Luachra, in time, extended their influence right into Corca Dhuibhne early in the twelfth century, so much so that the Corca Dhuibhne, as a people, seem to have disappeared without a trace. The Ciarraí Luachra brought their saints with them, particularly Brendan as patron, and devotion to the other saints became overshadowed. Also, Brendan was accepted as the patron of the diocese of Ardfert, and he was advanced to the detriment of the other saints, whose memory slowly faded. The Normans who followed seem to have taken to Brendan, too, who by now had become a famous saint with many legends centered around him and his voyages.

Appendix II

A Chara Uasail
My Dear Friend. . . .
We have a hand-written account from Paddy na hInise himself, fourteen
pages, dated 29 August 1933, in which he tells us about himself and his
people and their connection with the Inis. We are not sure why he wrote
it, but it would seem, from the date and some of the information, to be in
connection with the court case when he was seeking to establish ownership
of the Inis. After close examination it is clear that it is Paddy's handwriting,
which shows that he had both writing and reading, and, moreover, that in
Irish, however he came by it. I am very grateful to Eilís Uí Chéileachair
who let me see the manuscript.

An Blascaod Mór,
Dún Chaoin.
29–8–33.

My Dear Friend,
Here for you is an account. There is a man in this village who is over eight
years and four score and he tells me, that the islands were in the possession
of my Great-Grandfather that is Tadhg Ó Guithín and Seán Ó Guithín,
his son. Seán Ó Guithín went with the rent to the master who was on it,
That is Bess Rice, but Bess did not accept the rent because he had it not
dead exact. He came home, raised his sails and went over the ocean to
America, himself and his Wife. He left his father and the rest of them
behind him on the Stone (in the Inis). He gave a while there and came back
to the Inis, himself, his Wife and his family. He had a son whose name was
Seán Óg Ó Guithín. He married a woman from the Blasket and when he
married the father went back to America. Seán Óg had a sister married on
the great Blasket to a man of the Dálaighs at that time. Seán Óg was
drowned around the Inis and his wife came back home to the Blasket.
Then Cáit and her husband went back. Cáit was the sister of Seán Óg who
had married Muiris Ó Dála and their descendants are in the place since.
Cáit is my mother and I am Pádraig Ó Dála, and none of those people were
ever interfered in any way with until me who is being driven out now.

When my people went to the Inis they hadn't permission from anyone nor did I ever hear that they had. When my father and mother changed back to the Inis after Seán Óg's drowning they brought back two cows with them. My father was no sooner settled down when he lay into hard work breaking the ground and building fences. It wasn't long until the family were falling back on him. He had four sons, Mícheál and Pádraig Seán and Muiris. We used to be sowing potatoes and oats and turnips and every other Sort of cultivation in it. That's how we Were living our lives happily until my brothers were grown up as Men and they thinking of making out for themselves. Mícheál and Seán went to America and Maurice shortly afterwards. When they had all gone the work was too hard for me my father was too Old and my mother not too well. I myself had to bring back all the stock and sell them at the Dingle market. Then my father was very old and my mother and the fear of Death coming on them and they at me to bring them into a place somewhere near to the Priest. There was a gentleman from England on the Inis at the same time and He Presented us with it when he was leaving. My father told me to bring the hut east to the Blasket and that it would do me until they Would have died themselves. I brought back the hut and put it up on the Blasket. My father and mother were with me there but I used go back every Summer to the house. It is that Hut that I brought from the west with me that I still use as a house. After a while after that I bought four Bullocks and put them on the Inis and they were there for a Year and a half. I brought the four of them in a boat to Dingle and when I was taking them out from the boat onto the Dingle quay the leg of one of them got broken and the one who bought it was your father, Jonathan Moriarty. I had no stock in it then but a few goats. I used be fishing there every Summer and keeping up the house and it was often in a terrible state before me after the winter. There was a while then without any stock except the goats. The Blasket people then put sheep on it and it wasn't long until it was full up, and the Little garden that I used sow every Summer the sheep used destroy it on me. I came then and I put out every one of the Blasket sheep and I put sheep in it again and I bought sheep from the Mórach himself to put there. When I had fat sheep it's John Moore who used to buy them from me and who bought them this Year. There was nowhere suitable then to Shear the sheep or To Catch them except a place that was too dangerous down in the cliff. I had to myself make a suitable place and spend my own money on it as well as drawing the stones on my back a long way from Home. When I had the fold made I made another suitable place for the growing of willows because they grow well there. My sheep used be going over the Cliff then and I had to fence it off. I cut turf there every year, and I haven't a sod of the land of Ireland except the Inis. That is How I make my Livelihood. I bring back my donkey there every summer and I bring onions and mangolds and hay back home from it every Autumn. It is a year and twenty since my mother died. I never got permission To be in the Inis and I never heard that my father ever had permission either.

When Bess Rice died Sam Hussey was the agent for Lord Cork. All the islands paid no Rent at that time, Innis na Bró Innis Mic Faoileáin Innis Thuaidh Ort, Beag Innis, Oileán Buídhe, Oileán na n-Óg. Sam Hussey gave all the Islands to Caillear except to pay the rent on them but my ancestors were always in possession. When Caillear lost possession it is Moore and Moriarty who came into possession about thirty-five years ago.

Mícheál Ó Baodhléir from Ard na Cainnthe sent seven sheep grazing to me about nine years ago. They spent the year on grass and he gave me a sheep and lamb as payment. Sean Ó Casatha and Seán Ó Carna also sent sheep to me and each of them gave me a sheep and lamb as payment.

I am keeping up the Landing place every year and except for that no boat could safely dock there. It's very often *naomhógs* from the Blaskets sail in there when they are caught in a storm, and only for me being there they would Die with the hunger. I asked the Government to fix up the Landing for me, but they didn't do it, although they didn't refuse me. When the Mórach was shearing on Inis na Bró this year I had a little talking with the boys who Were shearing for him about the lamb which was owed to me which I didn't get from them.

There are signals between myself and the people in the Lighthouse on the Tiaracht and whenever anything goes wrong with them I go to their assistance. It is us who got the man who fell over the cliff this year.

Every account I have written down here and much more that I haven't written the four oldest in the Blasket are going to be my witnesses that they Have knowledge of what I have written in the account. Those people are: Eoghan Ó Suilleabháin whom is four score and eight years, Mícheál Ó Suilleabháin four score and four years and Seán Ó Ceárna four score Years.

There is no person in Corca Dhuibhne, old or young who does not know that there are always people living in the Inis and that no one ever put them out until this and we are the people who are now being put out of possession.

Tadhg Ó Guithín

Seán Ó Guithín (who spent some time in America)

Seán Óg Ó Guithín (He was drowned)
His daughter, Cáit = Muiris Ó Dála

Pádraig Ó Dála
The Inis was in the possession of my great grandfather Tadhg Ó Guithín,
and his son Seán Ó Guithín. It was Seán who offered the rent to Bess Rice.
Sean went to America and left his father Tadhg in possession of the Inis.
Seán returned to the Inis. Sean's son, that is Seán Óg Ó Guithín, and Seán
left the Inis to him and went back to America. Seán Óg was drowned and
his widow went back to the Great Blasket. Then Cáit Ní Ghuithín and her
husband Muiris Ó Dála moved to the Inis. Cáit was the sister of Seán Óg,
and they were my mother and father.

P. Ó Dála.

Appendix III

During those years before the famine, about the time that Seán went to America, and afterwards in the famine years, Bess Rice ruled over her tenants with a strict hand. She was a descendant of the Rice family, who owned a castle in Burnham, where Coláiste Íde is located today. They were evicted after the Cromwellian war, and the land was granted to Frederick Mullins, who was later given the title Lord Ventry. Bess Rice died in 1870, as mentioned in this piece in the *Tralee Chronicle:*

DEATH OF MISS RICE OF DINGLE

Died at Dingle on the 6th inst., after a long and painful illness, which she bore with Christian patience and resignation, Miss Eliza Rice, at the advanced age of 77 years. [Which means that she was born in 1793 or 1794.] She was the daughter of the late Patrick Rice Esq., of the 'Harbour' [ie. Cuan] near Dingle and Johanna Hickson of Hillville, Castlegregory. The death of this benevolent and charitable lady leaves a void in the old families of Dingle not likely ever to be filled up, she having been the almost sole surviving member in the ancient sept of the Rices of Fawne and Dingle. Miss Rice's death has caused universal regret amongst the people of this locality, to whom her noble qualities of head and heart endeared her.–May she rest in peace.

Tralee Chronicle, Tuesday, 11 January 1870.

Appendix IV

Here is a short account of Muiris and Cáit's family as far as can be ascertained at this time:

Catherine, Cáit, Cáit na hInise, born 23 December 1860, on the Great Blasket. She was the girl who was friendly with Tomás Ó Criomhthain. She went to America about 1880. She contracted TB there, returned home and died on 16 June 1885.

Eibhlín, Neil (Nell), Neil Mhuiris Mhóir, Neil na hInise. Born on the Blasket. We're not sure of her date of birth, though 1860 is given, which seems unlikely. She married Robert Mitchell from Ceathrú, Dunquin. They went to live in Dingle. One of their sons was Mícheál Mitchell, better known as An Fiagach.

Máire, Máire na hInise, Mary, born on the Blasket, 1863. She went to America and settled in Chicago.

Mícheál, Maidhc na hInise, Maidhc Mór. Went to America. Went into the American Army. He was the eldest son, as Tomás relates: " 'The devil!' says Mícheál, the eldest son he had, 'leave those to Tomás Dhónaill.' "[1]

Johanna, Joan, Siobhán. Born on the Great Blasket in November 1865. She was a good singer according to Tomás.

Maurice and Tomás, twins, born 1868 on the Great Blasket. Both died very young.

Anne, Áine, Neans. Born on the Great Blasket in the year 1871. Married Peats Mhuiris Ó Catháin from the Blasket, also known as An Líathach. They left the Blasket for Baile Eaglaise in the parish of Dún Urlann. She died in 1935 and is buried in Dún Urlann.

Honora, Nóra, Narrie na hInise. Born on the Great Blasket in 1871. She married Seán Sheosaimh de hÓra from Clogher, Ballyferriter, Shrove Tuesday, 13 February 1892, the same day as Peig Sayers and Patsy Flint Ó Guithín married. Seán Sheosaimh was called An Seanduine, a name that often followed the eldest son in the family.

It would seem that Áine and Nora may have been twins.

Seán and Nóra's family was as follows:

> Cáit (Kate), she married a farmer from County Kildare, a man named Byrne.

Séamus (Jimmy), he was a guard in Kildare.

Muiris (Maurice), went to Hartford, Conn. Did not marry.

Mary, also went to Hartford and did not marry.

Eilís (Lisa), who married Paddy Mitchell from Ceathrú, Dunquin. They had one daughter, Máirín (Main), who married Mícheál Ó Lúing (Mikey Long, Mikey Phádraig), from Baile an Treasna, Ventry.

Seán (Seáinín), who married Peig Ní Chaomhánach, and have a family, Niamh, Aoileann and Úna.

Elizabeth, Eilís na Beannaí. She was born on the Beannaigh, a headland of the Blasket, on 2 June 1873, as her mother, Cáit, was being conveyed from the Inis to the Blasket to have her baby, which shows that the Ó Dálaighs had moved to the Inis by that time. At the age of nineteen, Eilís went to America in 1892 on the *Majestic* to New York, from there to Chicopee Falls. We have no further account of her up to the present.

Pádraig, Paddy Mhaurice, Paddy na hInise. Born on the Inis in April 1876. He was the only one of the family that remained at home on the Inis; he later changed to live on the Blasket.

John, Seán, John Mór na hInise. Born on 27 July 1880. He went to Boston on the *Tutonic* and from there to Chicago.

Maurice, Maurice na hInise. Born on the Inis, June 1882. Baptised on 11 June in the church in Ballyferriter. Went to America and settled in Chicago where he married. Died in 1920.

The earliest entry in *Liber Baptizatum Parochium: Kilmelckidar, Morhin, Kilquane, Dunurlin et Dunquin*, 1808–1828, that deals with the Blaskets, is an entry, not for the *Insula Magna*, but for *Insulae fili Kyliani* for Catherine Gueehin, daughter of Johannis Gueehin and Maria Duana for the 5 April 1808. Catherine Gueehin is the first of thirteen entries from the Inis between 1808 and 1882, every baby taken across the sea to Ballyferriter to be baptised.

Inisvickillane Entries in the Register of Baptisms, Ballyferriter.

Year	Child	Parents
1808	Cáit Guiheen	John Guiheen & Máire Ní Duane.
1818	Brian Sheehy	James Sheehy & Joan Bowler.
1822	Gobnait Shea	Denis Shea & Helen Guiheen.
1827	Margaret Shea	Denis Shea & Helen Guiheen.
1844	Mary Guiheen	Seán Mhaurice Liam Guiheen & Mary Moore.
1866	Patrick Guiheen	Séan a' Mhóraigh Guiheen & Léan Kearney.

1868	Mary Guiheen	Séan a' Mhóraigh Guiheen & Léan Kearney.
1870	Séan Léan Guiheen	Séan a' Mhóraigh Guiheen & Léan Kearney.
1872	Cáit Léan Guiheen	Séan a' Mhóraigh Guiheen & Léan Kearney.
1874	Maidhc Léan Guiheen	Séan a' Mhóraigh Guiheen & Léan Kearney.
1876	Patrick Daly	Maurice Daly & Cáit a'Mhóraigh Guiheen
1880	John Mór Daly	Maurice Daly & Cáit a'Mhóragh Guiheen
1882	Maurice Daly	Maurice Daly & Cáit a'Mhóraigh Guiheen

Here is a short biographical note on some of the Inis people

Neans na hInise

Neans Daly, daughter of Maurice Mór na hInise Ó Dálaigh, married Peats Mhuiris Ó Catháin, who was called *"An Líathach,"* probably from the word *"liath"* meaning grey-haired. He was a brother of Maurice Mhuiris Ó Catháin of the Blaskets. They married in 1889 and had a large family.

1 Mícheál, born 1890, of whom we have no account,

2 Máire, born 1891, who died in 1905,

3 Seán, born 1892, who emigrated to the States,

4 Muiris, born 1894, who went to England,

5 Mártan, born 1895,

6 Hanna, born 1897,

7 Pádraig, born 1904,

8 Cáit, birthday not known, all of whom, other than Muiris, emigrated to USA.

9 Bríd (Bríd Neans), birthday not known, married Eoghan Ó Gráda, a writer in Irish who lived in Dublin. They had a son, Paddy Neans, or Paddy an Líathaigh, a fine gentle person, who died young. They had a daughter Kate, or Kate Neans, who went to America.[2]

Muiris, Maurice a' Líathaigh returned from England, as did Seán from the States. They left the Island and went with their father to live in Baile Eaglaise. Neans died in 1935. Peats died on Christmas Day, 1941.

An Fiagach. Mícheál Mitchell

Mícheál Mitchell was son of Nell na hInise (Dálaigh) and Robert Mitchell from Cill Uru in the parish of Ventry. The father and mother moved to Dingle at an early age and spent their lives there. Mícheál went to America as a young man but returned in the thirties as, it seems, he was not getting on too well there. In that respect he would be an example of the many who went there at the time, both ill suited and ill prepared for the life that lay before them. Many of them, unable to deal with the new style of life, fell by the wayside and were not heard of again. The odd one succeeded in making his or her way back home again, where they tried to pick up the pieces. Mícheál was one of those. He was lucky in having an elder sister, Kate, settled in the States before him. She thought he stood a better chance of survival if he returned home and provided the money for his passage back to Ireland and to the Blaskets where his mother was born.

Seán Mhaidhc Léan Ó Guithín and Seán Mhaurice Mhuiris Ó Catháin helped him to settle in by renovating the Líathach's old house and reroofing it with rushes from the Leaca Dhubhach.

He probably got the name "Fiagach" (the wild one) from being a wild character. Still, he always dressed very well, and is easily recognisable in old photographs from his hat. He had a merry disposition and was always in league with Paddy Beag in thinking up new tricks and plans.

He was as healthy as a trout, but had a great liking for the drink. He used to fish single-handed around the Inis in a little *naomhóg*.

After some time another cousin, John a' Líathaigh, who had come home to Baile Eaglaise, came to live on the Blasket. Muiris Mhaidhc Léan remembers:

> The Fiagach, the Líathach and Muiris Sheáin Eoin (Peaití's father) bought a *naomhóg* between them, and they went fishing lobster to Inisvickillane. They would stay there for the week and return to the Island on Saturday. When on the Inis, they would sleep in Poll na Mine on the Inis Strand.
>
> The Frenchman used to come and buy the lobsters from them; about once a week or once a fortnight he came. He would bring fishing nets, knives, oilskins, oil hats, pots, barrels and the likes, and a bottle of whiskey for Paddy an Oileáin, and he would swap them for lobsters. The Island people were very grateful to him.[3]

Lockley describes the Fiagach in *I Know an Island*. Lockley and Paddy na hInise had arrived in on the Inis strand with his son, Paddy Beag and he was there before them:

> The lonely fisherman Mitchell was working on the beach there, mending a hole in his small, threadbare canoe with tar, heated over a turf fire. He peered at us uncertainly, a timid look in his weatherworn face. Mitchell is another man who has come back from America to

248

end his days, like Eugene and his brother, in the peace of lobstering and turf-cutting at home.[4]

He had a brother, Silvie, who worked in Latchford's on the Main Street in Dingle. Silvie was a name that followed the Mitchells.

When his father died in Goat Street in Dingle, his mother, Neil, came to the Ceathrú to the Connor household where she ended her days. She was related to the Connors through the Mitchells, Donncha Ó Conchubhair's wife being a Mitchell from Cill Uru in Ventry. Donncha Ó Conchubhair was also known as *Dud,* Mollie O'Connor's father. The Fiagach came out from the Blasket for a while to be with his mother, and stayed also in Connor's house in Dunquin. This was around the year 1943.[5]

The Fiagach became famous in local circles. Muiris Bric remembers meeting him briefly when he was a boy in Gorta Dubha in the fifties:

> He had the carriage of a young man both in his walk and in his standing—as straight as a rush. But he had a hat on his head, and a stump of a pipe stuck out of his mouth. When he passed the gap in the field, I noticed that he had a white, brushy moustache under his nose, which was stuck out in front of him cutting the wind with its point. His shoulders were stretched back, and he had a kind of flannel shirt on him under his short jacket. He had nail boots on his feet but he carried them as though they were a pair of slippers.
>
> "Morrow, Paidí," says he to Dad, and he slipped the top of his fingers across the peak of his hat. "Morrow, lad," says he to me, without looking and without breaking his stride.

His father explained who they had:

> That's the Fiagach for you, Maurice—a fine healthy man from Dún Chaoin. It is said he goes to the stream every Sunday morning in the year. He washes his shirt, squeezes it out on the bank, and puts it back on for Mass.
>
> I said nothing, but I remember him as well today as though it was yesterday I saw him, and I never saw him again . . .[6]

A young Blasket girl, Eibhlís Ní Shúilleabháin, writes about him in January 1932, and shows a little of the man himself as well as the kindness and understanding of the island girls to an old man:

> Last night we went into Mitchell's house, you know him (the poor man). He is living alone in the small unfurnished house. His mother

living in town, an old age pensioner, supports him. Mary and two more girls and myself walked in to him. His bed is in one corner of the house near the fire. A spring bed and an old mattress without much clothes. A cup and saucer, an old tea pot and a small kettle, also a tin gallon to boil the potatoes. He had no flower [flour] last night, no bread only potatoes. He made a big fire but the turf was very wet and he hung the tin on it with some potatoes. He had a job, I tell you trying to make a fire of it, and he did in the end and about ten o'clock that time he ate six or seven of the potatoes. The candle was nearly out so we had to come home and leave him alone. We sometimes bring him bread and things because if he were anyway comfortable he'd tell us many stories. He is out of groceries now and the next fine day he'll go out again. He'll go to town to his mother. Poor Mitchell, he has no sense at all. After all he travelled.[7]

It would seem that he returned to the Island and to the Inis after his mother's death, and remained there till the final evacuation in November 1953. He is pictured, and easily recognisable in his trilby in a photograph taken on that occasion, firstly, on leaving the Island and then arriving at Dingle quay.

He was given a share in a recently evacuated house in Baile na Rátha, Dunquin, the old home of the Kavanaghs, who moved to Badgers Hill, County Kildare, sharing the home with two other islanders, Eoghan Sheáin Eoghain Uí Dhuinnshléibhe and his half-brother, Séamus Mhéiní Uí Dhuinnshléibhe.

He ended his days in the County Home, Killarney.

Peaidí Léan Ó Guiheen

Paddy was born on Inisvickillane and married a Dingle girl. They lived first in the Colony and then in a little house in Goat Street at the corner going into Fearanakilla House. They then got one of the new cottages in Ashmount near the hospital. He had a boat, *The Molly*, and he used to be fishing.

They had at least two in the family, Jack, called Jack Phaddy Léan. Jack became a very good rugby player for Dingle. He was a fine strong man and he went to America.

They had a daughter, Treasa. She went to England and married there. She comes home on her holidays frequently.

It was Paddy Léan who gave the prayers to be found elsewhere in this book.[8]

Cáit Léan Guiheen (Kate Léan)

She went to America and never returned. She married a man of the Kearneys from Fahan there.

She seems just to have had one child, a son, who became a priest, Fr Michael Kearney. He was ordained on 15 June 1935. He made two trips to Dunquin back in the fifties while he was on his way to Rome on both occasions. He presented Seán and Muiris Mhaidhc Léan with a radio, the first radio they ever had. He read mass in Dunquin and presented the priest, Fr Tomás Ó Muircheartaigh, with a set of mass vestments. It would appear to have been the only time that mass in English was allowed in Dunquin church, but he was given permission because his people came from the parish. He was made a monsignor afterwards, but he died young. There is a picture of him hanging on the wall in the house where Muiris Mhaidhc Léan lived in Baile na Rátha.[9]

There is a good chance that it was Kate Léan Ní Ghuithín who is described here by Seán Tom Ó Cearnaigh:

> We went out once that there was a girl from the Island looking to go to America, and if so, there were three or four outside on the mainland to be with her as they knew each other and they would like to be together for the company.
>
> She was looking out for a week before this to get out. It was the beginning of May, and the weather wasn't settled, and there was a big high swell, and the weather very broken, and no day coming that you could go out to Dunquin, and we were waiting until the sea would improve.
>
> The chance finally came.
>
> So, this day, we went out, and the wind was behind us sideways, and we raised our sail on the *naomhóg*, and we had the oars as well as the sail. On our way out what should come from the south but a steamer on its way to Limerick, and she going well down and her mast well below the great sea waves.
>
> . . . We saw a couple of sailors . . . and they gripping the iron railings in case a wave should sweep them in. We passed by her end, and when the *naomhóg* would rise on the back of a breaker with sometimes the steamer below us in a clash or sea glen, as though she were in a trough between two breakers–we used be looking down on the deck, and the next minute she would have risen and we would be down in a glen between the sea backs . . .

251

When it arrived in Limerick it was put in the paper that it was the greatest wonder he had seen in his life, an open boat from the Blasket going across over to Dunquin that day, and they themselves thinking at the time of turning back south again because the sea was too rough for them.

When we got out on the land we spent about half an hour waiting for it to calm, a space to get back in, but we did it.

A girl of the Guiheens it was who was going to America, and she had two brothers in the *naomhóg* that day, along with another boy of the Guiheens and myself.

The girl wasn't sea-sick that day. Sure, she had plenty of experience of the passage in and out, as had everyone in the Island at that time. The girl never returned to the Island since. She married over there.[10]

Seán Sheáin Uí Ghuithín

Seán was a son of Seán Léan Ó Guithín (Tim) born on the Inis in 1870. 'Tim' was a nickname often applied to members of the Guithín family. Muiris Mhaidhc Léan knew him well, an uncle of his father's. He married Máire Ní Dhálaigh from Baile na hAbha, Dunquin. Seán Léan didn't live to be old. They had a house a little to the south of the King's house, between it and the Fiagach's house. They had one son, Pádraig Ó Guithín (Paddy Tim), a really fine-looking strong specimen of a man. He spent a lot of time in Baile na hAbha with his relations. He didn't live to be old, and when he died Máire left the island and came home to Baile na hAbha.

Nóra Ní Dhálaigh, Narraí na hInise

It is clear that the Dálaigh family were unusual in many ways:

Muiris Ó Dálaigh from the Inis had a daughter, a sister to Paddy na hInise [Nóra] and she could go up high on a rope. She went a couple of times or three up to the hawk's nest in Inis na Bró and took away the eggs with her. The men were afraid to go up, but she had no such fear, even with a fearful cliff there. She married in Clogher afterwards. I'd say there was twenty nine feet in the rope and another forty to the bottom of the cliff.[11]

Appendix V

The End of an Era

The Guiheens Bid Farewell to the Great Blasket

Myself, Seán and Maraisín Mharas Mhuiris Ó Catháin were the last people on the Island. We spent the Christmas there. We had a sheep hanging on the wall. We had flour too and enough turf. Seán had the gun and wild geese landed in Seáinín Mhicil's field. They usen't be there at all, but now they came. Seán succeeded in shooting two of them. We boiled them but they weren't too tasty. I supposed they needed to be hung for a few days. But, still we weren't hungry. Maraisín Mhuiris was living in the Puncán's house, Tomás Ó Cearnaigh. The Puncán's wife had left it to him when they left. But Maraisín came to our house and the three of us were together. The only difficulty we had was the light. We had not a drop of paraffin. What we did was to get one of the plates of wax that used come in on the sea during the war and melt it on a saucer. There used to be big bales of cotton coming in on the tide as well and we had one. We were able to make a wick out of it and dip it into the wax and have it hanging from it like a cresset. We had light then even though it was dim enough.

We had intended to go out to the mainland for the Christmas, but the weather was too broken and we had to stay. Wren's Day itself was still too broken, but the day after was alright.

We took three rams and a donkey with us, and a side of sheep that remained over. Although we were lonely, we weren't too bad, because we knew that we would go in again to tend the sheep when the weather would improve.

That was the 27th December 1953, and I was almost thirty-four years of age.[1]

The Ó Dálaighs Bid Farewell to the Great Blasket

Tom and Paddy, sons of Paddy na hInise, spent their whole life on the Great Blasket until they left in 1953. The early death of their mother at twenty-eight was a great blow to them. Henceforth they would spend much time on the Inis with their father, far from the company of neighbours. It left them quiet and a little private in themselves, and neither of them married, though Paddy was very friendly with the schoolmistress on the island, Nóra Ní Shé, who was from the parish of Moore some dozen miles from Dunquin. They didn't attend school much, and they were old enough even when they received their confirmation. Nóra had actually taught the two brothers, though there was little between their ages.

> Nóra, who wrote her own account of her life as teacher on the Blasket, doesn't directly refer to Paddy Beag in her book, nor is there any mention of love between them. Or is there? Perhaps if we read between the lines: "There are no days that raised my heart more, there are no days that I love more to remember than the joyful and happy days that I spent on the gentle banks of Inisvickillane, and on the wild stack of the Tiaracht."[2]

And again: "I enjoyed the day I spent on the Tiaracht and Inisvickillane. I was as happy and content sitting back in the end of the *naomhóg* in the evening as if I were returning from the city of London. Let God not compare the two places."[3]

It seems that the romantic age hadn't arrived yet and this was similar to Tomás Ó Criomhthain and Cáit Ní Dhálaigh's life some fifty years previously. It was rumoured also that Tom, the brother, was very friendly with Neilí Sheáin Lís Ní Shúilleabháin, the writer Muiris's sister, but marriage was out of the question in view of the fact that they were closely related.

They had the natural learning. Tom was very good on the fiddle, and Paddy was a fine musician as well. Tom held the fiddle against his chest rather than under his chin, a style that seems to have originated with the old home-made fiddles, on account of their being heavier than the usual ones. Paddy played the flute and the Jew's harp and could be full of fun and sport. Both were great fishermen and strong, hardy men, heavily built, but not tall. They were very good with their hands and highly thought of in the building of *naomhógs*. In the late thirties and forties, it was in the old house of the Sullivans, the home of Muiris the writer, that they built them. The house was empty by that stage and the Sullivans either scattered or were dead and buried.

Tom and Paddy continued going in to the Inis from Monday to Saturday during the fishing season. They would always shrink from the limelight, even when it became fashionable to make television programmes on the Island people. Maria Simonds-Gooding remembers a visit she paid to the Inis:

On one visit–I must have been staying in a tent, because Tom and Paddy were in their house–Éamon de Buitléar and Pat Hayes arrived. Charlie had asked Éamon to erect his tent as he was going to arrive later. When Éamon was coming down in the helicopter, Tom and Paddy were tarring the roof with the brush. They said they were going over to the south side to shear their sheep. Éamon asked if he could go over later and film them. When Éamon came with his camera, they literally leapt over the wall and hid rather than be filmed.[4]

The Ó Dálaighs were very reluctant to leave the Blasket, and when they did leave, Tom and Paddy the father came out first and Paddy the son remained until December 1953. They settled down in one of the four houses that the County Council had made available for them in Baile na Rátha beside the school. It was there that I got to know them when I arrived to teach in Dunquin School in the autumn of 1970. I would see them heading for the hill up the Clasach to bring home the turf with the donkey and panniers, or looking in at the Blasket or the Inis through the telescope on a sunny evening, or sowing potatoes on a spring day. I would also see them at their work building *naomhógs* in the long hut outside. As Danny Mac Síthigh mentions in *Fan Inti:*

Tom and Peaidí used to build their *naomhógs* in a low stone, felt-roofed shed beside the dwelling house in Baile Na Rátha. They would be in no hurry at their work; they would spend time at it. They were highly trained and knowledgeable as boat builders. They were skilled in every way, and there were very few things they could not accomplish with their two hands. Tom could make a fiddle, make a model of a little *naomhóg*, execute a piece of sculpture on a flagstone or beat out a ring from a piece of bright metal. They were outstanding in the making of a four-oared *naomhóg* and I would place them on top of all in the peninsula in the making of them.
They could not be beaten.[5]

Incidentally, it was Tomás Ó Dálaigh who made the *naomhóg* in which Danny Sheehy and Ger Ó Ciobháin (Kavanagh) from Gorta Dubha rowed around the coast of Ireland in the summer of 1975. The complete account of that memorable voyage can be read in Ger's book, *Cogarnach Ár gCósta*, published by Cló Dhuibhne.

There are examples of the Dálaigh craftwork still in their old home, in Baile na Rátha, Dunquin, now the home of Ed Barrett and his wife, Jennie Shields, from Boston. Included are:

> A wall mirror. A small rectangular mirror, with a fishing frame surround with a further frame superimposed on the first.
>
> Lantern: Made from wood with glass sides, and a door which can be opened to insert a candle. It has a small chimney on top to release the smoke, and a handle to hold. It had the advantage of being able to be used both inside and outside. It could be used to show light when out tending the sheep and for hunting rabbits and birds at night. One of the families in the States had such a lantern, probably made there, and they still use it on special occasions like Christmas and birthdays.
>
> Table. Made from red deal, probably sea wrack.
>
> Settle bed. Made also from red deal as above, ornamented with knobs on the sides.
>
> Four oars.
>
> Two beds, called *tester beds*, also of red deal, built up on three sides to give protection from the breeze to the sleeper.[6]

We do not know which of the family made them, since they were all good carpenters. Tom was very skilled in making those small models of *naomhógs*, exact replicas of the original, and there are a number of them around still. He also made models of the "kittiwakes," bigger fishing boats. He could also make the *Claddagh rings*, with the heart clasped by the two hands, from a half-crown, with no tools except a nail and little hammer.

They remained shy of publicity. They were seabirds that could not be happy on land. I don't think they ever spoke on Raidió na Gaeltachta, but RTÉ did succeed in making a programme on the three of them–Paddy, Tom and Muiris (Deálaí)–on the Inis in 1973. They were speaking to Doireann Ní Bhriain, who lived for a year or more in Baile Bhiocáire close by and got to know them well.

Feargal Mac Amhlaoibh, who knew them well, says they were never in dull form. Like many of the Islanders they had a great fear of ghosts. Peig Sayers got the blame for that. She used to spend the nights telling ghost stories and was a master at the art, so much so that they became a reality on the Island.

An American cousin, Dolores Quinn, granddaughter of Maurice from

Chicago, came to visit them in 1986. She really wanted to meet the descendants of the Ó Dálaigh who had stayed at home, and reforge the links. But that wasn't too easy at the beginning.

"They eventually agreed to meet with her after many requests in 1986, and Tom gave her a 3ft. replica of a currach–one of her big highlights."[7]

The father, Pádraig Ó Dálaigh, Paddy Mhaurice or Paddy na hInise, died on 15 November 1963 and is buried in Teampall Dhuinín, the old graveyard in Dunquin.

Paddy, or Paddy Beag, the son, was born in 1908 and died on 25 January 1982, aged 74. Paddy Beag and Tom had been building a *naomhóg* in the long shed. The body had been completed and all that remained was to cover it with the canvas. Then Paddy died unexpectedly. The *naomhóg* remained unfinished. Tom would not lay another hand on it. It remained so until Tom himself died. Then the family presented the unfinished *naomhóg* to the Blasket Island Heritage Centre where it still remains on show.

Tom was born on 20 December 1907 and died on 20 July 1989, aged 82.

You would never see a puffin on the mainland. They stay near the Islands, and in particular around Inisvickillane. The story in Tigh Kruger after Tom's funeral was that a puffin had flown out from the Inis to Dunquin as far as Tom's house on the day he died. It circled the house three times and then flew back home to the Inis.

It knew it was the end of an era.

The third brother, Muiris (Deálaí), was born in January 1910 on the Island and was baptised on the tenth day of that month. He was still a young child when his mother died. His father, Paddy, sent him over to his aunt, Nóra, in Clogher, and it was here that he was reared.

He became a fisherman while still young, sailing from Cuas na Nao in Clogher. He also became a skilled builder and a well-known musician. He had the music from the two sides; the de hÓras (Hoares) were also known as good musicians and singers. Clogher was a well-known village for music, and all could be heard singing at the time of milking. Muiris, or Deálaí, as he was usually called, played the button accordion.

"There's no one as good as Deálaí," people would say, the best musician to play for sets.

He was well-known as a singer too with "*An Baile atá Lámh léi siúd*," a song of emigration composed by An Spailpín, Séamus Ó Muircheartaigh (Moriarty), from Ard na Caithne. He was in great demand for dance music, very measured and suitable for dances. There are some tunes named after him like "*Port Dálaigh*" and "*Rogha Dhálaigh.*" He could often be found in the local pubs, at house dances and *ball nights*.

Nóra, or Narrie na hInise, had a daughter Lisa, a first cousin to Muiris, who had married Paddy Mitchell of Ceathrú, Dunquin. Paddy died young in the year 1959, and Muiris spent a time living with Lisa and helping when her husband was failing and again after his death. It was while there that he got to know a local girl, Neil Ní Chonchubhair (Connor), also from Ceathrú. They married in 1958 and lived at Baile na Rátha, Dunquin.

Muiris was the only one of the three brothers that married.

Deálaí and Neil had three daughters, Eilís, Máire and Nóra. I taught them in Dunquin School.

Neil died in 1982. Muiris died 4 October 1990. He was 80.

He had a fine traditional funeral, with music, song and dance, as he richly deserved.

The three brothers and Neil are buried in Dunquin graveyard awaiting the resurrection.

Sources and Booklist

Armstrong, E.C.R. "Stone Chalices, so called," *Proceedings of the Royal Irish Academy*, vol. XXVI, section C. Dublin: Hodges, Figgis and Co., 1906–1907.

B 30. Cartlann na Gaeilge, Roinn na Nua-Ghaeilge, University College Dublin.

Barrington, Richard Manliffe. "Report on the Flora of the Blasket Islands, Co. Kerry," *Proceedings of the Royal Irish Academy*, vol. III, Science, Dublin, 1883.

Barrington, T.J. *Discovering Kerry*, Dublin: Blackwater Press, 1976.

Brick, Tom. *Memoirs of an Emigrant to USA, Spring, 1902*. Private papers. Typed copy, 1970.

Census of Ireland, 1901 and 1911. Thanks to Leslie Matson who made a study of it.

Crane, C.P. *Memories of a Resident Magistrate*. London: Constable, 1938.

Creedon, Ted. "Blaskets' Grey Seal Colony Recovering after Cull," *The Kerryman*, 24 November 2005.

Cuppage, Judith, ed. *Suirbhé Seandálaíochta Chorca Dhuibhne*. Ballyferriter: Oidhreacht Chorca Dhuibhne, 1986.

de Brún, Pádraig. "John Windele and Father Casey," *Journal of the Kerry Archaeological and Historical Society*, no. 7, 1974. Also "A Census of the Parish of Ferriter, January 1835."

Dornan, Brian. *The Inishkeas, Mayo's Lost Islands*. Dublin, Four Courts Press, 2000.

Flower, Robin. *The Western Island*. Oxford: Oxford University Press, 1985 (first published 1944).

Flower, Robin, trans. *The Islandman*. See O'Crohan.

Foley, Patrick.: *The Ancient and Present State of the Skelligs, Blasket Islands, Donquin and the West of Dingle . . .* Dublin: 1903.

Foley, Patrick. *The History of the County Kerry*. 1907.

Hamlin, Ann and Hughes, Kathleen. *The Modern Traveller to the Early Irish Church*. Dublin: Four Courts Press, 1977, reprint, 2004.

Hayden, Tom and Harrington, Rory. *Exploring Irish Mammals*. Dublin: Dúchas, Town House, 2000, 2nd ed. 2001.

Í Chearnaigh, Seán Sheáin. *An tOileán a Tréigeadh*. Dublin: Sairséal agus Dill, 1974.

Í Chearnaigh, Seán Sheáin. *Iarbhlascaodach ina Dheoraí*. Dublin: Sáirséal agus Dill, 1978.

Irish Folklore Commission, now Department of Folklore, UCD, collections.

Jennings, Stanley. *An Blascaod Mór*, in Ó Conaire, Breandán, ed. *Tomás an Bhlascaoid*. Indreabhán, Conamara: Chó-Iar Chonnachta, 1992.

Lewis, Samuel. *Topographical Dictionary of Ireland*. London: S. Lewis, 1837.

Lockely, R.M.; Lucas, James, illus. *I Know an Island*. London: George G. Harrap & Co. Ltd., 1938. Reprinted 1948.

Lockley, R.M. *The Private Life of the Rabbit: An Account of the Life, History and Social Behaviour of the Wild Rabbit*. London: André Deutsch, 1964.

Mac Airt, Seán, ed. *Annals of Inisfallen*. Dublin: Institute for Advanced Studies, 1951.

Mac Cárthaigh, Criostóir and O'Reilly, Barry. "The Great Blasket Village," *History and Architecture*, 1991. Survey in Great Blasket Centre, Dunquin.

Mac Conghail, Muiris. *The Blaskets–A Kerry Island Library*. Dublin: Country House, 1987.

Mac Mathúna, Ciarán: Programme RTÉ, *Mo Cheol Thú*. On Inisvickillane, featuring Seán Cheaist Ó Catháin, Déirdre Mac Mathúna, Tommy Peoples, Seán Ó Riada and Ceoltóirí Chualann, and speakers, Eugene O'Malley, Charles J. Haughey, Pádraig Ua Maoileoin and Séamus Forde. Broadcast, 1987.

Mac Síthigh, Domhnall (Danny Sheehy). *Fan Inti, Naomhóga ó Chorca Dhuibhne go Cabán tSíle*. Dublin: Coiscéim, 2003.

Mac Síthigh, Tomás. *Paróiste an Fheirtéaraigh, Stairsheanchas an Cheantair i dtréimhse an Ghorta Mhóir*. Dublin: Coiscéim, 1984.

Matson, Leslie. *Méiní: The Blasket Nurse*. Cork: Mercier Press, 1996.

Matson, Leslie. *Blasket Lives: Biographical Accounts of One Hundred and Twenty Five Blasket People*. Research presented on floppy disc, 2005, not published yet.

Mhac an tSaoi, Máire. "*An tOileánach* by Tomás Ó Criomhthain (1856–1937)," in Jordan, John, ed. *The Pleasures of Gaelic Literature*. Cork: Mercier Press, 1977.

Moore, Michael J. "Irish Cresset-Stones," *Journal of the Royal Society of Antiquaries of Ireland*, vol. 114, 1984.

Morrissey, James, ed. *On the Verge of Want*. Dublin: Crannóg Books, 2001. A unique insight into living conditions along Ireland's western seaboard in the late nineteenth century.

Ní Aimhirgín, Nuala. *Muiris Ó Súilleabháin*. Maynooth: An Sagart, 1983.

Ní Ghaoithín, Máire. *An tOileán a Bhí*. Dublin: An Clóchomhar Tta., 1978.

Ní Ghuithín, Máire. *Bean an Oileáin*. Dublin: Coiscéim, 1986.

Ní Shúilleabháin, Eibhlín and Ní Loingsigh, Máiréad, eds. *Cín Lae Eibhlín Ní Shúilleabháin*. Dublin: Coiscéim, 2000.

Ní Shúilleabháin, Eibhlís. *Letters from the Great Blasket* Dublin and Cork, Mercier Press, 1978, reprint 1979.

Ó Bric, Muiris. *Spotsholas na nDaoine*. Dublin: Coiscéim, 1995.

Ó Catháin, Seán Faeilí. *Seal le Faeilí*. Baile Átha Cliath: Coiscéim, 1989.

Ó Caoimh, Tomás. "*Mocheallóc Mac Uibhleáin of the Corco Dhuibhne*," in *Tuosist 6000*, Tuosist History and Newsletter Committee, Lárach, Co. Kerry, 1999.

Ó Catháin, Muiris. *Ar Muir is ar Tír*. Maynooth: An Sagart, 1991.

Ó Cinnéide, Seán. "*Logainmneacha*," *An Caomhnóir*, no. 26, December 2005.

Ó Cinnéide, Seán. *"Logainmneacha"*; Uí Ógáin, Ríonach, *"Ceol, Rince agus Amhráin,"* in Ó Muircheartaigh, Aogán, ed. *Oidhreacht an Bhlascaoid.* Dublin: Coiscéim, 1989.

Ó Ciosáin, Mícheál, ed. *Céad Bliain, 1871–1971.* Ballyferriter: Muintir Phiarais, 1971. Reprinted 2006.

O'Clery, Michael. *The Dingle Peninsula Bird Report 2002–2004.* Corca Dhuibhne Branch, BirdWatch Ireland, 2005.

Ó Coileáin, Seán. *"An tOileánach: Ón Láimh go dtí an Leabhar"* in Ní Chéilleachair, Máire, ed. *Ceiliúradh an Bhlascaoid, 2. Tomás Ó Criomhthain 1855–1937.* Dingle: An Sagart, 1998.

Ó Conaire, Breandán, ed. *Tomás an Bhlascaoid.* Indreabhán, Conamara: Cló Iar-Chonnachta, 1992.

Ó Criomhthain, Seán, *"Báfar Mé"* and Ó Criomhthain, Tomás, *"[An Mórdhach] Ón mBlascaod"* in Ó Criomhthain, Seán and Tomás; Ó Fiannachta, Pádraig, ed. *Cleití Gé ón mBlascaod Mór.* Dingle: An Sagart, 1997.

Ó Criomhthain, Tomás. *Allagar na hInise.* First printing 1928. New edition edited by Pádraig Ua Maoileoin, Dublin: Government Stationery Office, 1977.

Ó Criomhthain, Tomás and Ua Maoileoin, Pádraig, ed. *Allagar II.* Dublin: Coiscéim, 1999.

Ó Criomhthain, Tomás; Ó Conaire, Breandán, ed. *Bloghanna ón mBlascaod,* Dublin: Coiscéim, 1997.

Ó Criomhthain, Tomás; Nic Pháidín, Caoilfhionn, ed. *Dinnseanchas na mBlascaod.* Dublin: Cois Life, 1935; reprint 1999.

Ó Criomhthain, Tomás; Ua Maoileoin, Pádraig, ed. *An tOileánach.* Dublin: Talbot Press, 1973.

Ó Criomhthain, Tomás; Ó Coileáin, Seán, ed. *An tOileánach.* Dublin: Talbot Press, 2002.

Ó Criomhthain, Tomás and Mac Congáil, Nollaig, ed. *Scéilíní ón mBlascaod agus Blúirín as "Cín Lae Eibhlín Ní Shúilleabháin."* Dublin: Coiscéim, 2004.

Ó Criomhthain, Tomás; Ó Duillearga, Séamus, ed. *Seanchas ón Oileán Tiar.* Dublin: The Folklore of Ireland Society, 1956.

Ó Cróinín, Seán and Ó Cróinín, Donncha. *Seanachas Ó Chairbre I.* Dublin: The Folklore of Ireland Council, 1985.

O'Crohan, Tomás; Flower, Robin, trans. *The Islandman.* Dublin and Cork: Talbot Press, 1937. Oxford: Oxford University Press, 1951, reissued, 2000.

Ó Dálaigh, Pádraig: *A Chara Uasail.* Great Blasket, Dunquin, 29 August 1933. Ó Dálaigh papers. Not published. With kind permission of Eilís Ní Dhálaigh (Bean Uí Chéileachair), Dunquin.

Ó Dálaigh, Seán ("the Common Noun"). *Clocha Sgáil.* Dublin: Muintir Fhallamháin/ Government Publications Office, 1930.

Ó Dálaigh, Seán ("the Common Noun"). *Timcheall Chinn Sléibhe,* Dublin: Government Publications Office, second printing 1937.

Ó Danachair, Caoimhín. "Holy Wells of Corcaguiney, Co. Kerry," *Journal of the Royal Society of Antiquaries of Ireland,* vol. XC, part I, 1960.

Ó Dubhda, Seán. *"Meascra ó Chorca Dhuibhne,"* Béaloideas, The Journal of the Folklore of Ireland Society, vol. XXXI, 1963.

Ó Dubhshláine, Mícheál. *An Baol Dom Tú? Muintir Chorca Dhuibhne agus an Ghaeilge.* Dublin: Conradh na Gaeilge, 2000.

Ó Dubhshláine, Mícheál. *Óigbhean Uasal ó Phríomhchathair Éireann.* Dublin: Conradh na Gaeilge, 1992.

Ó Dubhshláine, Mícheál. *A Dark Day on the Blaskets.* Dingle: Brandon Press, 2003.

Ó Fiannachta, Pádraig, ed. *Irisleabhar Mhá Nuad 1985.* Maynooth, An Sagart.

Ó Gaoithín, Mícheál. *Is Trua ná Fanann an Óige.* Dublin: Government Publications Office, 1953.

Ó Guithín, Mícheál. *Beatha Pheig Sayers,* Dublin: F.N.T. 1970.

Ó Háinle, Cathal. *"Tomás Ó Criomhthain agus Caisleán Uí Néill"* in Ó Fiannachta, Pádraig, ed. *Irisleabhar Mhá Nuad 1985.* Maynooth: An Sagart.

O'Hanlon, Canon John. *Lives of Irish Saints.* Dublin: James Duffy, 1875.

Ó hÓgáin, Dáithí. *An File.* Dublin: Government Stationery Office: 1979, 1982.

O'Leary, Paddy and Snodgrass, Lee. "Archaeological Survey of the Blasket Islands, Co. Kerry, A Preliminary Report–1976." Private.

Ó Rahilly, T.F. *"Notes on Irish Placenames,"* in *Hermathena* vol. 48, 1933.

O'Shea, Kieran. *The Diocese of Kerry, Formerly Ardfert: Working in the Fields of God.* Strasbourg: Éditions de Signe, 2005.

Ó Siochfhradha, Pádraig *(An Seabhac). Triocha-céad Chorca Dhuibhne.* Dublin: Comhlucht Oideachais na hÉireann, Teor for the Folklore of Ireland Council, 1939.

Ó Súilleabháin, Muiris. *Fiche Bliain ag Fás.* Maynooth: An Sagart, 1976, second edition; first edition 1933.

O'Sullivan, T.F. *Romantic Hidden Kerry.* Tralee: *The Kerryman,* 1931.

O'Toole, Edward. *Whist for Your Life, That's Treason:Recollections of a Long Life.* Dublin: Ashfield Press, 2003.

Quinn, Dolores A. *Island Heritage, The Daly and Guiheen Families.* Twin Lakes, WI, USA, 1997. Privately published.

Rhys, John. "Notes on the ogham-inscribed stones of Donaghmore, Co. Kildare, and Inisvickillane, Co. Kerry," *Journal of the Royal Society of Antiquaries of Ireland,* series V, vol. XXXIII, 1903.

Ryan, Seán. *"The Red Deer of Killarney on Inishvicillaun,"* appendix III, *The Wild Red Deer of Killarney.* Dingle: Mount Eagle, 1998.

Sayers, Peig; Ní Mhainín, Máire agus Ó Murchú, Liam P., eds. *Peig, A Scéal Féin,* Dingle: An Sagart, 1998.

Smith, Charles. *The Ancient and Present State of the County of Kerry.* London, 1756.

Stagles, Joan and Ray. *The Blasket Islands, Next Parish America.* Dublin: O'Brien Press, 1980.

Stagles, Joan. "Nineteenth-Century Settlements in the Lesser Blasket Islands," *Journal of Kerry Archaeologican and Historical Society,* no. 8, 1975.

Synge, John M. *John M. Synge in West Kerry.* Dublin and Cork, The Mercier Press. 1979.

Thomas, Leslie. *Ghosts in the Sun.* London: Arlington Books, 1968.

Tyers, Pádraig, ed. *Leoithne Aniar.* Ballyferriter: Cló Dhuibhne, 1982.

Ua Maoileoin, Pádraig. *Ár Leithéidí Arís.* Dublin: Clódhanna Teoranta, 1978.

Uí Bheaglaoí, Cáit. *Craobh Ghinealaigh na mBlascaod.* Copy in Ionad an Bhlascaoid.

Uí Chonchubhair, Máirín. *Flora Chorca Dhuibhne, Aspects of the Flora of Corca Dhuibhne.* Ballyferriter: Oidhreacht Chorca Dhuibhne, 1995.

Uí Dhubhshláine, Áine and Kirby, Ruairí. *Fístéip na hIdirbhliana, Bealtaine/* television programme, Dingle, Christian Brothers' School, 2002–03.

Viney, Michael. "The Wild Island," *The Irish Times,* 13, 14, 15 September 1965.

White Marshall, Jenny and Walsh, Claire. *Illaunloghan Island.* Bray: Wordwell, 2005.

Acknowledgements

I would like to extend a special thanks to my old companion, Muiris Mhaidhc Léan Ó Guithín, of Inis stock, who has always most generously shared his memories and information with me. I would also like to thank the many others who helped me in so many ways, particularly the following:

Danny Sheehy

Tom Neilí Ó Mainín

Cáit Feiritéar (An Bhab), RIP 8 June 2005

Seán Mhaidhc Léan Ó Guithín, RIP

Charles J. Haughey, RIP and his wife, Máirín

Marie Sheehan, Dublin

Maire Mhaidhc Léan Ní Ghuithín, Bean Labhrás Uí Chiobháin, RIP

Roibeárd Ó Cathasaigh, Coláiste Mhuire gan Smál, Luimneach

Maria Simonds-Gooding

Colm Ó Bric, Dún Chaoin

Lís Ní Dhálaigh, Bean Uí Chéileachair

Máire Áine Ní Dhálaigh, Baile na Rátha, Dún Chaoin

Nóra Ní Dhálaigh, Bean Mhuiris Uí Mhurchú, Baile an Fheirtéaraigh

An Dochtúir Breandán Ó Ciobháin, Ventry

Seán Ó Ciobháin (Touí), An Ghráig

Mícheál de Mórdha, Ruth Ní Longáin Uí Ógáin, Donncha Ó Conchúir
    and Dáithí de Mórdha, Great Blasket Centre, Dunquin

Tomás Ó Dálaigh, Tom na hInise, RIP

Pádraig Ó Dálaigh, Paddy Beag, RIP

Muiris Ó Dálaigh (Deálaí), RIP

Tomás Ó Dálaigh, Coumeenole, RIP 2004

Ray Stagles, Wokingham, England

Leslie Matson, Waterford

Seán Ó Ceallaigh, Dublin, of Guithín stock

Brother Mícheál Ó Catháin, Dún Laoghaire, Dublin

Éamonn de Brún agus Pádraigín Ní Laoire, County library, Tralee

Cáit Uí Mhurchú, RIP, and Niamh Doyle, Dingle library

Jill agus Ian Crosher, Ballyferriter

Patty Haimerl, Debendorf, Germany, of Daly stock
Breandán Mac Gearailt, Márthain
Frances Uí Chinnéide, Dún Chaoin
Suzanne Mooney, Dingle
Seán de Lóndra, An tSeantóir, Dún Chaoin, RIP
Dr Seosamh Ó Dálaigh, Dún Chaoin, RIP
Páidí Curran, Dingle, RIP 11 August 2005
Eibhlín Bn. Uí Chathaláin, Springfield, Mass. (Eibhlín Pheats Tom), Blasket Islander, RIP
Thomas Moore (Tommy Tom Devin), Springfield, Mass.
Máire Bean Uí Shíthigh (Máire Ní Scanláin), Baile Eaglaise
Larry Slattery, Dún Chaoin
Simon Ó Faoláin, Ballyferriter
Seán Mac an tSíthigh, Baile Eaglaise
Eibhlín Bean Uí Shé, An Cheathrú (Eibhlín Lynch)
Máirín Ní Dhálaigh, Potadóireacht Dhún Chaoin, Baile an Teampaill
Cáit Uí Bheaglaoí
Tom Fitzgerald, ex-Senator, Dingle
Dolores Quinn, RIP, of Daly stock
Fr Tomás Ó hIceadha, Ballyferriter
Cristóir Mac Cárthaigh, and Ríonach Uí Ógáin, Roinn Béaloideas Éireann, University College, Dublin
Dr Bo Almquist
Ed Barrett and Jennie Shields, Baile na Rátha and Boston
Dr Conchúir Ó Brosnacháin, Dingle
Fr Tomás Ó Caoimh, Tralee
Isabella Mulhall, The National Museum, Dublin
Fr Eoghan Ó hEochaidh, Inchicore, Dublin
Feargal and Áine Mac Amhlaoibh
Isabel Uí Uallacháin, Oidhreacht Chorca Dhuibhne
Terri Peterson, Missouri, of Daly stock
Seán Ó Braonáin, Dún Chaoin and Dublin
Transition year students of Meánscoil na mBráithre Críostaí and Meánscoil Na Toirbhirte, 2002–2003 for their DVD, *Scannánaíocht na nÓg*

Notes

Notes to Chapter I

1 Tom Daly, Coumeenole, RIP, from (*An File*) Mícheál Ó Gaoithín.
2 Tomás Ó Criomhthain, Caoilfhionn Nic Pháidín (ed.), *Dinnseanchas na mBlascaodaí* (Dublin: Cois Life, 1999); Introduction by Tomás Ó Criomhthain (1935).
3 Máire Ní Ghuithín, *An tOileán a Bhí* (Dublin: An Clóchomhar, 1978), p. 83.
4 Dr. R.P. McCabe. An account from McCabe, Delaney and Associates, Consulting Civil and Structural Engineers.
5 Seán Ó Cinnéide, Aogán Ó Muircheartaigh (ed.), *Oidhreacht an Bhlascaoid* (Dublin: Coiscéim, 1989), p. 128.
6 Pádraig Ó Siochfhradha *(An Seabhac)*, *Triocha-céad Chorca Dhuibhne* (Dublin: Comhlucht Oideachais na hÉireann, Teo., The Irish Folklore Commission 1939), pp. 87–90.
7 Seán Ó Cinnéide in Aogán Ó Muircheartaigh (ed.), *Oidhreacht an Bhlascaoid*, p. 131.
8 *Ibid.*
9 Charles Smith, *The Ancient and Present State of the County of Kerry* (London: 1756), pp. 97, 98.
10 Dandno.
11 Pádraig Ó Siochfhradha *(An Seabhac)*, *Triocha-céad Chorca Dhuibhne* (Dublin: Comhlucht Oideachais na hÉireann, Teo., The Irish Folklore Commission 1939), p. 87.

Notes to Chapter II

1 Muiris Ó Catháin, *Ar Muir is ar Tír* (Maynooth: An Sagart, 1991), p. 51.
2 Tomás Ó Criomhthain, Caoilfhionn Nic Pháidín (ed.), *Dinnseanchas na mBlascaod* (Dublin: Cois Life, 1997), p. 60.
3 *Ibid.* p. 64.
4 *Ibid.*
5 *Ibid.*
6 *Ibid.* p. 58.
7 *Ibid.*
8 E.S.A. Baynes, *A Revised Catalogue of Irish Macrolepidopters*, 1964. Handwritten note in the book: "19 seen, 9 caught between 1961/64 on Inisvickilaun, H.C.H. [Henry Huggins]."

9   Seán Sheáin Í Chearnaigh, *Iarbhlascaodach ina Dheoraí* (Dublin: Sáirséal agus Dill, 1978), p. 116.

10   Seán Ó Cinnéide, Aogán Ó Muircheartaigh (ed.), *"Logainmneacha,"* *Oidhreacht an Bhlascaoid*, (Dublin: Coiscéim, 1989), p. 135.

11   Tomás Ó Criomhthain, *Dinnsheanchas na mBlascaodaí*, p. 59.

12   Seán Sheáin Í Chearnaigh, *Iarbhlascaodach ina Dheoraí*, pp. 112–13.

13   Tomás Ó Criomhthain, *Dinnsheanchas na mBlascaodaí*, p. 60.

14   C.P. Crane, *Memories of a Resident Magistrate* (London: Constable, 1938), p. 75.

15   Tomás Ó Criomhthain, *Dinnsheanchas na mBlascaodaí*, p. 55.

16   C. P. Crane, *Memories of a Resident Magistrate* (London: Constable, 1938), pp. 43–44.

17   Seán Ó Cinnéide, *Oidhreacht an Bhlascaoid*, pp. 136–37; *Feasta*, November 1985, February 1979 and February 1983.

18   Seán Sheáin Í Chearnaigh, *Iarbhlascaodach ina Dheoraí*, pp. 116–17.

19   Muiris Ó Súilleabháin, *Fiche Bliain ag Fás* (Maynooth: An Sagart, 1976, second edition; first edition 1933), p. 62.

20   Letter from George Thomson, 8 March 1983.

Notes to Chapter III

1   Máire Ní Ghaoithín, *An tOileán a Bhí* (Dublin: An Clóchomhar, 1978), p. 83.

2   Charles Smith, *The Ancient and Present State of the County of Kerry* (London: 1756), p. 98.

3   T.J. Barrington, *Discovering Kerry* (Dublin: Blackwater Press, 1976), p. 32.

4   G.V. Du Noyer, RSAI, *Antiq. Handbook Series* vi, 1905, p.115.

5   Peter Harbison, *Pilgrimage in Ireland: The Monuments and the People* (London: Barrue & Jenkins, 1991).

6   Kieran O'Shea, *The Diocese of Kerry, formerly Ardfert: Working in the Fields of God* (Strasbourg: Éditions de Signe, 2005), p. 8.

7   T.F. O'Sullivan, *Romantic Hidden Kerry* (Tralee: *The Kerryman*, 1931), p. 581.

8   *Journal of the Royal Society of Antiquaries of Ireland*, March 1903, pp. 79–87.

9   *Ibid.*

10   Patrick Foley, *The Ancient and Present State of the Skelligs, Blasket Islands, Donquin and the West of Dingle . . .* (Dublin: 1903), pp. 83–87.

11   Information: Charles J. Haughey.

12   *Ibid.*

13   Charles Smith, *Ancient and Present State*, p. 98.
14   T.F. O'Sullivan, *Romantic Hidden Kerry*, p. 580.
15   Charles Smith, *Ancient and Present State*, p. 98.
16   John Ganley. Field notes.
17   W.F. Wakeman, *Catalogue of the Petrie Collection*, vol. II, 1867.
18   E.C.R. Armstrong, *Proceedings of the Royal Irish Academy*, vol. XXVI, 1906–07, p. 322; Michael J. Moore, "Irish Cresset-Stones," in *Journal of the Royal Society of Antiquaries of Ireland*, vol. 114, 1984, pp. 98–116.
19   R.A.S. Macalister, *Corpus Insularum Inscriptionum Celticarum* (Dublin: 1945).
20   John Ganley. Field notes.
21   Caoimhín Ó Danachair, "Holy Wells of Corcaguiney, Co. Kerry," *Journal of the Royal Society of Antiquaries of Ireland*, vol. XC, 1960, cui 1.
22   Jenny Marshall and Claire Walsh (eds.), *Illaunloughan Island: An Early Medieval Monastery in County Kerry* (Dublin: Wordwell, 2005), pp. 46–53.
23   Pádraig Ó Dálaigh, *A Chara Uasail*, Ó Dálaigh papers. Not published.

Notes to Chapter IV
1   David Dickson, *Old World Colony: Cork and South Munster 1630–1830* (Cork: Cork University Press, 2005), p. 65.
2   Breandán Ó Conaire (ed.), *Tomás an Bhlascaoid* (Inverin, Connemara: Cló Iar-Chonnachta, 1992), p. 20; *Calendar of the Orrery Papers*, pp. 53–64. These accounts are written in letters which Orrery sent to his friend John Kemp from Dingle dated 20 August 1735. It is likely that Edward is a son of Piaras Firtéar.
3   Charles Smith, *The Ancient and Present State of the County Kerry* (London: 1756), p. 97.
4   *Tralee Chronicle*, 11 September 1847.
5   Sir Ralph Payne-Gallway, *The Fowler in Ireland* (London: 1882), p. 288.
6   *Journal of the Kerry Archaeological and Historical Society*, no. 7, 1974. p. 52.
7   Joan Stagles, "Nineteenth-Century Settlements in the Lesser Blasket Islands," in *Journal of the Kerry Archaeological and Historical Society*, no. 8, 1975, p. 79.
8   Tomás Ó Criomhthain, Caoilfhionn Nic Pháidín (ed.), *Dinnseanchas na mBlascaodaí* (Dublin: Cois Life, 1999), p. 55.

9   Baptismal Register, Ballyferriter.
10 Seán Sheáin Í Chearnaigh, Irish Folklore Commission, vol. 1406, pp. 43–44.
11 Letter from George Thompson to Charles J. Haughey, 22 May 1983.
12 Muiris Ó Súilleabháin, *Fiche Blian ag Fás* (Maynooth: An Sagart, 1976, second edition; first edition 1933), p. 105.
13 Robin Flower, *The Western Island* (Oxford: Oxford University Press, 1985), p. 121. (First published 1944.)
14 Tomás Ó Criomhthain, *An Lóchrann* (October 1931), p. 7.
15 Breandán Ó Conaire (ed.), *Tomás an Bhlascaoid* (Inverin, Connemara: Cló Iar-Chonnachta, 1992), p. 20; *Calendar of the Orrery Papers,* pp. 53–64.
16 *Ibid.*

Notes to Chapter V
1   Charles Smith, *The Ancient and Present State of the County of Kerry* (London: 1756), pp. 255–56.
2   Tomás Ó Criomhthain, Séamus Ó Duilearga (eds.), *Seanchas ón Oileán Tiar* (Dublin: Irish Folklore Commission, 1956), p. 184.
3   Pádraig Tyers, *Leoithne Aniar* (Ballyferriter: Oidhreacht Chorca Dhuibhne, 1982), p. 10.
4   *Ibid.*
5   Máire Ní Ghaoithín, *An tOileán a Bhí* (Dublin: An Clóchomhar, 1978), pp. 83–84.
6   *Proceedings of the Royal Irish Academy,* vol. 8, 1861–64; and T.F. O'Sullivan, *Romantic Hidden Kerry* (Tralee: *The Kerryman,* 1931), p. 582.
7   Tomás Ó Criomhthain, Seán Ó Coileáin (eds.), *An tOileánach* (Dublin: Talbot Press, 2002), pp. 88–89.
8   *Ibid.,* p. 92.
9   *Ibid.,* p. 93.
10 Máire Ní Ghaoithín, *An tOileán a Bhí* (Dublin: An Clóchomhar, 1978), p. 83.
11 Tomás Ó Criomhthain, Séamus Ó Duilearga (eds.), *Seanchas ón Oileán Tiar* (Dublin: Irish Folklore Commission, 1956), pp. 187–88.
12 *Ibid.,* pp 188–89.
13 Dáithí Ó hÓgáin, *An File* (Dublin: Oifig an tSoláthair, 1982), p. 301.
14 Information: Muiris Mhaidhc Léan Ó Guithín.
15 Tomás Ó Criomhthain, Séamus Ó Duilearga (ed.), *Seanchas ón Oileán Tiar* (Dublin: Irish Folklore Commission, 1956), p. 189.

16   Pádraig Tyers, *Leoithne Aniar* (Ballyferriter: Oidhreacht Chorca Dhuibhne, 1982), pp. 12–13.

Notes to Chapter VI

1   Peig Sayers, Ní Mhainín/Ó Murchú (ed.), *Peig, A Scéal Féin* (Dingle: An Sagart, 1998).
2   Mícheál Ó Dubhshláine, *An Baol Dom Tú? Muintir Chorca Dhuibhne agus an Ghaeilge* (Dublin: Conradh na Gaeilge, 2000).
3   Mícheál Ó Ciosáin (ed.), *"Cuimhne na Sean ar Thógáil na Séipéal, Seosamh Ó Dálaigh, Séipéal Dhún Chaoin," Céad Bliain*, 1871–1971 (Muintir Phiarais, 1971. Reprint 2006), pp. 253–56.
4   Building no. 19 (OPW). The Great Blasket Village.
5   Tomás Ó Criomhthain, Nollaig Mac Congail (ed.), *"Inis Uaigneach na Mara," Scéilíní ón mBlascaod agus Blúirín as "Cín Lae Eibhlín Ní Shúilleabháin"* (Dublin: Coiscéim, 2004), p. 62.
6   *Tralee Chronicle,* 10 May 1870.
7   *Ibid.*, 20 May 1870.
8   Pádraig Ó Dálaigh, *A Chara Uasail,* 29 August 1933, The Great Blasket, Dunquin. Ó Dálaigh papers.
9   *Liverpool Echo, Cork Examiner,* August 1866; *An Caomhnóir,* January 1990.
10   www.cil.ie/flat_areaEQLlighthousesAMPLighthouseIDEQL17 _entry.html
11   Pádraig Ó Dálaigh, *A Chara Uasail,* p. 12.
12   Seán Sheáin Í Chearnaigh, *Iarbhlascaodach ina Dheoraí* (Dublin: Sáirséal agus Dill, 1978), pp. 63–66.
13   Tomás Ó Criomhthain, Séamus Ó Duilearga (ed.), *Seanchas ón Oileán Tiar* (Dublin: Irish Folklore Commission, 1956), p. 185.
14   *Ibid.*, p. 189.
15   Tomás Ó Criomhthain, *Scéilíní,* p. 63.
16   R.M. Lockley, illustrations James Lucas, *I Know an Island* (London: George G. Harrap & Co. Ltd., 1938; reprint 1948), p. 116.
17   *Ibid.*, p. 113.
18   Tomás Ó Criomhthain, Seán Ó Coileáin (ed.), *An tOileánach* (Dublin: Talbot Press, 2002), p. 124.
19   Muiris Ó Dálaigh (Deálaí), 1990, speaking to the author.
20   Tomás Ó Criomhthain, Séamus Ó Duilearga (ed.), *Seanchas ón Oileán Tiar* (Dublin: Irish Folklore Commission, 1956), p. 190.
21   *Ibid.*, p. 185.

22 James Morrisey (ed.), *On the Verge of Want* (Dublin: Crannóg Books, 2001), p. 194.

23 *Ibid.*, p. 204.

24 T.J. Barrington, *Discovering Kerry* (Dublin: Blackwater Press, 1976), p. 92.

25 Tomás Ó Criomhthain, Séamus Ó Duilearga (ed.), *Seanchas ón Oileán Tiar* (Dublin: Irish Folklore Commission, 1956), p. 191.

26 Tomás Ó Criomhthain, *"Inis Uaigneach," Scéilíní*, p. 63.

27 Seán Ó Dálaigh ("the Common Noun"), *Timcheall Chinn Sléibhe* (Dublin: Government Publications Sales Office; second edition, 1937), pp. 49–55.

28 Tomás Ó Criomhthain, Seán Ó Coileáin (ed.), *An tOileánach* (Dublin: Talbot Press, 2002), p. 199.

29 *Ibid.*, p. 124.

30 *Ibid.*

31 Tomás Ó Criomhthain, *"Inis Uaigneach," Scéilíní*, p. 62.

32 Tomás Ó Criomhthain, Séamus Ó Duilearga (ed.), *Seanchas ón Oileán Tiar* (Dublin: Irish Folklore Commission, 1956), p. 185.

33 Maria Simonds-Gooding, "An Artist's Impression of the Blaskets, 'Máire Mhaith,'" *An Caomhnóir,* January 1990, p. 8.

34 Tomás Ó Criomhthain, Séamus Ó Duilearga (ed.), *Seanchas ón Oileán Tiar* (Dublin: Irish Folklore Commission, 1956), p. 195–96.

Notes to Chapter VII

1 Tomás Ó Criomhthain, Nollaig Mac Congáil (ed.), *Scéilíní ón mBlascaod agus Blúirín as "Cín Lae Eibhlín Ní Shúilleabháin"* (Dublin: Coiscéim, 2004), p. 63.

2 *Ibid.*, p. 63.

3 Tomás Ó Criomhthain, Seán Ó Coileáin (ed.), *An tOileánach* (Dublin: Talbot Press, 2002), p. 183.

4 *Ibid.*, pp. 124–25.

5 *Ibid.*, p. 127.

6 *Ibid.*

7 *Ibid.*, p. 129.

8 *Ibid.*, pp. 129–30.

9 *Ibid.*, p. 133.

10 Máire Ní Ghearailt (teacher), 22 August 1935, Corca Dhuibhne, Dunquin Parish, School: The Great Blasket, *Bailiúchán na Scol*, vol. 418, p. 209. And, *Beauty an Oileáin*, CD of music and song from the Blaskets, Céiríní Cladaigh, directed by Ríonach Uí Ógáin.

11   Pádraig Ua Maoileoin, *Ár Leithéidí Arís* (Dublin: Clódhanna Teo., 1978), pp. 5–6. Pádraig Ua Maoileoin from Maidhc Mhicil Ó Súilleabháin, Islander, Baile na Rátha, Dunquin.

12   Tomás Ó Criomhthain, Seán Ó Coileáin (ed.), *An tOileánach* (Dublin: Talbot Press, 2002), p. 134.

13   *Ibid.*, p. 135.

14   C.P. Crane, *Memories of a Resident Magistrate* (London: Constable, 1938), pp. 26–27.

15   Tomás Ó Criomhthain, Seán Ó Coileáin (ed.), *An tOileánach* (Dublin: Talbot Press, 2002), p. 135.

16   *Ibid.*, p. 137.

17   *Ibid.*, p. 137.

18   *Ibid.*, pp. 137–38.

19   *Ibid.*, p. 138.

20   *Ibid.*, p. 172.

21   *Ibid.*, p. 173.

22   *Ibid.*, p. 173.

23   *Ibid.*, p. 174.

24   I got this from Tom Neilí Ó Mainín, February 2005. See also, Tomás Mac Síthigh, *Paróiste an Fheirtéaraigh, Stairsheanchas an Cheantair i dTréimhse an Ghorta Mhóir* (Dublin: Coiscéim, 1984), pp. 128–29.

25   Tomás Ó Criomhthain, Seán Ó Coileáin (ed.), *An tOileánach* (Dublin: Talbot Press, 2002), pp. 174–75.

26   *Ibid.*, p. 175.

27   *Ibid.*, pp. 176–77.

28   *Ibid.*, p. 177.

29   *Ibid.*, p. 179.

30   *Ibid.*

31   *Ibid.*, pp. 179–80.

32   *Ibid.*, p. 183.

Notes to Chapter VIII

1   Tomás Ó Criomhthain, Seán Ó Coileáin (ed.), *An tOileánach* (Dublin: Talbot Press, 2002), p. 124.

2   Tomas O'Crohan, Robin Flower (trans.), *The Islandman* (Oxford: Oxford University Press, 1951), Foreword.

3   Tomás Ó Criomhthain, Seán Ó Coileáin (ed.), *An tOileánach* (Dublin: Talbot Press, 2002), pp. 125–26.

4   *Ibid.*

5   *Ibid.*, p. 186.

6   *Ibid.*, p. 187.

7   *An Sguab,* August, 1924, p. 162, from Seán Ó Criomhthain, the son of Tomás. *An tOileánach,* Seán Ó Coileáin, pp. 190, 191. Seán tells us he got the song from an old man but it is certain he got the song from his father. Also, *An Lóchrann,* July 1909, at "An Giolla Rua."

8   Tomás Ó Criomhthain, Seán Ó Coileáin (ed.), *An tOileánach* (Dublin: Talbot Press, 2002), p. 191.

9   John Jordan (ed.), *"An tOileánach," The Pleasures of Gaelic Literature* (Cork: Mercier Press, 1977), p. 36.

10   Máire Ní Chéilleachair (ed.), *"An tOileánach: ón láimh go dtí an leabhar," Ceiliúradh an Bhlascaoid, 2* (Dingle: An Sagart, 1998), p. 36. Statement from *An Seabhac.*

11   Edward O'Toole, *Whist for Your Life, That's Treason: Recollections of a Long Life* (Dublin: Ashfield Press, 2003), p. 110.

12   John Jordan, *The Pleasures of Gaelic Literature,* pp. 25–38.

13   Tomás Ó Criomhthain, Seán Ó Coileáin (ed.), *An tOileánach* (Dublin: Talbot Press, 2002), p. 340; and Mícheál Ó Dubhshláine, *A Dark Day on the Blaskets* (Dingle: Brandon Books, 2003), pp. 144–45.

14   Tomás Ó Criomhthain, Seán Ó Coileáin (ed.), *An tOileánach* (Dublin: Talbot Press, 2002), pp. 248–50.

15   *Ibid.*, p. 249. The O'Shea family from Valentia were the fishermen who were in charge of the *naomhóg.* Tomás tells us in *An Lóchrann,* August 1918, and in Tomás Ó Criomhthain, Breandán Ó Conaire (ed.), *Bloghanna an Bhlascaoid* (Dublin: Coiscéim, 1997), p. 22: "During this time three of the O'Shea family from Valentia were fishing amongst us. They were fine dancers and one was an excellent lilter."

16   Tomás Ó Criomhthain, Seán Ó Coileáin (ed.), *An tOileánach* (Dublin: Talbot Press, 2002), p. 250.

17   Eilís Ní Shúilleabháin, *Letters from the Great Blasket* (Dublin and Cork: Mercier Press, 1978; second edition, 1979), p. 24.

18   Tomás Ó Criomhthain, Pádraig Ua Maoileoin (ed.), *Allagar na hInise* (Dublin: Government Publications Sales Office; first edition 1928, second edition 1977), "30.1.1921," pp. 267–68.

Notes to Chapter IX

1   Information: Danny Sheehy.

2   Siobhán Ní Mhainín, Cillaruith, Irish Folklore Commission, Ms. 325.

3   Irish Folklore Department, Ms. 1249, p. 65.

4   Tomás Ó Criomhthain, Nollaig Mac Congail (ed.), *Scéilíní ón*

mBlascaod agus Blúirín as "Cín Lae Eibhlín Ní Shúilleabháin" (Dublin: Coiscéim, 2004), pp. 63–64.

5   "The Drowning of Collier's Bull," *Béaloideas*, 1963, p. 148.

6   Tomás Ó Criomhthain, Séamus Ó Duilearga (ed.), *Seanchas ón Oileán Tiar* (Dublin: Irish Folklore Commission, 1956), p. 185.

7   Peats Tom Ó Cearnaigh, *"Turas Callshaothach ag triall ar Phlúr,"* *Béaloideas* 1963, pp. 143–45.

8   *Long's Ledger,* Dingle, from the Archive, The Great Blasket Centre, Dunquin.

9   Máire Ní Ghuithín, *Bean an Oileáin* (Dublin: Coiscéim, 1986), pp. 31–32.

10   R.M. Lockley, illustrations James Lucas, *I Know an Island* (London: George G. Harrap & Co. Ltd., 1938, reprint 1948), p. 33.

11   *Calendar of the Orrery Papers*, p. 53–64; Breandán Ó Conaire (ed.), *Tomás an Bhlascaoid* (Inverin, Connemara: Cló Iar-Chonnachta, 1992), p. 20.

12   Tomás Ó Criomhthain, Pádraig Ua Maoileoin (ed.), *Allagar II* (Dublin: Coiscéim, 1999), p. 89.

13   Information: Seán Mhaurice Mhuiris Ó Catháin, 1 February 1989.

Notes to Chapter X

1   Information: Muiris Ó Dálaigh (Deálaí).

2   Letter from Brendan O'Keeffe to Charles J. Haughey.

3   Tomás Ó Criomhthain, Pádraig Ua Maoileoin (eds.), *Allagar na hInise* (Dublin: Government Publications Sales Office; first edition 1928, second edition 1977), p. 142.

4   Tomás Ó Criomhthain, Seán Ó Coileáin (ed.), *An tOileánach* (Dublin: Talbot Press, 2002), p. 127.

5   Tomás Ó Criomhthain, Caoilfhionn Nic Pháidín (ed.), *Dinnseanchas na mBlascaodaí* (Dublin: Cois Life, 1999), pp. 192–94.

6   Seán Ó Cróinín, Donncha Ó Cróinín, *Seanachas ó Chairbre 1* (Dublin: Irish Folklore Commission, 1985), p. 474.

7   Mícheál Ó Dubhshláine, *An Baol Dom Tú? Muintir Chorca Dhuibhne agus an Ghaeilge* (Dublin: Conradh na Gaeilge, 2000), p. 161. (From Hannah Daly tape.)

8   Breandán Firtéar, *An Spailpín* (programme 2). RTÉ, Raidió na Gaeltachta, 2005.

9   Muiris Ó Catháin, *Ar Muir is ar Tír* (Maynooth: An Sagart, 1991), p. 22.

10   Tomás Ó Criomhthain, Séamus Ó Duilearga (ed.), *Seanchas ón Oileán Tiar* (Dublin: Irish Folklore Commission, 1956), pp.195–96.
11   T.F. O'Sullivan, *Romantic Hidden Kerry* (Tralee: 1931), p. 243.
12   National Census 1901.
13   Leslie Matson, *Méiní: The Blasket Nurse* (Cork: Mercier Press, 1996), p. 35.
14   Thomas W. Brick, *Memoirs of an Irish Immigrant to U.S.A.* (private papers, typed copy, 1970), p. 25.
15   Leslie Matson, *Méiní: The Blasket Nurse* (Cork: Mercier Press, 1996), p. 37.
16   Karen P. Corrigan, *"I gcúntais Dé múin Béarla do na Leanbháin: eisimirce agus an Ghaeilge sa naoú aois déag,"* in Patrick O'Sullivan (ed.), *The Irish in the New Communities,* vol. 2 (London and Leicester: Leicester University Press, 1992), p. 143.
17   Seán Ó Dubhda, Questionnaire of The Irish Folklore Commission, 1955, Ms. 1407.
18   Thomas W. Brick, *Memoirs of an Irish Immigrant to U.S.A.* (private papers, typed copy, 1970), p. 3.
19   Breandán Firtéar, *An Spailpín*
20   *Páipéirí an Bhlascaoid,* The Great Blasket Centre, Dunquin.
21   Information from Patty Haimerl.
22   *Ibid.*
23   American Newspaper, without name, dated in pen "May, 1945," Kruger's papers.
24   Muiris Mhaidhc Léan O Guithín, 7 November 2003, in conversation with the author.
25   Dolores Quinn, *Island Heritage* (Private 1997).
26   Information from Patty Haimerl.

Notes to Chapter XI
1   Tomás Ó Criomhthain, Séamus Ó Duilearga (eds.), *Seanchas ón Oileán Tiar* (Dublin: Irish Folklore Commission, 1956), p. 196.
2   Robin Flower, *The Western Island* (Oxford: Oxford University Press, 1985), p. 123. (First edition 1944.)
3   Pádraig Ó Dálaigh, *A Chara Uasail,* 29 August 1933, The Great Blasket, Dunquin. Ó Dálaigh papers. Not published.
4   *Ibid.*
5   *Ibid.*
6   Letter from George Thomson to Charles J. Haughey, 8 March 1983.
7   Pádraig Ó Dálaigh, *A Chara Uasail.*

8   John M. Synge, *John M. Synge in West Kerry* (Dublin and Cork: Mercier Press, 1979), p. 44.

9   Tomás Ó Criomhthain, Séamus Ó Duilearga (ed.), *Seanchas ón Oileán Tiar* (Dublin: Irish Folklore Commission, 1956), pp. 196–97.

Notes to Chapter XII

1   Tomás Ó Criomhthain, Nollaig Mac Congail (ed.), *Scéilíní ón mBlascaod agus Blúirín as "Cín Lae Eibhlín Ní Shúilleabháin"* (Dublin: Coiscéim, 2004), p. 76.

2   Tomás Ó Criomhthain, Pádraig Ua Maoileoin (ed.), *Allagar na hInise* (Dublin: Government Publications Sales Office; first edition 1928, second edition 1977), p. 131.

3   Nóra Ní Shé, *Thar Bealach Isteach* (Dublin: Oifig an tSoláthair, 1940), p. 217.

4   Information: Danny Sheehy.

5   R.M. Lockley, illustrations James Lucas, *I Know an Island* (London: George G. Harrap & Co. Ltd., 1938; reprint 1948), pp. 110–11.

6   Seán Ó Cinnéide, Aogán Ó Muircheartaigh (ed.), *Oidhreacht an Bhlascaoid* (Dublin: Coiscéim, 1989), pp. 125–26.

7   T.J. O'Sullivan, *Romantic Hidden Kerry* (Tralee: The Kerryman, 1931), p. 574.

8   Seáinín Mhicil Ó Súilleabháin in conversation with Séamus Firtéar, on video made by the Folklore Department in the 1980s.

9   Information: Mícheál Ó Cruadhlaoich, 9 April 2006.

10   Tomás Ó Criomhthain, Pádraig Ua Maoileoin (ed.), *Allagar II* (Dublin: Coiscéim, 1999), pp. 42–43.

11   John M. Synge, *John M. Synge in West Kerry* (Dublin and Cork: Mercier Press, 1979), pp. 42–43.

12   Information: Séamus Touí Ó Ciobháin.

13   Seán and Tomás Ó Criomhthain, Pádraig Ó Fiannachta (ed.), *"Báfar Mé," Cleití Gé ón mBlascaod Mór* (Dingle: An Sagart, 1997), pp. 90–91.

14   Tomás Ó Criomhthain, Pádraig Ua Maoileoin (ed.), *Allagar II* (Dublin: Coiscéim, 1999), pp. 60–61.

15   Seán and Tomás Ó Criomhthain, Pádraig Ó Fiannachta (ed.), *"Báfar Mé," Cleití Gé ón mBlascaod Mór* (Dingle: An Sagart, 1997), p. 93.

16   Tomás Ó Criomhthain, Pádraig Ua Maoileoin (ed.), *Allagar II* (Dublin: Coiscéim, 1999), pp. 19–20.

17   Eilís Ní Shúilleabháin, *Letters from the Great Blasket* (Dublin and Cork: Mercier Press, 1978; reprint, 1979), p. 79.

18   Seán and Tomás Ó Criomhthain, Pádraig Ó Fiannachta (ed.), *"Báfar Mé," Cleití Gé ón mBlascaod Mór* (Dingle: An Sagart, 1997), pp. 92–93.

19   *Ibid.*, pp. 98–105.

20   Leslie Thomas, *Ghosts in the Sun* (London: Arlington Books, 1968), p. 72.

21   Information: Paddy Curran, Dingle.

22   John M. Synge, *John M. Synge in West Kerry* (Dublin and Cork: Mercier Press, 1979), p. 42.

23   Tom Neilí Ó Mainín, *Tíorabháin*, 3 September 2004.

24   R.M. Lockley, illustrations James Lucas, *I Know an Island* (London: George G. Harrap & Co. Ltd., 1938; reprint 1948), p. 106.

25   *Ibid.*, p. 111.

26   Information: Danny Sheehy.

27   Information: Ray Stagles.

28   Information: Seán Ó Braonáin and Danny Sheehy.

29   Tomás Ó Criomhthain, Pádraig Ua Maoileoin (ed.), *Allagar na hInise* (Dublin: Government Publications Sales Office; first edition 1928, second edition 1977), p. 53.

30   *Ibid.*, p. 125.

31   *Ibid.*, p. 133.

Notes to Chapter XIII

1   Robin Flower, *The Western Island* (Oxford: Oxford University Press, 1985), pp. 117–18 (First published 1944.)

2   Seosamh Ó Grifín, Kinard, who wrote from the telling of Máire Bean Uí Grifín, Kinard, 74 years. Irish Folklore Department, 7 April 1951, Ms. 217, pp. 81–83. Per. Roibeárd Ó Cathasaigh.

3   Máire Ní Ghearailt (teacher), 22 August 1935, Corca Dhuibhne, Dunquin Parish, School: The Great Blasket, *Bailiúchán na Scol*, vol. 419, p. 44.

4   From Pádraig Ó Dálaigh, living in the Great Blasket and who was born and reared on Inisvickillane, about six or seven miles from this island. He is 60 years. He heard this story from his father, Muiris Mór Ó Dálaigh, when he was 76 years old. Eternal rest on his soul.

5   Máire Ní Ghuithín, from Pádraig Ó Dálaigh, aged 67. He was born on Inisvickillane, and he heard this story from his father sixty years earlier, when the father was 36 years of age and living on the Inis. Máire Ní Ghuithín wrote this down on 17 October 1936. Irish Folklore Commission, Ms. 201, p. 238.

6   *Ibid.* p. 239.
7   *Ibid.*
8   *Ibid.*
9   Muiris Ó Catháin, *Ar Muir is ar Tír* (Maynooth: An Sagart, 1991), pp. 50–51.
10   Information: Maria Simonds-Gooding.
11   Information: Feargal Mac Amhlaoibh, from Tom na hInise Ó Dálaigh.
12   Seán Sheáin Í Chearnaigh, Irish Folklore Commission, Ms. 1406, pp. 43–44.
13   Mícheál Ó Guithín, *Beatha Pheig Sayers* (Dublin: F.N.T., 1970), pp. 97, 98.
14   Information: Muiris Mhaidhc Léan Ó Guithín.
15   Pádraig Tyers, *Leoithne Aniar* (Ballyferriter: Oidhreacht Chorca Dhuibhne, 1982), p. 11.
16   *The Western Island* (Oxford: Oxford University Press, 1985), p. 116.
17   Information: Charles J. Haughey.
18   Robin Flower, *The Western Island* (Oxford: Oxford University Press, 1985), p. 116 (First published 1944.)
19   Seán Ó Cinnéide, Aogán Ó Muircheartaigh (eds.), *"Ceol, Rince agus Amhráin," Oidhreacht an Bhlascaoid* (Dublin: Coiscéim, 1989), pp. 126–27.
20   Seamus Heaney, "The Given Note," *Door Into the Dark* (London: Faber & Faber: 1972).

Notes Chapter XIV
1   Tomás Ó Criomhthain, Seán Ó Coileáin (ed.), *An tOileánach* (Dublin: Talbot Press, 2002), p. 57.
2   Samuel Murray Hussey, *Reminiscences of an Irish Land Agent* (London: Duckworth, 1904).
3   Patrick Foley, *The History of the County Kerry* (1907), p. 73.
4   T.J. O'Sullivan, *Romantic Hidden Kerry* (Tralee: The Kerryman, 1931), p. 267.
5   Patrick Foley, *The History of the County Kerry* (1907), pp. 234–35.
6   *Kerry Sentinel*, 13 October 1871.
7   Information: Danny Sheehy.
8   Information: John Moore.
9   R.M. Lockley, illustrations James Lucas, *I Know an Island* (London: George G. Harrap & Co. Ltd., 1938; reprint 1948), p. 112.
10   *Ibid.*
11   *Ibid.*

12   *Ibid.*, pp. 113–14.
13   *Ibid.*, p. 115.
14   *Ibid.*
15   *Ibid.*, p. 117.
16   *Ibid.*, pp. 117–18.
17   *Ibid.*, p. 119.
18   *Ibid.*, pp. 119–20.

Notes to Chapter XV
1   Information: Eibhlín Pheats Tom Ó Cearnaigh (Eilín Bean Uí Chathaláin), Springfield Mass., February 2004.
2   Breandán Ó Conaire (ed.), *Tomás an Bhlascaoid* (Inverin, Connemara: Cló Iar-Chonnachta, 1992), pp. 188–89.
3   Máire Ní Ghuithín, *Bean an Oileáin* (Dublin: Coiscéim, 1986), pp. 82–83.
4   Letter from Brendan O'Keeffe to Charles J. Haughey.
5   Information: Charles J. Haughey.
6   Information: Maria Simonds-Gooding.
7   Information: Charles J. Haughey.

Notes to Chapter XVI
1   Michael Viney, "The Wild Island," *The Irish Times*, 13, 14, 15 September 1965.
2   Information: Maria Simonds-Gooding.
3   Seán Sheáin Í Chearnaigh, *Iarbhlascaodach ina Dheoraí* (Dublin: Sáirséal agus Dill, 1978), pp. 116.
4   *Ibid.*, p. 113.
5   *Ibid.*, p. 114.
6   *Ibid.*, p. 116.

Notes to Chapter XVII
1   Information: Charles J. Haughey.
2   Information: Charles J. Haughey, John Kennedy and Máirín Feirtéar.
3   Information: Charles J. Haughey.
4   *Ibid.*
5   Information: Larry Slattery, Dunquin.
6   Information: Pat Connor, Baile Dháith.
7   Information: Charles J. Haughey.
8   *Ibid.*
9   *Ibid.*

10   *Ibid.*

11   Information: Tadhg Ó Coileáin, Dingle.

12   Information: Dan Bric.

13   Information: Danny Sheehy.

14   Information: Maria Simonds-Gooding.

15   Information: Danny Sheehy and Charles J. Haughey.

Notes to Chapter XVIII

1   Charles J. Haughey on the programme, *Mo Cheol Thú* (RTÉ Radio 1).

2   A song by the author.

3   Information: Charles J. Haughey and Lís Ní Dhálaigh.

4   Charles J. Haughey on the programme, *Mo Cheol Thú* (RTÉ Radio 1).

5   Letter from Charles J. Haughey to George Thomson, 10 January 1985.

6   Seán Haughey, "Sunset on Inis Mhic Uibhleáin".

7   Information: Charles J. Haughey.

8   *Ibid.*

Notes to Chapter XIX

1   Charles Smith, *The Ancient and Present State of the County of Kerry* (London: 1756), p. 206.

2   *Ibid.*, p. 99.

3   Letter from Joe Thompson to Charles J. Haughey.

4   Information: Muiris Ó Dálaigh (Deálaí), 30 November 1988.

5   Michael O'Clery, *The Dingle Peninsula Bird Report 2002–2004*, Friends of BirdWatch Ireland in the Dingle Peninsula, pp. 19–20.

6   Richard Murphy, *Collected Poems* (Wake Forest University Press, October 2000), p. 107.

7   BirdWatch Ireland, Joint Nature Conservation Committtee, National Parks and Wildlife Service and INTEREG llc Atlantic Programme.

8   Information: Séamus Touí Ó Ciobháin.

9   BirdWatch Ireland, Joint Nature Conservation Committtee, National Parks and Wildlife Service and INTEREG llc Atlantic Programme.

10   *Ibid.*

11   *Ibid.*

12   *Ibid.*

13   *Ibid.*

14   *Ibid.*

15   *Ibid.*

16   *Ibid.*

17 *Ibid.*

18 *Ibid.*

19 Information: Charles J. Haughey.

20 Information: Joe Thompson.

21 Seán Ó Dálaigh ("the Common Noun"), *Clocha Sgáil* (Dublin: Government Publications Sales Office, 1930), p. 115.

22 Tomás Ó Criomhthain, Seán Ó Coileáin (ed.), *An tOileánach* (Dublin: Talbot Press, 2002), pp. 118–19.

23 Information: Charles J. Haughey.

24 Tom Hayden and Rory Harrington, *Exploring Irish Mammals* (Dublin: Town House, 2000; second edition 2001).

25 Charles Smith, *The Ancient and Present State of the County of Kerry* (London: 1756), p. 203.

26 Tomás Ó Criomhthain, Seán Ó Coileáin (ed.), *An tOileánach* (Dublin: Talbot Press, 2002), pp. 121–122.

27 Tomás Ó Criomhthain, Nollaig Mac Congáil (ed.), *Scéilíní ón mBlascaod agus Blúirín as "Cín Lae Eibhlín Ní Shúilleabháin"* (Dublin: Coiscéim, 2004), pp. 133–34.

28 Máire Ní Ghuithín, *Bean an Oileáin* (Dublin: Coiscéim, 1986).

29 Tom Hayden and Rory Harrington, *Exploring Irish Mammals* (Dublin: Town House, 2000; second edition 2001).

30 Patrick Foley, *The Ancient and Present State of the Skelligs, Blasket Islands, Donquin and the West of Dingle . . .* (Dublin: 1903), p. 73.

31 R.M. Barrington, "1881 Report on the Flora of the Blasket Islands, Co. Kerry," *Proceedings of the Royal Irish Academy* 1883, pp. 368–91.

32 *Ibid.*

33 *Ibid.*

34 *Ibid.*

35 *Ibid.*

36 A letter to the *Kerry Sentinel* on 13 January 1880, from the parish priest of Ballyferriter, Fr Liam Egan (1870–1890).

37 Tomás Ó Criomhthain, Seán Ó Coileáin (ed.), *An tOileánach* (Dublin: Talbot Press, 2002), p. 99.

38 Music: *Na Filí*, by Tomás Rua Ó Súilleabháin, *An Claidheamh Soluis* 8 August 1931/*An Lóchrann*, August, 1918/*Bloghanna ón mBlascaod*, pp. 200–01.

39 *An Lóchrann*, August 1918.

40 R.M. Barrington, "1881 Report on the Flora of the Blasket Islands, Co. Kerry," *Proceedings of the Royal Irish Academy* 1883, pp. 368–91.

41 Information: Charles J. Haughey.

42   Information: Joe Thompson.

43   R.M. Lockley, illustrations James Lucas, *I Know an Island* (London: George G. Harrap & Co. Ltd., 1938; reprint 1948), p. 113.

44   Information: Joe Thompson.

Notes to Chapter XX

1   Information: Charles J. Haughey.

2   *Ibid.*

3   *Ibid.*

4   Report by Seán Ryan on the red deer for Charles J. Haughey, 1990.

5   Information: Charles J. Haughey.

6   *Ibid.*

7   *Ibid.*

8   *Ibid.*

9   Seosamh Ó Grifín, Kinard, who wrote from the telling of Máire Bean Uí Ghrifín, Kinard, 74 years. Irish Folklore Department, 7 April 1951, Ms. 217, pp. 81–83. Per. Roibeárd Ó Cathasaigh.

10   Pádraig Tyers, *Leoithne Aniar* (Ballyferriter: Oidhreacht Chorca Dhuibhne, 1982), p. 91.

11   Information: Charles J. Haughey.

Notes to Chapter XXI

1   Pádraig de Brún, "John Windele and Father Casey," in *Journal of the Kerry Archaeological and Historical Society*, no. 7, 1974, p. 99.

2   *Tralee Chronicle*, 28 May 1858.

3   Mícheál Ó Gaoithín, *Is Trua ná Fanann an Óige* (Dublin: Government Publications Sales Office, 1953), p. 21.

4   Seán Ó Dálaigh ("the Common Noun"), *Clocha Sgáil* (Dublin: Government Publications Sales Office, 1930), p. 67.

5   *Ibid.*

6   Tomás Ó Criomhthain, Caoilfhionn Nic Pháidin (ed.), *Dinnseanchas na mBlascaod* (Dublin: Cois Life, 1997), p. 51.

7   Patrick Foley, *The Ancient and Present State of the Skelligs, Blasket Islands, Donquin and the West of Dingle . . .* (Dublin: 1903).

8   Seán Ó Dálaigh ("the Common Noun"), *Clocha Sgáil* (Dublin: Government Publications Sales Office, 1930), pp. 60–66. Séamus Touí Ó Ciobháin reckons the story came from Paddy na hInise.

9   Information: Charles J. Haughey.

Notes to Chapter XXII

1   Tomás Ó Criomhthain, Séamus Ó Duilearga (ed.), *Seanchas ón Oileán Tiar* (Dublin: Irish Folklore Commission, 1956), p. 166.
2   Paddy O'Leary and Lee Snodgrass, "Archaeological Survey of the Blasket Islands, Co. Kerry, A Preliminary Report–1976. Inish Vicillane," pp. 11–13. Private account.
3   *Béaloideas*, 1963, pp. 147–48.
4   Muiris Ó Catháin, *Ar Muir is ar Tír* (Maynooth: An Sagart, 1991), pp. 25–27.

Notes to Chapter XXIII

1   *Journal of the Royal Society of Antiquaries of Ireland*, March 1903.
2   Mícheál Ó Guithín, *Is Trua ná Fanann an Óige* (Dublin: Government Publications Sales Office, 1953), p. 44.
3   Information: Tomás Ó Mainín (Tom Neilí), Tíorabháin, grandson of Tomás mentioned here.
4   Information: Seán Ó Cíobháin (Seáinín Touí), Gráig, grandson of Taimí mentioned here.
5   Pádraig Ó Duinnshléibhe, "Kruger agus an Blascaod," in Tadhg Ó Dubhshláine (ed.), *Is Cuimhin Liom Kruger* (Maynooth: An Sagart, 1994), p. 76.
6   Information: Tomás Ó Mainín (Tom Neilí).
7   Information: Colm Ó Bric, Dunquin, the son of Séamus mentioned here.

Notes to Appendix I

1   Pádraig Ó Siochfhradha *(An Seabhac), Triocha-céad Chorca Dhuibhne* (Dublin: Comhlucht Oideachais na hÉireann, Teo., The Irish Folklore Commission 1939), p. 110.

Notes to Appendix IV

1   Tomás Ó Criomhthain, Seán Ó Coileáin (ed.), *An tOileánach* (Dublin: Talbot Press, 2002), p. 177.
2   Leslie Matson, *Blasket Lives: Biographical Accounts of One Hundred and Twenty Five Blasket People,* 2005, p, 26, not published yet.
3   Muirs Mhaidhc Léan Ó Guithín, Dunquin.
4   R.M. Lockley, illustrations James Lucas, *I Know an Island* (London: George G. Harrap & Co. Ltd., 1938; reprint 1948), pp. 111–112.
5   Eibhlín Bean Uí Shé (Eibhlín Lynch), Ceathrú, Dunquin.

6 Muiris Ó Bric, *Spotsholas na nDaoine* (Dublin: Coiscéim, 1995), pp. 60–61.
7 Eilís Ní Shúilleabháin, *Letters from the Great Blasket* (Dublin and Cork: Mercier Press, 1978; reprint, 1979), p. 64.
8 Muiris Mhaidhc Léan Ó Guithín, Dunquin, RIP, and Páidí Curran, Dingle, RIP.
9 Information: Muiris Mhaidhc Léan Ó Guithín, Dunquin, RIP.
10 Seán Ó Dubhda, *Meascra ó Chorca Dhuibhne, Béaloideas 26,* Turas Callshaothach, pp. 145, 146.
11 Seán Ó Dubhda, The Irish Folklore Commission, vol. 1549, February 1959.

Notes to Appendix V
1 Information: Muiris Mhaidhc Léan Ó Guithín, Dunquin, RIP.
2 Nóra Ní Shéaghdha, *Thar Bealach Isteach* (Dublin: Oifig an tSoláthair, 1940), p. 217.
3 *Ibid.*, p. 220.
4 Information: Maria Simonds-Gooding.
5 Domhnall Mac Síthigh, *Fan Inti* (Dublin: Coiscéim, 2004), p. 156.
6 Many thanks to Ed Barrett and Jennie Shields who gave me permission to study these items.
7 Information: Patty Haimerl.

MÍCHEÁL Ó DUBHSHLÁINE

A Dark Day on the Blaskets
The Drowning of Dónal Ó Criomhthain and Eibhlín Nic Niocaill on the Blasket Islands, 13 August 1909

"A wonderful piece of drama-documentary... entertaining and captivating. It's an evocative story, a portrait of a young woman and her times, and an engrossing description of a beautiful place at a turning point in its history." *Ireland Magazine*

"A fascinating insight into Blasket Island life, life on the mainland, and life in Dublin in the early part of the last century." *Kerryman*

ISBN 9780863223372

MÍCHEÁL Ó DUBHSHLÁINE

Inis Mhic Uibhleáin

"Bhí aithne ar Mhícheál Ó Dubhshláine mar phríomh-oide Scoil Dhún Chaoin, a coinníodh ar oscailt aineoinn pleananna na Roinne Oideachais. Scríobh sé trí leabhar a foilsíodh lena bheo agus bronnadh máistreacht oinigh air sa Stair Áitiúil. Críorann sé stair an oileáin úd ar le C.J. Haughey anois é, an t-oileán de na Blascaodaí ba mhó go raibh daoine ina gcónaí ann seachas an Blascaod Mór. Ní hamháin go dtugann sé oiread agus is féidir den stair agus den lonnú daonna ach cuireann sé san áireamh an ceol, an seanchas, an seandálaíocht agus an stair nádúrtha. Tá an insint seolta agus tá beaichte an scoláire sna tagairtí do na foinsí. Tá go leor foilsithe cheana féin faoin mBlascaod Mór agus faoi Chorca Dhuibhne: cloch ar an gcarn san é seo agus is saibhrede an ciste. Is é an trua an té a scríobh a bheith imithe ón saol." *Books Ireland*

ISBN 9780863223730

GEORGE THOMSON
Island Home: The Blasket Heritage

"Imbued with Thomson's deep respect for the rich oral culture and his aspiration that the best of the past might be preserved in the future." *Sunday Tribune*

"The body of the book consists of brief, luminous studies by Thomson of Blasket life and culture and the trail from there to all of cultural history." *The Irish Times*

ISBN 9780863221613

STEVE MACDONOGH
The Dingle Peninsula

"Far and away the best of the many books written about the area. A visitor who travels to Dingle without it is seriously deprived." *Irish Examiner*

ISBN 9780863222696

STEVE MACDONOGH
Dingle in Pictures

"Wonderful colour photographs reproduced to perfection and with informative captions. All the text is printed in English, Irish, French and German. Gorgeous!" *Ireland of the Welcomes*

"A beautiful book... We stopped at many places featured in its pages and found that Steve MacDonogh's photographs wonderfully reflected the beauty that was there." *Irish Examiner*

ISBN 9780863222795

THE BOOKS OF MANCHÁN MAGAN

Angels and Rabies: A Journey Through the Americas

"[Magan's] writing is unashamedly sensual and he has an engagingly confessional narrative voice; his adventures are as poignant as they are hair-raising." *Sunday Telegraph*

"Frightening, funny and lovable." *The Sunday Times*

"His writing is intimate and immediate, perceptive and humorous." *Books Ireland*

ISBN 9780863223495

Manchán's Travels

"Often humorous, at times hilarious, Magan... has an evocative and elegant turn of phrase." *New Statesman*

"Mad, brilliant and often hilarious." *The Irish Times*

"Magan has a keen eye for the hypocrisies of elite urban India and artfully evokes the 'fevered serenity' of the Himalayas." *Times Literary Supplement*

ISBN 9780863223686

Truck Fever

"Like *Lord Of The Flies* meets *Lost* meets *The Amazing Race*, *Truck Fever* is an insightful soap opera that does Africa, its radiant and impenetrable muse, justice." *Metro Life*

"An excellent writer, has a wonderful talent for transporting the reader into the heart of every experience. He is an intelligent observer of people and places, and his writing is sensitive and engaging. *Truck Fever* is a great read." *Sunday Tribune*

"*Truck Fever* is travel writing at its hair-raising finest." *Evening Herald*

ISBN 9780863223891

FRANCIS O'NEILL

*Chief O'Neill's Sketchy Recollections
of an Eventful Life in Chicago*

"Reminiscing in old age, the memoirs are not too sketchy and
are cleverly edited in headed sections and paragraphs, with
plenty of photos and document facsimiles throughout, making it
easy and enticing reading about not only a varied and
interesting life, but also the Irish-American community in
Chicago and beyond." *Books Ireland*

ISBN 9780863223785

SEAN O'CALLAGHAN

To Hell or Barbados: The Ethnic Cleansing of Ireland

"An illuminating insight into a neglected episode in Irish history,
but its significance is much broader than that. Its main
achievement is to situate the story of colonialism in Ireland in
the much larger context of worldwide European imperialism.
O'Callaghan's description of seventeenth century Barbados is a
powerful portrait of a society as brutal, corrupt and unjust as
anything the twentieth century has to offer. Yet it is precisely societies like colonial
Barbados and Virginia which lie at the root of our modern world. That is why
To Hell or Barbados is such a valuable book." *Irish World*

ISBN 9780863222870

ADRIAN HOAR

In Green and Red: The Lives of Frank Ryan

"The work is of a high standard, well documented, with index, a
list of sources and copious notes… there is hardly a dull
moment in the account from beginning to end."
Irish Independent

"Splendid… Instead of a cardboard cutout of an Irish hero, we
get a hugely complex and beautifully written portrait of a man who struggled
against his own marginality." *Scotland on Sunday*

"A readable and stimulating narrative." *Books Ireland*

ISBN 9780863223327